CHANGE

CHANGE

How to Make
Big Things Happen

DAMON CENTOLA

Little, Brown Spark
New York Boston London

Little, Brown Spark
Hachette Book Group
1290 Avenue of the Americas, New York, NY 10104
littlebrownspark.com

First Edition: January 2021

Little, Brown Spark is an imprint of Little, Brown and Company, a division of Hachette Book Group, Inc. The Little, Brown Spark name and logo are trademarks of Hachette Book Group, Inc.

The publisher is not responsible for websites (or their content) that are not owned by the publisher.

The Hachette Speakers Bureau provides a wide range of authors for speaking events. To find out more, go to hachettespeakersbureau.com or call (866) 376-6591.

ISBN 978-0-316-45733-0 (hardcover) / 978-0-316-70304-8 (int'l paperback)

LCCN 2020938668

Printing 1, 2020

LSC-C

Printed in the United States of America

For Susana and Milan

Contents

Contents

CHANGE

Preface

The science of networks is the study of how things spread. How do the connections we share with the people around us affect the way that diseases, ideas, trends, and behaviors move through communities and societies and around the world?

In the spring of 2020, as I was finishing work on this book, the world was suddenly transformed by two powerful new examples of things that spread very far, very fast. The first, of course, was the novel coronavirus, which emerged in a market in Wuhan, China, and, in a matter of weeks, spread throughout China, then to the Middle East and Europe, and from there to every corner of the world.

What made the virus so deadly and disruptive was how easily it could be transmitted. It was small, it was hard to kill, and it was airborne. You could catch it from someone standing a few feet away from you, and it lingered in the air for hours. What made the virus even more insidious was the fact that if you caught it, you could then spread it to others before you felt any symptoms, before you even knew you'd been infected. Every person was a potential source of contagion. Every contact was a mode of transmission. A hug. A handshake. Receiving a package in the mail. Accepting a piece of paper from your colleague. And so the disease spread rapidly, at choir practices and funerals and family reunions, through hospitals and nursing homes and meatpacking plants, between husbands and wives and between complete strangers. By June, more than six million people had been infected worldwide, a third of them in the United States. Once the virus took hold, it expanded exponentially.

But something else was spreading that spring. It wasn't a disease. It was a behavior.

Governments around the world reacted differently to the coronavirus pandemic—some responded much more quickly than others—but within a few months, public health advice worldwide had coalesced around four basic preventive measures: Wash your hands. Stay at home. Wear a mask. And stay at least six feet away from other people. As these directives took shape, a new question emerged: Would people follow them? Could the entire world change its behavior in such dramatic ways?

People looked first to their friends and neighbors. Were they wearing masks? Were they social distancing? Mostly, remarkably, they were. In many communities—small towns and large cities—the sidewalks were nearly empty. People stayed home. If they did go out, they usually wore face masks. And they afforded one another exaggeratedly wide berths as they passed on the street. In country after country, people changed the way they worked, socialized, went to school, raised children, and went on dates. New behavioral norms had sprung up, seemingly overnight, and they had propagated across the globe.

Gradually, these behaviors changed the course of the disease. After weeks of headlines full of death and despair, there was *good* news for the first time in months: the spread of the disease was slowing. New cases were going down. Hospital intensive-care units were emptying out.

And then the weather warmed. People began to weary of

the daily reminders to maintain their white-knuckled vigilance. Summer was arriving. And the new norms began to unravel.

Some people stopped wearing masks, others became less cautious about social distancing. Their friends and neighbors tried to figure out what to do. Which behaviors were acceptable? Which were overly cautious? Which were selfish or reckless? Different communities responded differently. Some groups wore face masks; others didn't. Some gathered together; still others kept their distance.

The disease, meanwhile, kept spreading the same way as before. Every person, every surface, every contact remained a potential source of infection. And the caseload continued to rise.

For nearly a century, scientists have believed that behaviors spread just like viruses do. But as the world saw in 2020, the spread of human behavior in fact follows very different rules than the spread of diseases.

Today, epidemiologists and public health experts can forecast the path of a virus, and they can use that science to develop policies to help slow it down. But how can we forecast the spread of new *behaviors*? How can we identify policies that will improve the uptake of positive behaviors? How can we recognize policies that will unintentionally cause those behaviors to unravel? Why do the rules of social influence seem to vary with culture and identity, and how can we ever hope to understand these complexities?

This book is an attempt to answer those questions. In the pages ahead, I'll show you what the brand-new science of networks tells us about how and why and when human behavior changes. I'll show you the factors that determine the spread of social change, explain why we've misunderstood them for so long, and reveal how they really work.

Behavior change, we now understand, is not like a virus, spreading through casual contact. It does follow rules, but learning these rules takes us beyond the spread of diseases to reveal a process that is deeper, more mysterious—and much more interesting.

Introduction

In 1929, Werner Forssman was a twenty-five-year-old heart surgeon with a big idea. He had invented a radical new lifesaving procedure that he thought would change the world. But the medical community met his idea with contempt: he was ridiculed by his colleagues, fired from his job, and driven from the field of cardiology. Thirty years later, Forssman was working as a urologist in a small town in the remote hills of Germany. One night at the local pub, he received a phone call with some startling news: his long-ago discovery had won the 1957 Nobel Prize in Medicine and Physiology. Today, cardiac catheterization is used in every major hospital around the world. How did Forssman's unpopular innovation become one of the most widely accepted procedures in medical science?

In 1986, American citizens could be incarcerated for up to five years for possessing marijuana—a jail sentence that would forever alter a person's prospects for financial success, marriage, and even political participation. Today, storefronts in shopping malls sell marijuana openly and pay federal taxes on the proceeds. How did a behavior that was both illegal and regarded as socially deviant become so acceptable that previously stigmatized "drug dealers" became part of the mainstream American business community?

In 2011, internet powerhouse Google launched its new

social-media tool, Google+. Although Google had over a billion users worldwide, the company struggled to transfer its dominance in the search-engine market to the social-media market. By 2019, Google+ was forced to shut its doors. During the same period, the start-up Instagram entered the arena. It reached one million users within two months. Within eighteen months the company was purchased by Facebook for $1 billion, and by 2019 Instagram had become a staple among social-media users. What did Google do wrong? And how did Instagram, with fewer resources and less time, outcompete the search-engine juggernaut?

In April 2012, the hashtag #BlackLivesMatter was first posted on social media in response to a jury's acquittal of the man who shot and killed seventeen-year-old Trayvon Martin. In the two years that followed, several police-related deaths of African American men and women were reported in the news and on social media, but by June of 2014 #BlackLivesMatter had been used only 600 times. Two months later, however, the death of eighteen-year-old Michael Brown in Ferguson, Missouri, triggered a revolution: within months, #BlackLivesMatter had been used more than a million times, and a national movement to protest police violence was underway. Six years after that, in response to the killing of George Floyd in May 2020, #BlackLivesMatter transformed again, this time into a global phenomenon, with solidarity protests in more than 200 cities worldwide and new federal legislation to reduce police violence. What happened to transform decades of overlooked police violence into a powerful, self-organized popular movement?

This book is about change. How it works, and why it so often fails. It's about the spread of unlikely innovations, the success of fringe movements, the acceptance of unpopular ideas, and the triumph of contentious new beliefs. And it's about the strategies that help them succeed. Those success stories all have one thing in common: the radical new ideas at their core all expanded and spread through social networks.

I have a unique perspective on these questions because I am a sociologist who studies the science of social networks. In fact, over the last couple of decades, my ideas have helped shape this new field. In the fall of 2002, I made a series of discoveries that altered our scientific understanding of social networks, and launched a new way of studying how change spreads. The resulting insights have helped to explain why social change can be hard to predict, and why it so often confounds our most trusted ideas about which strategies will work and which others will fail.

For decades, our standard ideas about social change have been based on a popular metaphor—that change spreads like a virus. Recently, we have all been reminded how a virus works: one person gets infected, they pass it on to one or two or three (or a hundred) others, and the contagion spreads through the population. The idea that "influencers" are the key to spreading innovations is based on the notion that well-connected individuals can play an outsize role in the spread of a disease— for instance in a viral pandemic. Similarly, the idea that *stickiness* is essential for a successful social-marketing campaign is based on the idea that certain viruses are particularly infectious.

These viral metaphors are useful when we're talking about the dispersal of simple ideas or information (headline news of a volcanic eruption, for example, or the marriage of royal celebrities). And those bits of information really *are* contagious: easy to catch, easy to transmit. But there's a big problem with the viral metaphor: to create real change, you need to do more than spread information; you must change people's beliefs and behaviors. And those are much harder to influence. Viral metaphors are able to describe a world where information spreads quickly yet beliefs and behaviors stay the same. It is a world of *simple contagions*—catchy ideas and memes that spread quickly to everyone but lack any lasting impact on what we think or how we live.

But social change is far more complicated. Innovative ideas and behaviors do not spread virally; simple exposure is not enough to "infect" you. When you are exposed to a new behavior or idea, you don't automatically adopt it. Instead, you have to make a decision about whether to accept or reject it. And that decision can often be complex and emotional.

My research, and that of many others in this field, has shown that as we consider whether to adopt a new belief or behavior, we are guided, much more than we realize, by our social networks. Through the hidden power of social influence, the network around us shapes how we respond to an innovation, causing us either to ignore it or to adopt it. This much-deeper process of social spreading is called *complex contagion,* and it has given rise to a new science for understanding how change happens—and how we can help *make* it happen.

When we discuss "social networks," it is important to remember that these networks are not necessarily digital. They have existed for as long as humans have been around. They include everyone we talk to, collaborate with, live near, and seek out. Our personal network makes up our social world. The *science* of social networks studies the web that binds these social worlds together—from neighbors living on the same street to strangers on different continents—and how social contagions can spread among them.

This book crystallizes over a decade of new research by myself and hundreds of other sociologists, computer scientists, political scientists, economists, and management scholars working to discover the most effective strategies for spreading complex contagions. But the idea at its heart is a simple one: successful social change is not about information; it's about norms. Social networks are not merely the *pipes* through which ideas and behaviors flow from person to person. They are also the *prisms* that determine how we see those behaviors and interpret those ideas. Depending on how a new idea comes to us, we may either dismiss it or jump on board.

Unlike perceptual bias, in which our eyes distort visual information, or cognitive bias, which distorts our reasoning about economic information, *network bias* is the way our social networks invisibly shape the beliefs we hold and the norms we follow.

The social network that links the members of a community together can inadvertently reinforce people's existing biases, preventing innovative ideas and movements from catching on. Yet with slight changes, the same network can instead trigger collective enthusiasm for an innovation, accelerating its adoption throughout the community.

My goal in this book is to help you unravel some of the mysteries of societal transformation by showing you how these social networks function. From protests in the streets to new management strategies in an organization—from the spread of healthy diets to the adoption of solar power—social networks are the force that drives the potential for social change.

In the pages ahead, I will take you to Silicon Valley, where you will see innovations unintentionally crushed by the very "influencers" who are supposed to help promote them.

We will visit Denmark and discover how a clever group of computer scientists deployed a network of autonomous Twitter bots to spawn human social networks that spread social activism to thousands of people.

You will venture behind the scenes at Harvard University, where network scientists pioneered and patented networking strategies to accelerate the adoption of innovative technologies.

Finally, I will show you how President Barack Obama used novel networking strategies to improve the quality of his presidential decisions.

When I began exploring these topics, I worked mostly in the realm of theory, studying the civil rights movement and the worldwide growth of social-media technologies. But a decade or so ago, I realized that if I really wanted to understand why social change succeeds or fails, I would need to find a way to test my theory of networks in the real world. In Parts II, III, and IV of this book, I will detail for you a series of large-scale social experiments I conducted, in which I directly manipulated the behavior of entire populations. Some of these populations were young professionals attending exercise classes at a local gym; others were Democrats and Republicans debating climate change; and still others were physicians engaged in clinical diagnosis. As you will see, these experiments revealed profound new truths about the nature of social change.

By the end of this book, you will understand how the science of networks can empower you to gain control of your own social network and the influence it has on you and others. And you will see how the social networks around you guide people's behaviors, their receptivity to innovations, and their ability to maintain healthy and productive cultural habits.

In the next chapter, I will begin by identifying popular myths and mistakes in our understanding of social change. But throughout the book, my focus will be on solutions. My ultimate goal in presenting this new perspective on social change is to allow readers from all walks of life to acquire the resources they need to create the change they want to see.

PART I

PERVASIVE MYTHS THAT PREVENT CHANGE

CHAPTER 1

The Myth of the Influencer: The (Un)Popularity Paradox

There is an old joke in brand-marketing circles.

On July 20, 1969, a group of advertising executives stayed late at the office—not because of crushing deadlines but because they wanted to witness a singular moment in history: the first walk on the moon. Along with them, an estimated 530 million people around the world watched Armstrong's televised image and heard his voice describe the event as he took "one small step for a man, one giant leap for mankind."

Everyone was in high spirits in celebration of this first-ever event, with the exception of one executive who walked away from the TV, shaking his head. When a colleague caught up with him and asked what was wrong, the executive looked at him sadly and said, "If only Armstrong was carrying a Coke."

That was the dominant thinking in the late 1960s: sales happened through big, top-down endorsements, traveling to passive audiences via one-way broadcast channels.

Now fast-forward several decades and imagine that you want to launch a new social innovation—a time-management app, a fitness program, a poetry collection, an investment strategy, or a political initiative. You are emotionally and economically invested in your campaign, and you want to ensure it spreads by word of mouth as quickly and as widely as possible. Whom would you choose to promote it: a highly connected social star such as Katy Perry or Oprah Winfrey who resides in the center of a vast social network? Or a "peripheral actor"—someone who is more modestly connected and lives on the network's fringe?

If you're like most people, you'll decide to pitch your change campaign to the social star, rather than the peripheral player.

And you'll be making a mistake.

The power of highly connected social stars (or, as we now call them, *influencers*) to spread innovations turns out to be one of the most enduring and misleading myths in social science. It has infiltrated the worlds of sales, marketing, publicity, and even politics. So much so, that even when an innovation spreads from the periphery to achieve worldwide influence, we still give the credit for its success to a social star.

The Oprah Fallacy

When Twitter launched in March 2006, the earth did not move. Its founders and a few early funders were excited about the technology, but the microblogging site was not the immediate blockbuster you might imagine, given that it now has more than 330 million users and has become a wildly popular marketing tool for businesses, nonprofits, and even politicians. Twitter merely crept along in its early months, spreading slowly.

So, what happened to transform it from another also-ran into one of the largest communication platforms in the world?

Twitter looks like the kind of technology that *New Yorker* writer Malcolm Gladwell and Wharton School marketing professor Jonah Berger refer to as "contagious." To jump-start

Twitter's growth, in 2007 its founders decided to promote it at the giant annual tech-and-media conference South by Southwest, aka SXSW, in Austin, Texas. SXSW is a weeklong paradise for film, music, and technology buffs who thrive on discovering avant-garde media and quirky new technologies.

Today SXSW is the largest music-and-media festival in the world, with more than fifty thousand annual attendees and talks by leading political and media figures such as Bernie Sanders, Arnold Schwarzenegger, and Steven Spielberg. Back in 2007, however, SXSW was still working its way from the fringe to the mainstream, and cool new technologies like Twitter were often debuted there as a way of doing preliminary market testing. Twitter was a big hit.

After that initial breakout, Twitter grew only incrementally until 2009, when its growth suddenly accelerated. The story commonly told about Twitter's explosion is that Oprah Winfrey deserves the credit. On April 17, 2009, Winfrey sent her first tweet on her talk show, before an audience of millions. By the end of the month, Twitter had grown to approximately twenty-eight million users.

This version of the Twitter success story is compelling and easy to grasp. It tells us that the key to success is to find the influencers and get them on board. It gives start-ups, and the people who invest in them, a road map for success. And it features a major star.

The problem is that this road map steers us off course. In fact, when it comes to the kinds of change we care about most, it leads to a dead end.

Oprah's adoption of Twitter was not the reason for Twitter's success; it was a *result* of it. By the time Oprah sent her first tweet, Twitter had already entered the fastest part of its growth curve. Starting in January 2009, Twitter was achieving exponential growth month after month, skyrocketing from under eight million users in February to approximately twenty million users in early April. In fact, Oprah adopted at the peak of Twitter's growth. Afterward the site kept growing, but at a *slower* rate.

A better question to ask about Twitter's success is not *How did they get Oprah to spread Twitter?* but rather *How did Twitter grow so big that Oprah herself got a boost from adopting it?* The answer to this question explains how small start-up companies, fringe political campaigns, and marginal interest groups can use people's well-established friendship networks to grow new movements into household names—and it involves the social periphery, *not* the social stars.

The Aerosmith Gesture

A revealing study conducted in the virtual-reality platform Second Life provides rich insight into how the spread of innovation accelerates when we target networks of peripheral actors—not the Perrys and Oprahs of the world, but our everyday friends and neighbors.

Just as in the real world, commerce has real value in Second Life. That was especially the case when Second Life was in its infancy. In February 2006, only three years after the site launched, a member of the Second Life community, Ailin Gaef (going by the Second Life alias Anshe Chung), earned enough credit inside the game's fictional economy to cash in her assets for more than one million real-world US dollars. Anshe's virtual activity had made Ailin into a real-life millionaire.

Thousands of entrepreneurs flocked to Second Life. People wanted to spread the word about their products and services to as many other users as possible—and get rich in the process. Their approach to success was the same as it would be in a real-world market: find the influencers and convert them into evangelists for your idea. In Second Life, as anywhere else, the traditional wisdom is *target the highly connected stars in the social network.*

There are lots of things to buy in Second Life—clothes, houses, pets, and food, for example. But it goes far beyond that. In Second Life, you can also buy behaviors.

Unlike in real life, if you want to adopt a new style of talking or a hip kind of handshake, you need to make a deliberate effort to *acquire* it. Sometimes that requires money—as much as $500 US—sometimes it doesn't. But it always requires some forethought and action.

One gesture that became popular in the fall of 2008 was the Aerosmith gesture, an animation in which your character throws its hands above its head and makes a horn shape with its index and pinky fingers, with its thumb outstretched for emphasis. A gesture like this needs to be officially added to your character's list of assets in order for you to use it. But the important thing about a Second Life gesture is that you don't really *want* to use it unless other people are using it, too.

It's the same in real life. Imagine greeting a friend at a bar with the Aerosmith gesture just as he extends his hand for a handshake. You'd feel ridiculous.

Given the established norm of shaking hands, how did the Aerosmith gesture become popular? In real life, this would be a difficult question to answer; it would be nearly impossible to trace exactly how many people were greeting their friends and colleagues with handshakes versus how many were using the Aerosmith gesture. In Second Life, however, analysts can not only count the number of players using the gesture, they can track the number of interactions each person has in a given day, see how each interaction transpired, and note from whom each person learned the Aerosmith gesture and at what point they started using it themselves. Which makes Second Life the perfect place to measure how social innovations spread.

In 2008, physicist Lada Adamic and data scientists Eytan Bakshy and Brian Karrer set out to use this digital precision to measure the person-to-person transfer of a new behavior. Conventional wisdom at the time said the first thing to do was to look for the influencers. In Second Life, as in the real world, there are social stars—the Oprahs of the metaverse, who are far more socially connected than everyone else. These people are in a position to exert a lot of social influence on the community. If a new behavior like the Aerosmith gesture is adopted by one of these prominent individuals, you might assume that it would then spread to a lot of other people very quickly.

As it turns out, the researchers found exactly the opposite of what they expected. The most highly connected users were in fact the *least* effective at spreading the Aerosmith gesture. Why? Surprisingly, because the more connected people were, the less likely they were to adopt the innovation. The more contacts that someone had who were *not* using the Aerosmith gesture, the less likely they were to make the effort to acquire it, or to start using it themselves.

The value of the Aerosmith gesture, like most assets in Second Life, hinges on its being commonly accepted by other people around you. Just like any greeting gesture—hugging, kissing on the cheek, high-fiving—you do not want to try it out in a new social situation if everyone you know is still shaking hands. You would rather wait until you're sure the gesture is a well-known greeting before you try it yourself.

Once a new social trend catches on, it's good to be on the frontier. But you don't want to adopt too early and be out there all by yourself—the lone high-fiver in a world of handshakers.

This is an example of what sociologists call a *coordination problem.* Any kind of social gesture you might adopt—from a high-five to a handshake—is a behavior that depends on coordinating with other people. The question for the researchers was: how many people must adopt the Aerosmith gesture before you will think the trend is popular enough that *you* decide to adopt it too? It turns out that the answer is relative: it depends on the size of your social network.

Adamic and her team discovered something that has since been confirmed in dozens of other settings, from Facebook to fashion. Namely, that we are typically influenced by the *percentage* of the people we know who are doing something, rather than the total number. Imagine you know only four people in Second Life. If two of them start using a new greeting gesture, you would be likely to start using it too. Fifty percent of your social network is a lot of social influence. But if you know 100 people in Second Life, two people adopting a new gesture is unlikely to have much of an effect on your behavior. You'll wait until you see more people adopting it before you decide to start using it as well.

In fact, the researchers found that a very popular person with about five hundred contacts was about ten times *less likely* to adopt the Aerosmith gesture than a moderately connected person with only fifty contacts. In other words, the more connected someone is, the harder it is to convince them that a new idea or behavior is legitimate. The more contacts they have, the more adopters it takes to change their mind.

The Reluctant CEO

Let's think about this in the real world. Say you want to spread an innovative technology like Venmo—a social media–based payment service that lets you split checks, repay debts, and share comments via a social feed. You are building the marketing strategy for Venmo, and you need to decide whom to target: a small group of people working at a tech start-up, each with a few hundred contacts, or the CEO of a nationally recognized brand with tens of thousands of contacts?

You've read enough by now to know the answer.

As prominent as that brand CEO may be, she is also paying attention to people's behaviors. She is keenly aware of how her decisions will look to her peers and clients. She got where she is, in part, by being highly socially perceptive. She will be thoughtful before adopting an unknown technology, and will look around to see how many of her peers and peer institutions have brought this technology on board. She is unlikely to take the reputational risk of adopting a highly visible product before many of her contacts do.

That brings us to the key reason why that über-influencer CEO is so hard to influence: Though her massive social network may connect her to a few people who have adopted the innovation, she is far more likely to know many more people who have *not* adopted it. I refer to these people as *countervailing influences*. The mere inaction of these people—their lack of adoption—sends a resounding message to the social star that the innovation has not yet been accepted.

These countervailing influences send a silent but remarkably strong social signal. They tell us how accepted an innovation is, and how likely it is to be seen as legitimate (or illegitimate) by our peers. Which is to say, a well-connected leader will be much more influenced by the countervailing influences coming from the overwhelming majority of her non-adopting contacts than by the positive signal coming from a small number of early adopters.

It is different for the start-up employees in the network's periphery. A small number of peer adopters would be much more influential for a more moderately connected person than they would for a highly connected CEO. Because people in the network periphery have fewer countervailing influences surrounding them, a few initial adopters constitute a far greater fraction of their social network. This makes the network periphery an easier place for an innovation to take hold. The more people in the periphery who adopt your innovation, the stronger the signal will be for everyone else. This is how social change gains momentum. Once an innovation starts to spread through the periphery, it can grow large enough that even highly connected influencers will be forced to sit up and pay attention.

This is exactly what happened with Twitter. It is also what happened in Second Life. Social stars who were reluctant to adopt a new behavior early on became avid users once the innovation reached a sufficient *critical mass* to convince them it was legitimate.

The story of Twitter's success is particularly instructive because of how starkly it cuts against our intuitions. Starting in 2006, it was ordinary people in San Francisco and the surrounding Bay Area who gave Twitter its big start, passing it on locally through their friendship and family networks. The new internet technology succeeded by traveling from block to block, neighborhood to neighborhood, across the city. As Twitter gained momentum, it expanded to similar regions of the country until finally reaching critical mass in January 2009. At that point, its popularity exploded. It only took a few months to grow from a few hundred thousand users to nearly twenty million active members. That kind of growth can make even a social supernova like Oprah Winfrey sit up and pay attention.

Opinion Leaders and the Influencer Myth

In the 1940s, television was a technology on the rise. For decades, radio had been the dominant means of disseminating everything from sports media to political slogans. Advertisers poured millions of dollars (billions in today's currency) into radio advertising in the hopes of reaching a massive consumer audience. Television looked to be no different. The secret to success was simple: write a catchy jingle and get it onto the airwaves.

The first inkling of a wrinkle in the plot came from the famous Columbia University sociologist Paul Lazarsfeld, whose work would revolutionize both politics and advertising. In 1944 Lazarsfeld coined the term *opinion leaders* to refer to a special group of people who were much more attuned to the media than everyone else. They became the social "influencers" from whom most other people learned about new media content. Lazarsfeld's idea disrupted the classical theory of broadcast media.

According to the established view, media messages traveled from broadcast stations to reach millions of people, directly influencing their opinions and behaviors. Audiences, in this view, were passive receptors, easily led. All an advertiser had to do was get its message on the airwaves and it could sell its product or promote its candidate with ease.

Lazarsfeld's discovery revealed a major flaw with this theory: in actuality, broadcast media influenced only a very small fraction of its audience. Most people were not swayed by these messages. But a core group of people—the opinion leaders— paid close attention to the media, and they influenced everyone else.

In 1955, Lazarsfeld and fellow sociologist Elihu Katz (whom

I've had the remarkable good fortune to have as a colleague at Penn) published a study that became the foundational work on opinion leadership, targeted marketing, political advertising, and influencer marketing.

Their idea was simple and revolutionary: although most media advertising fell on deaf ears, opinion leaders were the great hope for advertisers. These people were highly connected social stars who could spread advertisers' messages to the masses. When advertisers, politicians, and public-health officials sent out media signals, they needed to target opinion leaders. They were the gatekeepers to reaching and influencing broader society.

The implications were enormous: a small group of special people was the key to a trillion-dollar industry. Get the opinion leaders and you could get everyone.

Two decades ago, the idea (based in the work of Katz and Lazarsfeld) that highly connected influencers were the key to spreading everything from social movements to innovative technologies was crystallized in Malcolm Gladwell's ominous phrase, "the law of the few." Like Katz and Lazarsfeld, Gladwell theorized that social change depends on these *special people*—a small number of luminous social stars whose efforts are responsible for spreading new ideas and behaviors to the rest of us.

"The law of the few" is a notion that has become widely accepted partly because there are certain situations in which it works amazingly well.

Gladwell and others have recounted legendary stories of influential people such as the American revolutionary Paul Revere, whose terrific social connectedness enabled him to effectively spread the message about the arriving British invasion in 1775. Or fashion designer Isaac Mizrahi, whose status and popularity helped catapult an obsolete brand of children's shoe into a fashion craze among adults. Gladwell's point was to show how these special people were the key players in famous social "epidemics." These stories are compelling. Once we see the power of these well-connected people to shape the spread of information and ideas, it seems obvious that the success of any social-change effort would depend on their involvement.

Today we call this "influencer marketing." *Influencers* are the opinion leaders of the social-media age. And although the basic idea of influencer marketing is three quarters of a century old, it is still among the most popular practices used by industry leaders today.

But it is based in a myth—one I call the *myth of the influencer.*

This myth tells us that whenever we want an idea or a trend or a movement to spread, we need to find these special people. While this myth works perfectly well to describe certain events in history, it turns from fact to fiction when it switches from the spread of news to the adoption of Twitter, or from the success of a fashionable shoe to the growth of the US civil rights movement.

In the 1970s, sociologists discovered a new truth about the spread of information that would shift the dominant thinking—not only in the study of consumer marketing and political campaigns, but also in the fields of mathematics, physics, epidemiology, and computer science. It would irrevocably change the best practices for spreading ideas in management, education, finance, and government.

This intellectual revolution would come to be known as *network science.* The big idea was that highly connected social stars do not explain how influence spreads. Rather, the stars' contacts—and their contacts' contacts, and those people's contacts, and so on—all form a massive geometrical pattern that underlies every society. This pattern explains how media signals are disseminated, and why certain social-change initiatives either succeed or fail.

This pattern is technically referred to as the *topology* of a social network. It is crucial for deciphering everything about social change: how and when game-changing technological innovations take off; whether contentious political ideas reach the mainstream; and under what circumstances movements for cultural change spread through a society. The new scientific insight was that the social star is just one link in a chain of network connections. Sometimes the social star—as you would expect—is the most important link in the chain; social stars can indeed initiate a large-scale spreading process. But at other times, as in the spread of the Aerosmith gesture in Second Life or the spread of Twitter across the US, social stars are not very helpful for spreading innovations. What's more, they can actively prevent it.

The challenge for social stars arises when it is not just a piece of news spreading but a social change—a new idea or behavior that faces countervailing influences from non-adopters. Because highly connected people are often difficult to bring aboard a change campaign, they can form roadblocks in the social network, slowing the spread of innovations and new ideas. In fact, this happens quite often: many of the most far-reaching innovations have succeeded by following alternative routes—detours around the social stars—to spread through the social network. Ultimately, this makes highly connected social stars the very *last* step in the change process.

When it comes to social change, the myth of the influencer obscures the real pathways that have led challenging and even controversial social, commercial, and political initiatives to succeed. The first step to seeing how change really works is to stop looking for the special *people* in the network and instead start looking for the special *places*.

The Berlin Study

In the fall of 1989, the Soviet Union was on the brink of collapse. It was the most important geopolitical moment since the Second World War, and everybody knew it. East Germans were gathering daily along the massive wall that separated them from the free West, squaring off with Soviet police who pointed machine guns filled with live rounds into the crowd.

Live news coverage showed a major historical event unfolding before everyone's eyes. But how could it be studied scientifically?

In the weeks after the Wall's fall, the most advanced scientific investigation into the social tumult of the era was being conducted by a renowned German sociologist, Karl-Dieter Opp. His procedure was precise and easy to follow. He got in his car in Hamburg and drove 240 miles across the former East German border to Leipzig, ground zero for the protests. Once Opp reached Leipzig, he got out of his car and took a deep breath. He then started walking around and interviewing people. It was a decidedly low-tech approach—but it was, at the time, the cutting edge of sociological technique.

He asked them, "Why did you join the protest?"

"Weren't you afraid of being killed or imprisoned?"

He talked to more than a thousand Leipzig citizens. He asked them to take surveys, and furiously scribbled notes into his scientific journal.

Opp started publishing his findings almost immediately. They quickly became the preeminent scientific record of the fall of the Berlin Wall. By 1994, Opp had published more than half a dozen scientific papers explaining how these social protests happened, and why they succeeded. Opp showed that people do not join revolutions just because they are unhappy. It is not simply their anger over civil abuses that leads people to revolt. Nor is it their frustration with poverty, nor their dreams of wealth, nor even the promise of freedom.

Rather, the key factor is their social networks.

German citizens joined the protest at the Wall because they had friends and family who were joining. They did it together. It was a collective process of social coordination. Once people found out that citizens like them were showing up and taking a stand, they believed they could make a difference, and they wanted to be part of it too.

A few years earlier, in 1988, Stanford University sociologist Doug McAdam had used methods similar to Opp's to conduct the first scientifically rigorous study of the US civil rights movement. Historically and culturally, the civil rights movement differed dramatically from the East German protests. But McAdam found the exact same behavioral pattern that Opp did: the key factor that explained why US citizens took part in some of the most dangerous and important social protests of the 1960s was that others in their social networks took part too.

People like Rosa Parks became focal points for the civil rights movement during the Montgomery bus boycotts. She took a public stand against government oppression and motivated others to follow. But Rosa Parks was effective because she was not alone; she was part of a massive social network of citizens who coordinated their efforts to protest segregation in the American South.

In the months leading up to Rosa Parks's infamous arrest in 1955 for her refusal to sit in the back of a city bus—the section legally assigned to citizens of one race as opposed to another— at least half a dozen other women from Montgomery were likewise arrested for refusing to comply with racially segregated seating. Chances are you've never heard of Claudette Colvin or the other protestors, but they were just as brave and just as vital to the movement for racial equality as Rosa Parks. The difference in terms of their impact was that they did not have the support of a massive coordinating social network around them. They were simply not located in the right part of the social network to spark a revolution.

In any struggle for freedom, countless brave souls stand up valiantly against oppression. Most of them are quickly silenced by the regime. But that's only if they act alone. Social networks are the coordinating sinews that allow large numbers of regular people from many different walks of life to act together. When people act as a coordinated whole, then any one person's action — that of Rosa Parks, for example — carries with it a mass of anonymous people. That is how revolutions are sparked.

By 1994, sociologists had figured out that social networks are the crucial factor for social change. But not until the new millennium did we finally have a technology that would allow us to observe these networks in action. The resulting discoveries would set sociology on a collision course with nearly a century of social-science theory.

That technology was social media.

What Happened (and Didn't) in Tahrir Square

On January 18, 2011, twenty-six-year-old Egyptian activist Asmaa Mahfouz was planning a revolution. Just a few weeks earlier, the world had witnessed a spontaneous eruption of revolution in Tunisia that successfully overthrew the country's authoritarian regime. Mahfouz wanted Egypt to follow in Tunisia's footsteps. She was not alone.

Mahfouz was a founding member of the "April 6 Youth Movement," one of Egypt's leading activist groups. The previous spring, on April 6, her group had successfully mobilized large worker protests against the inhumane conditions suffered by Egyptian laborers. This success was met with harsh retaliation. Many of the protesters were jailed, and some were beaten. None of them escaped the wrath of Egypt's despotic leader, Hosni Mubarak.

Mahfouz was a popular and charismatic leader. She was savvy about social media, and she had successfully used her Facebook and Twitter accounts to gain tens of thousands of followers who supported her activism. In other words, she was a "connector" who stood at the center of a large social-media and activist community. Mahfouz had successfully organized protests in the past, and she was well positioned to organize another—particularly timely—protest against Mubarak's regime.

The recent success of the Tunisian revolution had given new confidence to activists in the Middle East. Revolution was in the air. Everyone could feel it.

The country was primed for action, and Mahfouz was the perfect person to set the powder keg ablaze. Not only was she well connected socially and technologically, but she was also a seasoned social organizer who had learned successful methods and techniques from earlier protest movements. Mahfouz's activism blog had tens of thousands of followers.

She announced to her massive audience that the time had come. Mahfouz rallied her followers to join her in Egypt's Tahrir Square on January 18. Her goal was to start an Egyptian revolution.

Her message had spread far and wide.

But her movement had not.

Mahfouz stepped into Egypt's Tahrir Square arm in arm with a small group of friends. But no one else was there. Except the police.

What went wrong?

Egyptian citizens knew they could trust Mahfouz. They knew her posts were sincere, her calls to action genuine. From everything we know about highly connected social stars, she would seem like precisely the right person to ignite a revolution.

But here's the catch: knowing that Mahfouz is a dedicated young activist also means knowing that she is different from most of us. Most of us have children, spouses, or elderly parents to think about, jobs to consider, or houses to protect. In other words, while we may admire the Mahfouzes of the world, we also know that they do not have the same concerns that we have. They are typically young and righteous and full of moral clarity. They are also far more willing to step into harm's way than most of us who have families and businesses and reputations to think about. Whereas activists may circulate their calls to action far and wide, rarely do they inspire tens of thousands of regular citizens to brave police retaliation and take to the streets.

So, what was different in Berlin, the US South, and Tunisia that enabled social revolutions there to catch on among ordinary people?

The events seven days later would reveal that it was social networks.

On January 25, Mahfouz and her friends again walked into Tahrir Square, but this time they were joined by tens of thousands of fellow Egyptians. It was one of the most shocking uprisings since the fall of the Soviet Union. The Tahrir Square protest grew into an Egyptian revolution that toppled the Mubarak regime.

In the years since, the world media, and many international human-rights organizations, have deservingly celebrated Mahfouz for her bravery and resolve. Mahfouz's posts were impassioned and compelling, and they undoubtedly placed her in harm's way. But that alone cannot explain the success of the revolution. Why were her posts leading up to January 18 so futile, while her efforts leading up to January 25 overthrew a government?

To understand what happened—not only in Egypt but also in Tunisia, Yemen, Morocco, and Libya—we need to look beyond the Mahfouzes of the world and their fervent calls for revolution; we need to understand how activism flowed out into the social networks of non-activists. How did the expansive social topology among Egyptian citizens actively coordinate them on a single action?

The story of Egypt's uprising is the story of social networks. It is the story of the modestly connected network periphery where most people live. Because the network periphery is so large and unexceptional, it can appear less significant than the networks of highly connected social stars. But the truth is just the opposite: when it comes to social change, the network periphery is where all the action is.

Many thoughtful people have speculated that social media was responsible for the success of the Arab Spring. Because of the way new-media tools such as Facebook and Twitter connected people across the Middle East, it is tempting to think that these social technologies allowed social stars like Mahfouz to enjoy greater reach and influence than they ever had before. But the wealth of scientific evidence from that year actually leads to a different conclusion.

In 2011, people's connections on social media were, as they are today, surprisingly prosaic. The contours of personal influence on social media are not that different from how social networks operated a few generations ago, well before the advent of social media. Over the last fifty years, network studies have all reported the same basic patterns of social ties: personal networks composed of friends, family members, neighbors, and coworkers. The networks that enabled the success of the civil rights movement in the American South in the 1960s are remarkably similar to those that led to the fall of the Berlin Wall in East Germany in 1989. And both are remarkably similar to the networks that triggered Arab Spring revolutions in 2011. The important difference with the Arab Spring was that—for the first time— we had a way to *measure* how these networks operate in real time.

In 2011, social media gave us an exceptionally powerful tool for studying social change—a lens through which social scientists could observe the spread of activism among leaders, friends, neighbors, students, teachers, business owners, and parents. Hashtags such as #jan25 became social contagions that unveiled the real-time spread of revolutionary action. Uploaded and time-stamped photographs documented the number of people in the streets, revealing correlations between social-media activity and protest marches, police violence, and escalating civil unrest. For the first time, social scientists had a precise record of how a social movement unfolded. And that record enabled us to see clearly, for the first time, that highly connected influencers were *not* at the center of the action.

Analyzing the Arab Spring

Zachary Steinert-Threlkeld is an energetic political scientist at UCLA. For nearly a decade, Steinert-Threlkeld has been dedicated to studying the social-media records of countries like Tunisia and Egypt, trying to understand how patterns of social connectivity may have contributed to the unlikely events that transpired in the spring of 2011. While completing his PhD at the University of California, San Diego, he examined more than thirteen million tweets to see whether a common pattern connected Egypt, Libya, and Morocco to all the other places where revolution had erupted. As it turned out, one did: in every case, whenever social-media activity translated into real social activism — that is, people marching in streets — the bulk of messages did not come from the highly connected stars in the social network. Instead, the greatest predictor of activism was coordinated online activity in the network periphery.

In late January 2011, the chain reaction among modestly connected groups of regular people in the periphery of Egypt's social network created a reinforcing pattern of engagement. A powerful social contagion spread.

As the Egyptian protests grew, citizens in the network periphery provided one another with information about police movements, protest hot spots, and the location of blockades. Their coordination was logistical, but it was also emotional. Citizens used hashtags such as #egypt and #jan25 to show solidarity with one another. They posted photos and shared firsthand accounts that spread awareness of the movement to people outside Cairo. Their messages, posts, videos, and chats triggered an emotional connection among friends and family — the feeling that they were part of a movement that surrounded them. That feeling mobilized them to take to the streets. These peripheral networks soon triggered a chain reaction of protest events that spread from one Egyptian city to another, from Cairo to Giza to Waraq Al Hadar.

The data from the Arab Spring showed the same historical pattern observed in the US civil rights movement and the East German protests, but with far greater clarity and resolution. It is also what Adamic and her team saw in the spread of the Aerosmith gesture in Second Life, and it is the same network signature that underwrote the explosive growth of Twitter across the US.

Several generations after Paul Lazarsfeld's discovery of opinion leaders, we finally have a new kind of data at our disposal. We can now say with confidence that the crucial networks of social change are not the hub-and-radiating-spoke patterns that surround highly connected "influencers," but rather the interlocking ties that permeate the network periphery. If social change is going to gain traction, it has to start there—among people who face the same choices and challenges that we do, people whose coordination and acceptance form an invisible but essential part of our daily routines. The network periphery is a powerful place. It is where the strong, broad currents of social change take hold and expand.

The Right Place

The myth of the influencer is a story of change that appeals to our love of heroes. It is romantic to think of one special person working against all odds to remake the course of history. The key flaw in that story is not the idea that one person can have an impact. Indeed, when I show you the science behind the #MeToo movement, you will see that it is true that a few people—and in some cases, a single person—can be the difference between the success or failure of a movement. The main distinction between my story and the one that has been told for over three quarters of a century is that these key people are not *special*. They are no different from the rest of us. In fact, they may even *be* us. They are simply the people located in the right part of the social network at the right time. At that moment, their actions can make all the difference.

This doesn't mean that I am going to tell you a story in which social change is merely a series of random events. If that were true, there would be no useful way to study it scientifically. And it would be impossible to make predictions.

Instead, I will show you why predicting social change is difficult...but not impossible. I will show you that "the right time and place" is not a random occurrence, but a measurable feature of social networks. And I will show you how to identify these essential network patterns, and how to target them.

The hero of this book is not a celebrity or a social star, but rather a *location* within our social networks. It is not a person, but a place. It is the kind of place where the confluence of social ties across different social groups strengthens bonds between families, partnerships across organizations, and solidarity within nations.

The science of social networks shows that these places also exist online. The hero of the Arab Spring revolutions was neither Twitter nor Facebook, but rather the pattern of community that formed in those virtual networks, creating surprisingly effective pathways for the expansion of social coordination. The rest of this book will show you how to identify these special places in our social networks, and how to use them to spread your own change initiatives. What you read will help you answer two questions that are at the forefront of what all parents, teachers, voters, businesspeople, policymakers, public-health workers, entrepreneurs, and activists want to know: How does change happen, and what can we do to help?

CHAPTER 2

The Myth of Virality: The Unexpected Weakness of Weak Ties

In the spring of 1347, the Black Plague landed in Marseille, France. Ship-borne rats from Sicily and Crete, carrying infected *Xenopsylla cheopis* — "Oriental rat fleas" — scurried into the city. The fleas' intestines were bursting with the plague bacterium. They injected a heavy dose of the disease directly into the bloodstream of everyone they bit, resulting in immediate infection. Within days the rats had infested the city, and so had the disease.

Once the plague had overtaken Marseille, it began to cascade outward across Europe. By mid-1348 it had spread west to Barcelona and east to Florence. The more cities it hit, the faster the wave front propagated. Six months later, every city in western Spain, southern Italy, and northern France had been reached. Paris had fallen, as had Rouen on the northern coast of France, as well as Frankfurt. Passengers sailing from northern France to London carried the disease across the English Channel. That autumn, the plague spread through London, and by late 1349 it had traveled all the way to Scotland. On the

Continent, the disease traversed the mountainous terrain of northeastern Europe, overtaking Prague, Vienna, and even Scandinavia. By 1351, one-third of Europe's population had died. Town by town, Europe had been ravaged.

The Importance of Weak Ties

The Black Plague is one of the most dramatic examples of disease propagation in European history. It also reminds us how different things are today. In the fourteenth century, communication networks were determined by the geography of the continent and low-tech transportation. Infected fleas traveled from town to town on infected animals carried by cart, wheelbarrow, carriage, and sometimes boat. Today, modern diseases don't waste time traveling by land or sea. Air travel has radically accelerated the spread of infectious disease. In 2009, the H1N1 virus spread across the globe in a matter of weeks—from New York to San Francisco to London, Rio de Janeiro, Sydney, Frankfurt, Tokyo, and Hong Kong.

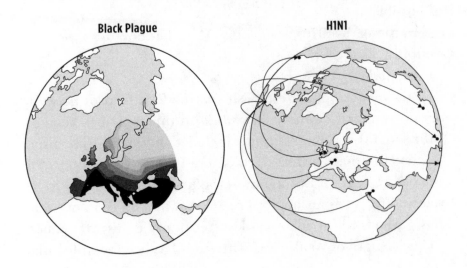

Black Plague   H1N1

In 2020, COVID-19 spread across the entire globe just as fast, and with far greater impact. So why did the Black Plague take years to conquer Europe, whereas modern diseases spread to all of the world's cities in a matter of weeks? The answer is obvious: faster, better transportation networks.

Now consider what that means.

It means that even though the pathways followed by the Black Plague look different from those followed by modern diseases such as H1N1 or COVID-19, the notion of *viral spreading* applies equally to all of them. Strictly speaking, the Black Plague is a bacterium and COVID-19 is a virus; but they are, of course, both diseases. Given the right travel options, the Black Plague and COVID-19 would spread in the same fashion—globally and quickly.

They are contagions that spread through close proximity, and they will both exploit expansive networks to travel much faster around the world.

What else that once spread slowly, over land and sea, might now spread quickly and virally, if we could just find better and faster networks to expose it to as many people in as many places as possible?

In the early 1970s, sociologist Mark Granovetter gave us a definitive answer:

Everything!

His answer helped establish the modern field of network science. In fact, Granovetter's work on this topic has been so influential that he was recently included among the Thomson Reuters Citation Laureates, considered the top contenders for the Nobel Prize in Economics—the first sociologist ever to be selected for such an honor. Preeminent among the work that has garnered him this well-deserved fame is his first paper, "The Strength of Weak Ties." This study has been so influential that it is the most-cited scientific paper today in the entire field of sociology.

Granovetter's idea is powerful and clear. It hinges on his elegant distinction between "strong" ties and "weak" ties. Your close friends and family are your trusted strong ties. They make up your inner social circle. Your casual acquaintances—the people you meet at a conference, in a class, or on vacation— are your weak ties. They make up your outer circle—the random connections in your orbit. And because they exist outside your usual orbit, they connect you to new people with whom you would likely never intersect otherwise.

It's not hard to see how the distinction between strong and weak ties applies to disease spreading. The Black Plague spread through strong ties—tightly knit social connections that linked people to their families, friends, and neighborhoods. But that's only because there *weren't* many weak ties in the 1340s: most people lived their whole lives in the same small community where everyone knew everybody else. Travel outside these communities was rare. It was a world of stasis, slow technology, and strong ties.

Of course, modern transportation and communication technologies have changed all that. We now intersect with people from all over the world all the time, whether we realize it or not. These random contacts have families and friends whose paths will likely never cross yours. Because these people exist outside your immediate social network, any contact you have with them gives you a rare connection to *their* social networks— to people whom you will, in all likelihood, never meet. These "weak" connections do not usually evolve into "strong" ones. Because you do not share friends or contacts with these acquaintances, the weak ties you make typically do not form lasting social bonds. But they are extremely effective at spreading viruses such as COVID-19 quickly and widely, across the globe.

The Redundancy Effect

Granovetter's groundbreaking work on weak and strong ties was based on his study of how people find information about job opportunities. Granovetter argued that while those we are connected to by strong ties obviously matter to us the most, those connected to us by weak ties are responsible for most of the large-scale spreading processes we are part of.

To see why Granovetter's idea has been so influential, think for a minute about the strong ties in your own life. These are the people you would not hesitate to lend money to, or whom you might ask to watch your kids for an evening. In other words, they are people you trust. One thing you will quickly notice about these familiar and trusted people is that their social networks overlap with yours. Many of your strong ties already know each other, and they also know many of one another's *other* contacts. Your strong ties are often closely tied together.

Granovetter explained that the overlapping structure of strong ties makes them inefficient for spreading information and ideas. Why? Because overlap leads to *redundancy*. If you try to use your strong ties to propagate a new idea, each person who spreads the word will probably wind up telling it to someone who has already heard it, whether from you or from a mutual friend. Even if the message is intuitive and "sticky" (more on that shortly), if it spreads solely through strong ties it will end up ricocheting around the same community of people without traveling very far.

In a competitive landscape, where your idea is fighting for attention against a sea of other ideas, redundancy is an especially big problem. Every time someone explains your idea to a person who has already heard about it, a network tie is "wasted."

That tie could carry your idea to someone new, but instead it takes it back to the same people who've already heard it.

Your network would serve you much better if each of your contacts could spread your idea to people who have never heard it before. Instead of wasting time bouncing around redundant networks, your idea could be transported by each new contact to far-flung places, where it could reach lots of new people much faster. The *weakness* of strong ties is that we wind up talking among ourselves, often preaching to the converted. The *strength* of weak ties is that they expose our ideas to a vast global network of fresh faces whom we may never meet in person, but who may nevertheless find out about our ideas. Weak ties provide *reach*.

Based on this crucial advantage of reach over redundancy, Granovetter concluded that the people you know through weak ties are the best people to enlist in your job-hunting efforts, your promotional campaigns, your product-advertising ventures, and your social initiatives. Weak ties are far-reaching channels that allow us to connect with many more people—and, more important, many different types of people.

Stanley Milgram's Postcards

In 1967, when Granovetter was just a graduate student, the stage was being set for his groundbreaking insights by another luminary in the history of social networks, Stanley Milgram.

In the early 1960s, Milgram had won international recognition for publishing his now-infamous studies of obedience and authority—often referred to as "the Milgram Experiments." By the mid-1960s, Milgram had parlayed his fame into a career move from Yale to Harvard that would allow him to turn his attention to a new problem: he wanted to discover the typical social distance between Americans.

This was a hot topic at the time. A lot of scientists were trying to figure out how to solve this puzzle of social networks. An enterprising group of mathematicians at the Massachusetts Institute of Technology had started interviewing hundreds of people in an attempt to derive the mathematical principles underlying Americans' social connectedness. Based on their calculations, the MIT mathematicians had speculated that most people were only two steps apart.

This was a good start, but Milgram noticed at least two major flaws with this approach. First, a lot of people's contacts are strong ties. This means that if you interview several hundred people from the same area who all know one another, it would not necessarily tell you much about how connected they were to the rest of the country. Second, there are often clear socioeconomic divides within people's social networks. As Milgram put it, "poor people tend to be among other poor people." As coarse as his phrasing was, he had a point.

Social networks in the 1960s were not a random mass of crisscrossing ties. People tended to live and work within small communities. Wealthier people tended to know wealthier people, and poorer people tended to know poorer people. These divides were not just economic. Racial segregation was a huge factor in American social networks, as was religious segregation. Any approach that sampled a small group of personal networks was unlikely to reveal anything about national connectedness. That is, not unless it could somehow also identify the weak ties that bridged from one social group to the next.

In his first year at Harvard, Milgram devised an unusual "experimental" approach to studying social networks. It was not a controlled experiment like a medical trial, in which one group of people gets a treatment and another group does not. Rather, Milgram's approach was more akin to a series of carefully repeated observations.

Milgram pitched his idea to the funders at Harvard's Laboratory of Social Relations. He asked them to consider whether it might be possible to measure the number of social steps between a random person in the middle of the country (say, a widowed grocery-store clerk in Omaha, Nebraska) and a stranger on the East Coast (say, a stockbroker living in Sharon, Massachusetts). Once Milgram had piqued their interest, he offered a solution.

If the laboratory funded him, he would randomly select several dozen people in the Midwest—a widowed grocery clerk, among others—and mail them each a packet of prepaid postcards. Each of these people would be given the task of sending their postcards to people who they thought might be able to forward the postcard message to a selected target person (the stockbroker in Massachusetts). But there was a catch: the senders in the Midwest couldn't just look the stockbroker up in the phone book and target him directly. They could send their postcards only to targets they knew *personally*. Because it was unlikely that any Midwest sender would know the Massachusetts stockbroker personally, Milgram hypothesized they would mail their postcards to people whom they imagined to be socially similar, or "close" to the Massachusetts stockbroker—for instance, someone who worked in the financial sector in Chicago, or someone who happened to live in the state of Massachusetts.

Milgram's idea was that once the original sources in the Midwest sent their postcards to their intermediate targets, these targets would then become the next round of senders. He speculated that this chain of senders and targets would keep going until the postcards finally reached their final destination — the stockbroker in Sharon, Massachusetts. Milgram might have asked the funders to ponder his proposal by trying to guess, "How many steps would there be in the chain of social connections from the Midwest to Massachusetts? How many sequences of postcards going from friend to friend—from sender to target—would it take to finally reach the stockbroker?"

Milgram's proposal observed a key principle of network science. If he ran this study once, the length of the social chain from the Midwest to Massachusetts might be an idiosyncratic feature of the personality of the grocery clerk, or the social habits of the stockbroker. But if he was able to repeat this process enough times with enough randomly chosen people, he would be able to reliably calculate an average distance across all of the different chains. This simple procedure would reveal approximately how far apart most Americans are from one another.

It was an ingenious proposal. Milgram got his requested funds—$680—and was off to the races.

The answer he found is now so famous that it has become legend: six degrees of separation. Some letter chains, stretching from Nebraska to New England, took only three steps. Others took seventeen steps. But the average distance was six.

Just as Milgram's remarkable findings were making headlines, Granovetter was beginning his graduate studies at Harvard. It took only four years for his piercing intellect to boil Milgram's work down to one fundamental insight into the nature of social networks.

Granovetter realized that weak ties are the crucial links that enabled messages to jump from one community to the next. They are the bridges that bind diverse communities together, turning a nation of racially and economically disjointed regions into a single connected network.

The scope of Granovetter's idea was staggering. Weak ties are not just people's interpersonal sources for information about new jobs. They are the backbone of national and transnational connectedness. They are the nonredundant links that reach outside people's communities and connect nations together. For this reason, they are also the fastest way to spread the word about a new product, change initiative, or political candidate.

In 1967, there were 200 million Americans. Milgram showed that there were only six steps between any of them. Granovetter soon explained why.

Today—thanks to the internet—weak ties are far more extensive. They link us to people we meet on dating sites, in health communities, in political chat rooms, in multiplayer games, through investment networks, and everywhere else we connect on social media. On a planet with seven billion people, weak ties bring everyone much closer together than anyone ever thought possible.

The impact of Granovetter's idea has only grown with the expansion of social media. From the Arab Spring to the Aerosmith gesture, the current wisdom is that everything that spreads effectively owes its success to the ability of far-reaching weak ties to escape local redundancy.

The Weakness of Weak Ties

Granovetter's idea of the power of weak ties comes from the science of infectious diseases. When it comes to biological pathogens, such as the COVID-19 virus or the measles, simple contact with one infected person—shaking hands or simply talking—can spread the virus. The more weak ties there are in an infected person's network, the easier it is for the disease to spread far and wide.

This is also true for information. In Milgram's study, for instance, it took only one contact between a painter in Council Bluffs, Iowa, and an editor in Belmont, Massachusetts, to propagate the message from the Midwest to New England. For decades, we have assumed that everything—not just germs and information but products, social norms, political movements, social technologies, and even religious beliefs—spreads the same way that infectious diseases do. Especially now, in our globally connected world, it seems clearer than ever that weak ties are the key to the successful spread of innovative technologies and social-change efforts.

Right?

Wrong.

When I began to conduct my own studies of how change happens, I was stunned to find that none of the data on the spread of social-media technologies, social movements, or social norms confirmed the importance of weak ties. In fact, quite the opposite. Technologies such as Twitter did not zip across the globe via weak ties. They spread through overlapping networks of *strong* ties, often geographically—from neighborhood to neighborhood, or from town to town. The distinctive network pathways that Twitter used to reach 300 million adopters in just a few years looked nothing like pathways of viral spreading. Twitter *did* spread with amazing speed, but it did not spread like a virus.

Nor did Facebook, or Skype. In fact, none of the successful communication technologies that dominate our wired world did. And these modern communication technologies are not exceptional. It's the same for modern social movements, such as the Arab Spring and Black Lives Matter; for modern social norms, such as the growing acceptance of same-sex marriage and the legalization of marijuana; and for the rapid growth of support for alternative political candidates. None of the major behavioral or social changes that have happened in the last half-century have spread the way viruses do. They have spread not through *reach* but through the phenomenon that, for years, network scientists believed to be the great enemy of effective contagion: *redundancy*. These findings overturn half a century of conventional wisdom—and they reveal the *limits* of weak ties.

Redundancy will not help to spread the measles. You can't get infected twice—it takes only one contact to do it. But when it comes to a new idea, the experience of being exposed to it from two, three, or four people within your network of strong ties—*that* changes the idea into a norm. It changes how you think and feel about it. And that is the overlooked power of redundancy.

The Twitter Quake

Near the end of 2005, it was clear that the internet startup Odeo was going to fail. Evan Williams, the ex-Googler who had helped start Odeo, realized that Apple's new iTunes podcasting platform had, overnight, made Odeo's podcasting technology obsolete. Evan and his colleagues—Biz Stone, Noah Glass, and Jack Dorsey—needed another idea. After weeks of unbridled hackathons and brainstorming sessions, Noah struck upon on a promising idea: a microblogging platform called Twttr.

Several key technological and marketing steps were essential for transforming this San Francisco start-up into the internet juggernaut we know today as Twitter. But the event that gave this technology its start was a natural one: an earthquake. In August 2006, just a few months after Twitter's official launch, an earthquake hit San Francisco. It was small by Bay Area standards— magnitude 3.6—but the scary thing about earthquakes is that once they start, you never know how big they're going to be. Within minutes of the first tremors, a service that had previously been used to post mundane updates about people's lunches had suddenly become a vital lifeline to friends and family. Twitter's server activity exploded, as messages came flying across the network, reporting real-time updates from neighborhoods that were hit, relaying information on tremors and aftershocks. Instantly, Twitter gained real social value for people in the Bay Area. They were glued to their accounts for the better part of the day.

It was an aha moment for the company and its investors. Within a few weeks, Twitter grew from a few hundred users to several thousand. It was a first glimpse of a key factor in Twitter's success—which would play out on a national scale two years later, during the 2008 US presidential election. Twitter's value was both social and topical: it was a compelling source of news and updates, but it was not like mainstream media, which sorts through and organizes each day's news. Instead, it was a real-time account of how unfolding events were being experienced by large numbers of regular people. Each person had a unique perspective to offer on events that mattered to everyone.

Whether the event was a parade, a concert, an earthquake, a protest, or an election, the immediacy of social feedback on unfolding events compelled people to pay attention to their Twitter feeds.

Unlike a television station, Twitter's particular value was that people could hear the news from other people they were interested in talking to. Twitter adopters were selective about their connections. How could this kind of selective social technology spread from a few neighborhoods in San Francisco to 300 million users?

Surprisingly, Twitter did not spread like COVID-19; it spread like the Black Plague. Twitter membership grew locally. It spread across the nation through strong ties.

In 2007, Twitter expanded throughout San Francisco. By February 2008, it had reached critical mass in the Bay Area and become one of the region's mainstream social technologies. But it had not yet exploded across the internet—or anywhere else, really.

It was spreading, but not like a virus.

It makes sense that Twitter first took hold in the Bay Area, since that's where the technology got its start. But on the Web, geographic locality is not a constraint. From San Francisco, it could go anywhere. Why wouldn't Twitter do what modern viruses do, jumping from San Francisco to other areas of high population density such as New York or LA?

If you look at the US map and chart the growth of Twitter from February 2008 through February 2009, you can see Twitter's runway to success written across the American landscape.

From San Francisco, Twitter expanded regionally. In March and April 2008, it reached critical mass in the nearby towns of San Mateo, Santa Clara, Mountain View, Santa Cruz, San Jose, and Berkeley.

Twitter was flowing out across the California countryside. In April 2008, Twitter looked like it would reach the small mountain town of Portola—just a few hours east of San Francisco—within a few days.

Then something weird happened. The technology stopped spreading geographically. It would be half a year before it finally hit critical mass in LA and San Diego, and a full year before it reached Portola.

Twitter was still growing, but not in California. Instead, it followed an entirely unexpected course that revealed something new about how innovations spread in the modern era.

Twitter's next major stop was not New York. Nor Chicago. Twitter leaped to Cambridge, Massachusetts.

This cross-country jump looks like a perfect example of Granovetter's theory of weak ties. The geographic part of Twitter's story appeared to be over. Now that it was bicoastal, Twitter seemed destined to expand like COVID-19, reaching every major city within a matter of weeks.

So it seemed. And so Twitter's founders hoped.

But again Twitter's growth defied common sense: its next stage of expansion was geographic once more. This time, Twitter membership thickened throughout the Boston area, spreading to nearby towns and suburbs, just as it had in San Francisco. It was once again flowing across the countryside just like the Black Plague.

This was a puzzling pattern of growth.

If Twitter was spreading geographically, how could it reach Boston, Massachusetts, before Portola, California?

It couldn't. Twitter must have been spreading across weak ties, like a virus.

But if it was spreading like a virus, why would it spread through the Bay Area before reaching any other cities? And once it spread to Cambridge, Massachusetts, why would it spread to the Boston suburbs and outlying towns of Massachusetts before reaching New York or LA?

In fact, Twitter was doing something different: it was following a new and invisible pattern of strong ties, a pattern that exists within local neighborhoods but also stretches across the country. Twitter was exploiting a unique feature of the modern era—networks of people who are socially close together but geographically far apart.

Twitter's nonstop trip from San Francisco to Boston was different from anything that network scientists had seen before. It was not like an airplane flight carrying a deadly virus, nor like a postcard carrying a novel piece of information. It was a social-recruitment campaign that grew its following by spreading almost exclusively through strong friendship networks, which were both local and remote.

To understand this uniquely modern pattern of network expansion, we need to consider this question: What do people in San Francisco have in common with people in Cambridge, that they *do not* have in common with people in the rural mountain town of Portola? Well, MIT, for one, and Stanford, Harvard, Northeastern, Berkeley, Boston University, and Tufts for a few others. These are top schools that in the late 1990s and early 2000s produced tens of thousands of commercially and technologically minded young graduates. A large number of them either stayed in Boston to work in the Tech Corridor along Route 128 or moved west to the promise of Silicon Valley. Separated by a continent, these graduates maintained a network of strong ties, forged both by their formative years in school together and by their shared professional ambitions. Many of these people knew one another and had friends in common. The social networks between Silicon Valley and Boston in the mid-2000s were densely interwoven, populated by people enthusiastic about the burgeoning world of social media who could reinforce one another's interests in using a new social technology.

More often than not, strong ties are local. It's natural that physical proximity is typically correlated with tie strength, and this correlation is an important reason why social contagions such as Twitter tend to spread geographically.

But strong ties can also be remote. A big difference between the social networks of Milgram's generation and those of the present is that today it is more common for strong ties to connect regions that are spatially distant. Strong ties are less bound by physical space now than at any other time in history.

This new pattern of strong ties offers essential insight into the nationwide expansion of not just Twitter but also Facebook, Skype, and other social technologies in the mid-2000s. All of these innovations gained their momentum through expansive networks of strong ties.

Facebook's Blue Circles

In 2016, three out of every four Americans were on Facebook. People varied in how frequently they used it, and how active they were once logged in. But with 239 million US citizens enrolled, it offered the largest, most comprehensive view of social networks in the country's history.

That summer, a team of young economists from Harvard, Princeton, New York University, and Facebook decided to use Facebook's unprecedented social-network data to revisit Milgram's classic question: How connected is our country? But this time they weren't taking a small sample. They were able to observe nearly the entire population.

Even before Milgram—since the 1940s—social scientists such as Paul Lazarsfeld and Elihu Katz had been trying to figure out how many connections people had, and what those connections looked like. It is an important question, for social connectedness is correlated with every major social outcome that Americans care about—from the success of the civil rights movement to the national rate of suicide to the financial well-being of the middle class.

Researchers have been able to demonstrate that it is not just the number of connections we have, but the *pattern* of those connections that makes a difference in our lives. People who live within more stable, reinforcing social networks tend to live longer, more successful lives. There are also notable economic advantages to forming an expansive network of weak ties that reach far and wide. But having *too many* weak ties is a sign of impoverished social capital. People need a balance, and one of the key features of both financial success and personal well-being is having a lot of strong ties in your network.

To find out how connected Americans are, the 2016 team of economists created a massive map of the US Facebook network. They expected to see an unruly tangle of lines crisscrossing the country—the chaos of American life in the age of social media. Instead, they found something very different: the vast majority of people's Facebook contacts were geographically close to them.

The digital map of the Facebook network these economists created is stunning to look at. (You can find a link to the map in the "Notes and Further Reading" section at the back of this book.) Put your cursor on any spot in the country and the map lights up bright blue in every area with social connections to the spot you chose.

One location on the map has, by far, more connections to other areas of the country than any other place. When you put your cursor on this spot, the entire country lights up. Can you guess what it is? Here's a hint: it's not New York. LA, or Chicago. The majority of people in those cities are heavily connected within their local communities.

The answer is Onslow, North Carolina.

Many of us have never heard of Onslow. But if you have family or friends in the Marine Corps, chances are that you know about Base Camp Lejeune. It's one of the primary training and deployment centers for the marines, and it's the reason why so many people come to Onslow. Or, more accurately, it's the reason why so many people go *through* Onslow. Facebook networks in this area have unrivaled national reach because people do not stay—they're just passing through. Their close friends and family—their strong ties—are elsewhere. By contrast, even college towns such as Austin, Texas, Berkeley, California, and Bloomington, Indiana, show a surprising density of connections within residents' immediate community. As connected as the world is today, people still build their networks where they live. Even on Facebook, people's lives are entrenched within the towns and cities where they socialize, date, and study, and where many of them ultimately settle. Onslow is an outlier.

Tip O'Neill, the former Speaker of the House of Representatives, famously said, "All politics is local." That's still true today—and true about more than politics. People care about their town and their neighbors. And the key to these connections is not just geography. It is strong ties.

Certain cities in the US are politically and culturally out of sync with the broader region around them. Austin, for example, is an island of liberal, avant-garde culture surrounded by a sea of conservative values. Austin's signature SXSW media extravaganza, where Twitter made its major debut, stands in stark contrast to the cattle ranches and oil derricks that surround it. Unsurprisingly, placing your cursor on San Francisco on the Facebook map does not light up much in the state of Texas. But it does create a glow around Austin. Twitter reached critical mass in Austin months before it reached any other part of the state.

The growth pattern of Twitter (as well as a host of other

twenty-first-century technologies) reveals a spreading process that is unique to strong ties. The diffusion pattern of these technologies *looks* entirely new. But the explanation has been there for centuries. It has simply been impossible to see clearly until now.

The Virus Template

There is a good reason why the viral theory has stuck around so long. For all of recorded history, the virus has been the template for our understanding of social spreading. Every major social contagion—of writing, of Christianity, and of the Black Plague— followed the same geographic contours, "infecting" one community and then progressing slowly to a neighboring one. It makes intuitive sense to suppose that everything else would spread the same way. And it makes sense that once modern transportation and communication technologies made it possible for diseases to travel faster and farther, through weak ties, everything else would spread that way too. But the most striking revelation from the new science of social networks is that many behaviors and beliefs spread a different way. And, what's more, they always have.

It was simply not possible to see the distinctive style of spreading exhibited by social contagions such as Twitter until the data were more accessible. In our globally networked world, diseases and information have been given the chance to spread in new ways through precisely measured and highly trafficked networks. So, too, have behaviors and beliefs. Our modern communication infrastructure has revealed, for the first time, the precise pathways that behaviors follow as they move through populations, and how distinctive these pathways often are when compared with the pathways taken by diseases and by simple informational contagions.

CHAPTER 3

The Myth of Stickiness: Why Great Innovations Fail

Ralph Waldo Emerson offered an inspiring view of product innovation and the opportunity it posed: "If a man has good corn or wood, or boards, or pigs, to sell, or can make better chairs or knives, crucibles or church organs, than anybody else, you will find a broad, hard-beaten road to his house, though it be in the woods." More colloquially, "If you build a better mousetrap, the world will beat a path to your door."

It is inspiring. Unfortunately, it is also wrong. The market has often rewarded a lesser innovation with greater success. Take the QWERTY and Dvorak keyboards. The QWERTY keyboard is the one you probably use every day. The much-less-popular Dvorak keyboard was developed by a psychologist in 1936 to increase the speed and reduce the strain of typing. From a design perspective, the Dvorak is far superior: 70 percent of keystrokes are in the home row, which means you can type thousands of words from the home row with minimal effort. You can type only a few hundred words from the home row of a QWERTY keyboard. One Dvorak enthusiast panned the QWERTY keyboard as "a pair of running shoes that are made of concrete."

And that enthusiast wasn't just a lone cranky brand loyalist, unwilling to change. From the 1930s to the 1970s, at least half a dozen scientific tests using human subjects found the Dvorak keyboard to be the superior design. Yet still, only about 10,000 diehard outliers use it today. Despite its obvious advantages, the Dvorak keyboard suffered a decisive loss to QWERTY.

The case of VHS and Beta videocassette recorders is similar. Experts agreed that Betamax was better designed and more cost-effective than VHS. Betamax knew it had a superior product and pushed hard to spread the word through expensive marketing and advertising campaigns. But it didn't work. VHS won out. Comparable stories of inferior products outcompeting superior ones are almost a cliché in economics. The dustbins of history are littered with "market imperfections"—examples of the market's failure to select the option widely acknowledged to have been the better choice.

So why does the "fittest" product—best-designed, highest-performing, and most cost-efficient—frequently *not* survive? The main reason is that success in the marketplace often has less to do with a company's *better products* than with its *better ways of using a network*. If an inferior product gains greater traction early on with individuals in the crucial network locations, a superior competitor will typically fail to dislodge it. The power of incumbency is huge.

Our natural inclination when we run up against this problem has been to go back to the drawing board, tweaking, redesigning, and repackaging the innovation to make it "stickier"—easier to use, more striking, more discussion-worthy or more exciting, and less expensive.

But innovators from Silicon Valley to South Korea have learned that catchy advertising, aggressive marketing, and impressive science are often not enough to change people's beliefs and behaviors. Cultural and social norms embedded in our networks can create enduring opposition to change. The story of change is not only a story of pioneering social innovations that disrupt markets and challenge the powerful. Remarkably, it is also a story of how the people who are most in need of new solutions often resist them. Promising social and technological innovations—such as sustainable farming techniques, renewable energy sources, new educational programming, and even lifesaving medications—are often resisted by the very people who need them the most. Regardless of how they're packaged, new products and ideas are not easily adopted when they threaten established beliefs and social norms.

Later in this book, we will explore new scientific discoveries showing how tipping points can be used to disrupt social norms. You will see how an innovation campaign on the brink of becoming a national fiasco instead became one of the most successful initiatives in US history. I will show you how social networks transformed this failed marketing effort into an amazingly effective product campaign—reaching 100 percent market saturation and saving thousands of families in the process.

First, though, I want to show you why notions of product "stickiness"—the idea that the success of an innovation depends on its having specific features, such as practicality, novelty, tangibility, and emotional triggers—can be misguided, leading entire product lines not only to fail but to *backfire*. You will see how the lessons learned from famous innovation campaigns— ranging from Google's attempt to a spread a wearable technology to the National Institutes of Health's attempt to spread a lifesaving medication—force us to think differently about why new behaviors do and don't catch on.

Google's Grapefruit Problem

In 2013, Google looked invincible. For over a decade, it had controlled the global search engine market, and its Web-based email client, Gmail, had recently overtaken Yahoo! Mail and AOL Mail as the top Webmail client in the world. Google was ready to expand again. It was time, Google's leaders decided, to make the move to hardware.

Their innovation was called Google Glass.

Glass is a cyborg technology. It is voice-activated digital eyewear that gives the user direct access to streaming internet content, along with enhanced real-time capabilities to interact with the environment, for instance by recording and photographing elements in a person's visual field. It sounds both scary and cool. Certainly futuristic. This is what Google leaders thought, too. And they marketed it that way.

They invited a special group of culturally avant-garde and technologically sophisticated users to be part of the initial pool of members who would beta test the product. These people were chosen to be influencers. They would act as the key point of entry for introducing the product to the broader population. It's exactly the kind of marketing strategy that most of us would imagine:

Step one: Find the people who are most likely to accept this futuristic new technology.

Step two: Get them to be the "early adopters."

Step three: Sit back and watch as these social elites (who could afford a $1,500 pair of glasses) spread the technology to everyone else.

It's Influencer Marketing 101. But Google didn't stop there. It wanted to make sure its product would be "sticky."

Google wanted it to be remarkable, memorable, discussion-worthy, and unexpected. All the things that are supposed to propel an innovation to success.

Google also wanted it to be high-status. Part of what made Glass remarkable, memorable, and discussion-worthy was that it embodied a new kind of socio-technical sophistication.

It's similar to a strategy that has been used for decades by companies such as BMW, Ferrari, and Rolex to secure and expand their market positions. Any consumer who can afford their products wants other people to know about it because it signals something about their wealth, discernment, and life-style. It broadcasts their status. In the case of Google's Glass technology, the product would also signal that adopters were on the cutting edge of digital culture.

Strangely enough, this multi-sector, trillion-dollar strategy is familiar to children around the world. Any child who grew up reading Dr. Seuss knows his classic story of Star-Belly Sneetches (who have "stars upon thars"). In that story, status differentiation separates the elite (Star-Belly) Sneetches from the regular (Plain-Belly) Sneetches. This seemingly innate fact of Sneetch society is cleverly exploited by an enterprising fellow with a social agenda. His big idea is to trick all of the Plain-Belly Sneetches into paying enormous sums to have replica stars imprinted on their bellies. Of course, there is a twist. He makes a series of profitable switches, in which he builds a machine to remove stars from the once-high-status Star-Belly Sneetches, making a starless belly the new "it" thing. Once the other Sneetches get wise and start to remove their stars, too, he then charges even more for the elites to have their stars put back on. After a few rounds of adding and remov-ing stars, everyone becomes so confused about which group is supposed to be elite that stars become meaningless, and the sta-tus system collapses. The entrepreneur's work is done.

Google's big idea was not to get rid of stars, but rather to market a new star of its own. Based on the "stickiness" playbook, Google marketed Glass as an edgy, elite, wearable technology, hoping that everyone would notice it, talk about it, and want it.

But even the best-engineered, best-marketed products can fail, even backfire, when they crash into social norms.

The specific group of early adopters Google selected was conspicuously different from most people. They were predominantly young, well-off, tech-savvy, and male. In other words, stereotypical "techies."

To prevent the Glass market from being limited to techies, Google promoted the product widely. Press releases, media events, and social buzz let everyone know that Glass was coming...and that they were going to want it.

All of which makes perfect sense.

And all of which completely backfired for Google.

Why?

Because Glass ran up against an unanticipated problem of social norms, which I call the *grapefruit problem*.

The Glass campaign had two ingredients that, individually, are useful for success. But when put together, they became lethal.

These two ingredients are *awareness* and *differentiation*.

When Glass came out, everyone heard about it—a lot. People knew that it was Google's big new push into wearable technology. Awareness was achieved.

But the only people actually *wearing* Glass were techies. They were culturally, economically, and socially distinct from all the other people who were not wearing Glass but knew about it (and knew they were supposed to want it). Google's product-release strategy created a sense of exclusivity. But it did not rouse feelings of aspiration—like wanting a Ferrari. Instead, it elicited—perhaps even manufactured—feelings of resentment.

Google's campaign crystallized a latent form of social differentiation.

Here's why it's called the grapefruit problem:

Alone, grapefruit juice is a healthy drink. And, alone, daily cholesterol medications such as Lipitor can be lifesaving. But put the two together and the interaction can be toxic, with potentially lethal effects.

For awareness and differentiation, it's the same idea. By itself, creating massive awareness can obviously be a valuable way to promote a new product. And likewise by itself, differentiation within a market—for example between tweens and teenagers—can be a useful way to attract the consumers you want, helping them distinguish your product from other similar products they may have seen.

But if you create massive awareness by targeting a broad swath of society while simultaneously drawing a line of social differentiation that separates the early adopters from the non-adopters, it can be deadly.

Google's strategy inadvertently (and much to their dismay) created a normative backlash.

As a reporter for *Wired* magazine wrote, "People get angry at Glass. They get angry at you for wearing Glass. They talk about you openly. It inspires the most aggressive of passive aggression."

Glass crashed head-on into social norms about decorum in face-to-face interactions, and about the appropriate uses of surveillance technology in public. Google's innovation became emblematic of a cultural divide that separated the people who would wear Glass (referred to at the time as "Glassholes") from people who would not.

It was a disaster. Not only was the entire product line canceled, but the company's overall reputation took a hit. Google's image was transformed. It went from a cool search-engine company that used its website to celebrate the contributions of women and minorities in the arts and sciences to a tech giant offering surveillance technology for the rich.

The product did not just fail. It backfired.

Glass was indeed sticky. Everyone who witnessed the product release — and the ensuing cultural backlash — talked about it and remembered it. Google has worked very hard to help people forget this memory.

Korea's Quantum Leap

In the 1960s, the world was changing. India, Taiwan, and Korea were becoming industrialized. They were each passing through a historic moment called the *demographic transition*—a rite of passage for many modern nations.

Generations earlier, the United States, Britain, Germany, France, and other Western nations had all undergone the same transformation. But it was different then. In the late nineteenth and early twentieth centuries, medical science and industrial technology were still relatively new; those countries' transition to modernization had been slow and incremental.

Not so in the 1960s. The first half of the twentieth century saw the remarkable marriage of science and industry, enabling the global distribution of vaccines for tetanus, pertussis, polio, diphtheria, and smallpox. Simultaneously, innovations in sanitation, water safety, and food production worked in concert to dramatically extend life expectancy.

These modern miracles posed a new problem for developing nations: population growth. In less developed countries, infant-mortality rates are typically quite high, requiring families to have many children just to maintain the status quo. This balance between high fertility and high mortality kept population levels stable.

In the 1960s, many nations entering the demographic transition suddenly had better health care and more rapid economic growth than any transitioning society in history. Paradoxically, this rapid influx of better sanitation, wider vaccinations, and greater food supplies threatened to precipitate a catastrophic loss of life. If all of these innovations arrived simultaneously before social norms about family planning could change, crippling overpopulation would result.

A century earlier, families had generations to evolve their expectations about family planning. During the slow process of industrialization in the West, modern ideas such as a distinct period of "childhood" were invented. Each incremental advance in medicine and food availability gradually ushered in cultural adaptations that changed household social norms.

At the turn of the twentieth century, the process of modernization in the US gave rise to progressive evangelists for women's rights and contraception. Activists such as Margaret Sanger, the founder of Planned Parenthood, worked for half a century to help slow birth rates in the US. Not until 1965 did the Supreme Court finally legalize the use of the birth-control pill (though only by married couples, not by single women). But nearly a century before legalization of the pill, birth control was common among women throughout the US—resulting in a 50 percent drop in national fertility rates from 1850 to 1900. By the 1960s, birth control was accepted in most parts of the country.

Korea didn't have that kind of time.

Within only a few years, Korea's infant mortality plummeted while food availability soared. Long-standing social norms still encouraged citizens to have large families of five or six children. But now all of those children would survive to have five or six children of their own—who would do the same in turn. The math was simple: forecasts showed that within two generations there would be massive overpopulation, with people starving in the streets.

Koreans needed birth control to become widely adopted, and they needed it to happen fast. To succeed, they would have to overcome an unprecedented social challenge. Traditional beliefs about gender roles, women's rights, and a family's duty to have many children were deeply entrenched in Korea's national culture. Expectations of high fertility permeated people's sense of social status and personal accomplishment.

Contraception was not an easy sell.

What's worse, the West could not provide a role model. Although new medical and technological innovations had come from the West, the West had never experienced this kind of rapid cultural transition. There was no precedent for solving Korea's problem.

At the time, India, Taiwan, Indonesia, Pakistan, and a host of other nations were facing similar challenges. All of them were hard at work developing aggressive contraception programs. Then, as today, the dominant strategy for public health messaging was broadcast media.

Countries such as Pakistan that relied primarily on broadcast-media strategies struggled to reach their fertility goals. But Korea achieved all of their policy goals *ahead of* schedule. Within twenty years, contraception had spread through the entire country. The success of Korea's campaign remains unrivaled, globally.

As a reference point, consider that the US government's "War on Drugs" began in the 1970s. In 2011, after nearly half a century of battle and billions of dollars spent, the US Congress conceded that not only had it failed to win the war, the problem of drug use had actually gotten worse.

What happened in Korea to transform the entire culture in twenty years?

The Korean birth-control program began simply enough. Villages throughout the country were offered a list of contraceptive options: the pill, condoms, diaphragms, intrauterine devices (IUDs), and even vasectomies.

In some villages, contraception successfully spread to large numbers of adopters, while in other villages it failed to catch on. People in the unsuccessful villages had access to all the same birth-control methods, and received all the same advertising messages and incentive offers, as people in the successful villages, but nothing changed.

A similarly puzzling pattern arose a couple of decades later in Kenya. In 1977, contraception was used by only 1.7 percent of Kenyan households. In the mid-1980s, the country pursued an aggressive nationwide policy of promoting contraception. In some villages it was incredibly successful, quickly reaching 40 percent of families, while in other villages there was little to no adoption.

Why were some villages so successful while others failed?

In Korea, Kenya, and a host of other nations undergoing the demographic transition, the same patterns were observed. The explanation for these varying outcomes from village to village was not the available method of contraception, nor the marketing approach, but the *social ties* within each village. These social networks determined success or failure.

There was a clear difference between the successful and unsuccessful villages. Successful villages all had a similar social-network pattern: there were clusters of strong ties among friends and neighbors. There were also strong ties *between* the various clusters. These redundant social connections were the reinforcing pathways that spread contraception from one cluster to the next, across different social groups in the village. Unsuccessful villages did not have these reinforcing networks.

In the Korean villages where diffusion succeeded, women tended to adopt the same contraceptive methods as their friends and neighbors. In fact, there was generally widespread agreement on the contraceptive method used within each successful village.

If you look at the Korea story through the lens of "stickiness"—with the belief that certain trends or technologies are inherently more appealing and catchy—what happened might seem fairly straightforward. You would likely conclude that some contraceptive options were simply more attractive than others. Perhaps they were easier to use, or more memorable, or more culturally appropriate than others. Regardless, they were easier to spread. Whichever method it happened to be, if it took off in one village, it should naturally be expected to have taken off in all villages.

But this is not what happened in Korea. While there was complete agreement on which contraceptive method everyone used *within* each village, there was no consistency *across* villages. Some villages were "IUD villages," whereas others were "pill villages" and still others were "vasectomy villages." The particular method of contraception was not the key to successful adoption.

Why wasn't the same birth control method adopted in every successful village? Because of the power of social norms.

Korean families learned about contraception from their friends and neighbors. Their decision to start using it was based on contact with peers who could give them information about contraception, discuss the advantages and disadvantages, and support their use of birth control. In the end, villagers' receptiveness to contraception was based not on the qualities of a particular contraceptive method but on their receiving social approval from other adopters. Whichever method a person's contacts adopted was the one she was likely to adopt, too. The contagion that spread through Korea's villages was not a particular birth-control product but rather the social acceptance of contraception in general.

The early adopters were tightly knit "women's groups" — friendship-and-advice circles in each village — in which local women could talk about contraception and share their experiences with it. Once the members of a women's group adopted a particular method of contraception, it spread from the early-adopting group to other social clusters in the village network.

The incredible success of Korea's birth-control initiative stands in stark contrast to Google's Glass campaign. Both of these initiatives challenged social norms. Korea's success and Google's failure show how social networks can either accelerate a change in a social norm — or block that change completely.

Google's Other Grapefruit Problem

In 2011, two years before Glass was released, Google made a major foray into social networks. Not by choice, but by necessity. Facebook was preparing to go public, and it was going to have the largest IPO valuation in history: $104 billion. In 2007, Microsoft had outbid Google for a 1.6 percent stake in the company, and now Google was feeling the pressure of being excluded from the market entirely.

It was Google's fourth attempt to get into the social-networks market. Orkut (2004), Google Friend Connect (2008), and Google Buzz (2010) had all failed. During this same span, Facebook was expanding at a record pace, and the photo-sharing start-up Instagram had also entered the arena. Within two months of Instagram's arrival it had reached one million account holders, and within eighteen months Facebook had purchased it for $1 billion.

Google is renowned for being one of the sharpest technology firms out there. For a young engineer on the job market in the 2000s, landing a programming position at Google was not just a good job but a mark of distinction. So with all of Google's talent and resources, why couldn't it figure out how to be competitive in the social-networks market, let alone dominate it?

In its final attempt, Google released a new social-networking platform, Google+. Google had a simple plan for generating awareness: it would sign people up automatically. Google+ was positioned as a "social layer" that would cut across all of Google's other products and services. If you had a Gmail account, you also had Google+. If you signed up for Google Contacts, or wanted to make comments on Google's video-sharing site, YouTube, you got Google+ too. In fact, very few people *didn't* have Google+. It seemed like a brilliant strategy for taking over the market.

Google reported staggering levels of early growth for its social-networking platform. Google+ was ubiquitous. You saw reminders about Google+ every time you used anything related to Google. The product achieved unprecedented awareness because most people had it—whether they had signed up for it or not.

Here's the problem with that strategy: if you create massive awareness for your product but people don't use it, all that awareness can backfire.

It's the grapefruit problem again.

This time the two critical ingredients were not awareness and differentiation; they were awareness and *lack of use.*

By itself, awareness is clearly a good thing for any product campaign. And, by itself, lack of use is not necessarily a problem, particularly if your product is just getting started. But if you combine massive awareness with widespread lack of use, it can once again be lethal.

Why?

Because if everyone in the world knows about your memorable, remarkable, discussion-worthy product, they will also be sure to notice if no one around them is using it. The more that people's awareness of a product outpaces its actual uptake, the stronger the implicit signal from all of those non-adopters that there's something wrong with it.

It's the problem of countervailing influences.

In chapter 1, I showed you how highly connected people are often aware of the large number of non-adopters in their network. These social signals can cause highly connected people to hesitate before adopting a particularly unusual, discussion-worthy, or noticeable innovation, because choosing to adopt is a decision that will be widely seen and commented on.

These countervailing influences do not prevent social stars from adopting later on, once the innovation has become more accepted. But they can delay a social star's decision until sufficient social proof exists. In chapter 1, you saw how this happened with the Aerosmith gesture in Second Life.

But the problem for Google+ was worse. For the Aerosmith gesture, a social star who learned about the innovative greeting before anyone else did could afford to wait and see if people accepted it, then adopt it once it became legitimated. But Google's massively successful awareness campaign exposed so many users to Google+ that everyone knew *that everyone else knew* about Google+—*and that they weren't using it.* Google had inadvertently manufactured worldwide social proof *against* its own technology.

This would be a problem for any innovation. But it's a particularly lethal problem for a social technology. A crucial difference between, say, an email client or a search engine and a social-networking platform is that the first two can be adopted without coordinating with anyone else. But a social technology *requires* social coordination. People need to make the move together.

The incursion of Google+ into the social-networks market challenged a very powerful incumbent—Facebook. The task of dethroning an incumbent technology is similar to the challenge of mobilizing a revolution. To successfully grow a social movement, activists need to enable regular people to coordinate with one another. Participants need to feel like they are all joining together. And as you saw in chapter 1, the best place to mobilize an insurgency is through strong ties in the network periphery.

Google's strategy was to mobilize the entire population in one fell swoop. Adoption of Google+ lagged so far behind awareness that it led not just to delay but to collapse.

In April 2019, Google+ closed its doors.

The Zimbabwe Experiment

Everyone still remembers Google+. And that it failed. Just as everyone remembers Glass—and how *it* failed. An important caveat for marketing strategies that rely on stickiness is not just the potential for failure, but the possibility of leaving a lasting memory that can undermine future campaigns.

Today, the National Institutes of Health (NIH) is facing a similar challenge—not with a wearable technology or a networking platform, but with lifesaving medications.

This story starts in 2001, when Zimbabwe was being devastated by the HIV/AIDS pandemic. At one point, one in four Zimbabweans was HIV-positive.

Scientists were working hard to find a solution.

There were lots of available strategies. Condom use and male circumcision were among the best-known ways to prevent HIV. But acceptance of condoms was low—no one wanted to use them—and circumcision campaigns had backfired. These programs were viewed as cultural profanities that violated villagers' religious beliefs. In some countries, aid workers met with such violent retaliation that officials had to evacuate their staff and come up with a new plan.

Scientists needed to find a way to make HIV prevention stickier.

That's exactly what they did. In 2005, researchers unveiled a crowning achievement in HIV prevention: it was called pre-exposure prophylaxis, or PrEP, and it was designed to save the world.

PrEP is a miracle drug. A single daily pill—the equivalent of taking a morning aspirin—essentially eliminates HIV transmission. Starting in 2009, physicians and the Zimbabwean government conducted a massive outreach effort to spread PrEP to affected villages. Excitement among program officials and researchers was palpable. The global implications for HIV prevention were huge.

The campaign followed the viral-marketing playbook perfectly.

The innovation was free. It was easily accessible. Villagers were encouraged to talk about PrEP with their friends and neighbors. Regular screenings and checkups reminded villagers to maintain their medication regimen.

The campaign drove the message home: PrEP is free, easy to use, and will save your life.

But it was shockingly ineffective.

Most villagers who were regularly interviewed as part of the program—and who reported to physicians that they were taking PrEP daily—had no traces of the medication in their bloodstream. They were actively resisting the innovation.

Why?

Their reasons tell volumes about why social-change campaigns fail.

People worried that their friends and neighbors would find out that they were taking the medication, and therefore suspect that they had already contracted HIV. If their neighbors saw them picking up the medication, or spotted the packaging in their home, it would be enough to start a rumor. Villagers knew well the stigma that surrounded HIV, and the social norms about how infected people were treated. They did not want to risk any misunderstandings or rumors about their HIV status—which would be difficult, perhaps impossible, to eradicate if they ever took hold.

Others worried that perhaps the medication might *give* them HIV. This may sound odd at first, but a significant fraction of Americans worry that the influenza vaccine will give them the flu. In Zimbabwe, this medical anxiety was compounded by the fact that even if PrEP did not lead to HIV infection, villagers knew that their friends and neighbors shared their fears that it might. If they took PrEP, their neighbors might think they stood an *increased risk* of contracting HIV. Coupled with the social norms stigmatizing HIV-infected individuals, there were clear social reasons why someone would not take the medication, regardless of how adamant the physicians were or how compelling its marketing was.

The physicians running the PrEP campaign were exasperated. What more could they do?

The myth of stickiness tells us that key product features

offer a solution. If an initiative fails, the solution is to redesign your innovation with these features in mind—make it easier to use, more striking or more memorable, less costly—or to spruce up your campaign by making the message more fun and more emotionally engaging.

But cultural and social norms are not so easily outsmarted.

Attempts to spread everything from vaccinations to environmental technologies to new management practices have faced the same challenge. The less familiar and more disruptive an innovation is, the greater the resistance to it will typically be. This is the primary reason why social change is so difficult.

So, what do we do?

The answer is not influencers, nor viral marketing, nor stickiness. It is *the infrastructure of contagion.* Social networks are not merely pipes that spread information or disease, but prisms that color how people receive new ideas and innovations. In the next chapters, we will explore how a contagion infrastructure can trigger an essential chain of network propagation, transforming a struggling initiative—for instance, to spread a new generation of social technology, grow support for a new political candidate, or increase the acceptance of new disease-prevention measures—into an explosion of social change.

PART II

THE CHANGEMAKER'S PLAYBOOK: HOW TO BUILD CONTAGION INFRASTRUCTURE

CHAPTER 4

How Change Happens: The Discovery of Complex Contagions

Every story of scientific discovery is a combination of two things: painstaking work and dumb luck. In biology, when Charles Darwin was a young naturalist, his voyage on the HMS *Beagle* just happened upon the Galápagos Islands. It was dumb luck that he stumbled upon one of the rarest places on earth, where evolutionary trajectories had taken a unique and conspicuous turn. Of course, dumb luck was not enough. Plenty of others had been to the Galápagos. Darwin, however, realized what he had found.

The discovery of complex contagions began with just such a moment of dumb luck.

When I started graduate school, the prevailing wisdom was that any word-of-mouth recruitment drive for a political campaign or social movement would spread the same way that a virus does. Activating weak ties—network connections that reach far across a population—would accelerate the pace of recruitment. Today, this idea *still* seems obvious to most people. It continues to shape the way most of us understand the processes of change and innovation.

In grad school, I set out to use Mark Granovetter's elegant weak-tie theory to understand the rapid, nationwide growth of the American civil rights movement in the 1960s. But to my surprise, what I discovered while poring over the extensive data collected years earlier by sociologist Doug McAdam was that the growth of the civil rights movement did not look anything like viral spreading. Far from it. Recruitment efforts involved not weak ties but strong ones. They spread most quickly through social networks with lots of social redundancy, rather than those with extensive reach.

I pulled on the thread of this idea to see how far it would go. How would the data on the civil rights movement compare with the spread of the women's suffrage movement? What about the spread of unionization across Europe? The growth of online communities? In each case, I saw the same patterns. Struck by this consistency, I widened the search. What about the spread of the Arab Spring revolutions? What about Black Lives Matter? What about #MeToo? The explosion of new technologies such as Skype, Facebook, and Twitter? Or the rapid rise of new political candidates? The more I pulled on this thread, the more the conventional view of how social change spreads unraveled before my eyes.

Eventually, a new picture came into focus. The reason Granovetter's theory of networks did not match the data is that it assumed *everything* spreads like a virus. But I could see with increasing clarity that that assumption was a mistake—and a costly one at that. The data showed another kind of contagion. Simple ideas sometimes *did* spread virally, through weak ties, but ideas that involved significant personal investment— everything from the world-historical social and political movements I was focusing on to many of the grassroots political campaigns and product-marketing efforts that happen every day—followed a path very different from the viral one. That's when I identified two very different kinds of spreading processes, *simple* and *complex*.

The Four Barriers to Adoption

We've already seen *simple contagions* in action in chapter 2. A virus is typically a simple contagion. It is the kind of contagion that spreads easily from one person to another. All it takes is contact with one "infected" person. A viral video is a simple contagion. So is gossip. And news. Or information about job openings (Granovetter's famous example). In fact, just about every kind of word-of-mouth spreading process is a simple contagion.

Simple contagions benefit from reach in the social network. This is why social stars are so useful for spreading simple contagions—they have a large number of far-reaching contacts. "Infecting" a highly connected individual suffices to spread the word fast—or, as we say, to make it "go viral."

Simple contagions have defined how we think about social spreading for over a century. They have become the default model for our innovation-and-change campaigns. The problem is that the dynamics of simple contagions apply only to the spread of simple ideas. Beliefs-and-behavior change spreads in a different way, and through different channels. Any change that involves real risk—financial, psychological, or reputational—requires more than simply coming into contact with a single random adopter or "carrier."

That realization led me to the discovery of complex contagions. Complex contagions are contagions that people *resist*. Sometimes resistance to innovation is easy to understand, like Korean villagers' reluctance to adopt birth control because it challenged their cultural norms about family planning. Other times, resistance is harder to anticipate, like Second Lifers' reluctance to adopt the Aerosmith gesture because it was not yet widely accepted. In either case, contact with a single adopter is not enough. People need to receive reinforcement (or "social proof") from multiple adopters to be convinced—and for the new behavior to propagate. The more resistance there is to a new idea or behavior, the more social reinforcement is needed to persuade people to adopt it.

Most of the behaviors we care about—investing in a market; choosing a political candidate, a career path, a neighborhood to live in, or whether to use birth control; adopting a costly technology; or joining a social movement—are complex contagions. They are complex because they involve risk. The higher the stakes of a decision and the greater the uncertainty, the more "proof" people require—in the form of confirmation from multiple peers—before taking the plunge.

So how can you determine whether an innovative idea or product will be simple or complex? How can you know ahead of time so that you can design your change strategy accordingly? The answer lies in the idea of *resistance:* the more resistance a new idea must overcome, the more likely it is to be a complex contagion.

In my research, I have identified four main sources of resistance that create complexity. Each one is a barrier to adoption. Knowing whether an innovation will encounter any or all of these barriers enables you to determine whether an innovation is simple or complex—and how much resistance it is likely to face. Just as important, identifying the particular barrier (or barriers) to adoption reveals the most effective strategy for helping an innovation succeed.

These are the four barriers to adoption:

- **Coordination:** Some innovations are appealing only if people use them *together.* If the value of an innovation or behavior depends on the number of other people who adopt it, then it requires social reinforcement to spread. Many popular communication technologies, from Skype and instant messaging (and fax machines before them) to free and easy-to-adopt media-sharing platforms such as Twitter and Facebook, are essentially useless until lots of people you know are using them. Their value hinges on the number of other users you know. The more people who adopt, the more valuable the innovation becomes and the easier it is to spread.

- **Credibility:** Some innovations encounter skepticism about their effectiveness or safety. The more people who adopt a behavior, the more social proof there is that it is not as risky as we might have feared. We become more inclined to believe that the behavior is worth the cost or the effort it takes to adopt it. Social confirmation matters when individuals or organizations decide to invest in expensive new technologies or time-intensive practices. Think of software firms deciding whether to adopt a new cloud-computing infrastructure, or overweight patients deciding whether to try a new diet. Before adopting, they want to be sure the innovation is credible. Repeated confirmation by trusted others overcomes the credibility barrier.

- **Legitimacy:** Some innovations require social approval before they will be adopted. The barrier here is the risk of embarrassment or a tarnished reputation. The more people who adopt a behavior, the greater the expectation that others will approve of the decision to adopt and the lower the risk of embarrassment or sanction. Think of fashion. Think of your willingness to try a new greeting, like the fist bump or the Aerosmith gesture. Think of putting a rainbow flag on your social-media profile to show support for same-sex marriage. As more people you know adopt an innovation, you perceive less social risk in doing likewise. Social reinforcement from respected peers overcomes the legitimacy barrier.

- **Excitement:** Some innovations and behaviors are appealing only when people are emotionally energized by one another. The more people who adopt a behavior, the more excited other people become about adopting it. This is how social effervescence grows. It is what fuels the spread of participation in a sporting event, or a protest march, or even the Arab Spring revolutions. The enthusiasm of those around us fires our own. And if we don't sense that excitement, we won't join in. Social reinforcement among energized peers is essential for these emotional contagions to spread.

Each of these barriers to adoption can be overcome by social reinforcement. That's something we all tend to seek in adoption decisions where the stakes are high and we want to mitigate risk, such as investing in a new market or switching to a new business platform. If we know several people who can vouch for the new market or business approach, we'll feel much better about diving in. It's the difference between being *aware* of an innovation and being convinced to *adopt* it.

But the same barriers to adoption that make these complex social contagions hard to spread—such as the need for legitimacy, or the requirement for social coordination—can also make behaviors more likely to "stick" once they are adopted. For instance, the legitimacy of a new augmented-reality game, like Pokémon Go, depends upon other people adopting it. You do not want to wander the streets playing augmented-reality games unless others see them as acceptable. But once you've received enough social encouragement to convince you that a game is not only acceptable but also exciting to play with others, that social support will keep you interested in playing as long as others do.

It's the same for new communication technologies, from videoconferencing to email: you need several contacts to adopt the technology before its social value becomes clear to you. But once a communication technology is widely used it becomes a social necessity, making it hard to abandon.

The takeaway here looks like a paradox: innovations that encounter the greatest resistance—because people are sensitive to issues of legitimacy, coordination, or social proof—are often the ones people are most committed to once they finally adopt them. This is what sociologists call *entrenchment*. Entrenchment often appears to be an obstacle to social change, but it is actually the key to achieving it.

Real social change is about creating entrenchment. Whether the product is a free, life-saving HIV medication or an expensive new gadget, people's resistance to change is often just a signal that they are looking for social confirmation. Once you come to understand resistance this way—not as an obstacle to change, but as an opportunity to create enduring commitment— it helps you to calibrate your change strategies.

The Power of Pals

In August 1914, the British Army was outmatched. It was the start of World War I, and Germany enjoyed a staggering 10-to-1 advantage in the size of its armed forces. Not only that, Germany's army was built on professional soldiery, while Britain's troops were largely volunteers.

For Britain, raising a competitive infantry seemed a daunting prospect. The only hope was to recruit far and wide across all social classes—but this idea ran against the well-established norms of British society. Traditionally, only a small number of officers (drawn from the gentry) and enlisted men (drawn from the lower classes) chose to enter the armed forces. Men from the professional classes, such as bankers and merchants, were not typically recruited to fight.

Britain's War Office knew all this would have to change if they were to have any chance of winning the war. But it was a challenged effort from the start.

The first point of resistance was obvious: war is terrifying. Anyone who joined the fight faced a very real existential threat. Second, even for the brave, enlisting in the army was not traditionally seen as socially acceptable. For men with families—and particularly for men in the professional classes—there was genuine discomfort at the idea of violating one's social rank and position to join the infantry.

The former lord mayor of Liverpool, Lord Derby, realized that the solution was not to target people as individuals, but to target their social networks. He suggested that the secretary of state for war, Field Marshal Lord Kitchener, should grow his army through people's strong ties.

Derby's innovation, the "Pals Battalions" campaign, was remarkably effective.

Kitchener's campaign promised that people who enlisted together would also fight together. This strategy targeted residential neighborhoods and professional communities that had previously enforced the strong social norms *against* professional men enlisting. Kitchener transformed these strong ties into the opposite: the sources of social proof that would encourage men to join the army. Emotional excitement and feelings of solidarity spread easily through these networks. Enlistment became not only legitimate but expected. The campaign turned people's reasons for *resisting* the call to arms into their main reasons for *responding* to it.

Strikingly, this same approach had been used for centuries by insurgents. In Africa, Central America, and India (where Kitchener had served), neighborhood-based recruitment campaigns were used to build revolutionary uprisings against colonial governments. Taking a page out of the revolutionaries' playbook, Kitchener hoped instead to use neighborhood mobilization to galvanize support for the national military, town by town.

And it worked. In towns and cities across the country, the national war effort was energized. Citizens' close social bonds became the backbone of Britain's army. Neighborhood parochialism became the source of Britain's international power.

The first major success was the "Stockbrokers Battalion": a group of 1,600 London stockbrokers and City of London employees who enlisted within the first week of Kitchener's push. Two days later, 1,500 citizens from Liverpool enlisted. Within three days, three more battalions of Liverpudlians joined up. The city of Manchester soon followed suit, raising four battalions of local merchants and businesspeople.

Within a month, more than fifty towns across the United Kingdom had raised battalions to join the war effort. By the end of the first year, half a million men had enlisted. Cities began competing to see who could raise the greatest number of troops. Just as Kitchener had hoped, mobilizing for war had become a matter of local pride.

The recruitment effort was so successful that the soldiers flooding into recruiting stations soon overwhelmed the national treasury. Britain's federal budget could not keep up with the expense of feeding and housing its own troops.

Now strong ties came to the rescue again. Municipal governments and local businesses voluntarily pitched in to help finance the war effort. Citizens from each city donated food and money earmarked for the recruits from their hometown. The neighborhood recruitment campaign had produced a groundswell of national excitement that was palpable and contagious.

Even secondary schools and sports organizations mobilized battalions. Three battalions of professional soccer players answered the call. One professional club from Scotland, Heart of Midlothian F.C., marshaled not only its starting players and its reserve team but also its boardroom and staff members, along with a substantial number of local fans.

During the first two years of the war, enthusiasm for the Pals Battalions spread to every corner of the country. All told, more than two million men enlisted. It was the largest volunteer army that Britain had ever raised.

The Geometry of Networks

The key to understanding the success of the Pals Battalions—or to understanding the spread of any complex contagion—is the pattern of network connections that underlie strong ties and weak ties.

Do you remember Stanley Milgram's message-sending experiment? He started by placing messages in people's social networks in the Midwest, then observed how many steps it would take for the message to spread from this "seed" person to a randomly chosen "target" person in Sharon, Massachusetts.

When I was in graduate school, I began to think about the Pals Battalions the same way—as a spreading process that flowed from "seeds" outward into the social network. A crucial difference was that Milgram's postcards constituted a simple contagion: they spread through weak ties. But the Pals Battalions involved a much deeper commitment than merely sending a postcard. They were complex contagions that spread through strong ties. In this respect, the Pals Battalions had something in common with Twitter, the Arab Spring, the Aerosmith gesture, and contraception in Korea: all were complex contagions.

This led me to a puzzle that consumed my work for the next few years. What did the networks on Second Life that spread the Aerosmith gesture have in common with the British neighborhood networks that spread the Pals Battalions nearly a century earlier? They each seemed so different. What did the friendship networks linking San Francisco with Cambridge, through which Twitter expanded, have in common with the online social connections that mobilized the Arab Spring? What was it about these networks that allowed complex contagions to spread so effectively?

You already know that there are two types of social networks—strong ties and weak ties. Each one has its own geometry.

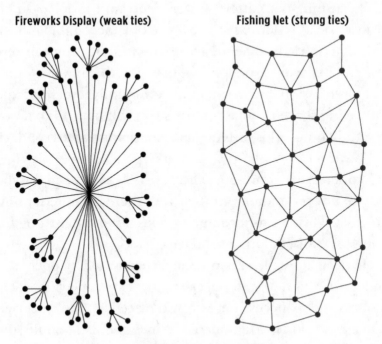

(Images adapted from Baran [1962])

The geometry of weak-tie networks looks a lot like a fireworks display. Each person is at the epicenter of their own "explosion," and their weak ties reach out randomly in every direction. Each tie jumps to a different, sometimes faraway place. There is very little social redundancy in weak ties. These people tend not to be connected to one another's friends.

The geometry of strong-tie networks looks more like a fishing net. These networks have the appearance of an interlocking sequence of triangles and rectangles. This pattern, often referred to as *network clustering,* is distinctive for its abundance of social redundancy. People are connected to one another's friends.

Our real-world networks are a combination of these two patterns. In fact we experience these two different patterns almost every day, but the effect of each one is quite different.

The fishing-net pattern fosters trust and intimacy. This is because social redundancy makes people accountable. In this kind of network, if someone treats you unfairly, you can report their bad behavior to people whom you both know in common. In any professional or residential community, everyone knows that having shared contacts means you will be held to account for your actions. This fosters social cooperation and solidarity.

Conversely, people in a fireworks pattern have very few, if any, contacts in common. These people are acquaintances. Without any redundancy in their ties, there is limited intimacy and trust. This network geometry does not offer a strong foundation for cooperation or solidarity.

Here's a thought experiment: What would happen if you conducted Milgram's message-sending experiment in each of these network patterns? Let's say you placed a "seed" message in each network, just as Milgram did. Which geometry would spread the message faster? Granovetter offered a clear prediction: on geometry alone, the fireworks network would spread the social contagion much faster than the fishing net.

It seems obvious. The fireworks network looks like speed incarnate. We can imagine how a message would spread from any location to reach the center, then spread out from there to reach everyone else. By contrast, in the fishing net the message would have to lumber along from neighbor to neighbor, suffering a lot of redundancy along the way.

But is this true for a complex contagion? What if you were trying to spread a contagion that provoked some resistance, or required social coordination—for instance, if you were building a following for a new social technology like Twitter, or recruiting citizens to a dangerous uprising like the Arab Spring? What about entrepreneurs spreading new management practices and investment strategies? Or activists recruiting people for civic celebrations and political movements that feed on emotional excitement? Do these social contagions spread faster in the fireworks pattern?

I wanted to find out. I wanted to design the same kind of experiment that Milgram had invented forty years earlier. Unlike Milgram, though, I didn't want to send a message to one person, but rather to spread a social innovation to *everyone*. My goal was to test Granovetter's idea—to see whether the fireworks network really would spread social innovation more effectively. Or whether, contrary to the weak-tie theory, the fishing net would do a better job.

I based my design on the paradigm of a medical trial. But instead of comparing the outcome of people who received a drug with the outcome of people who didn't, I would compare the outcome of an entire population connected in a fishing-net pattern with the outcome of an entire population connected in a fireworks pattern. Like Milgram, I would "seed" each network with a social contagion, then watch how it spread. But instead of spreading a simple message, I would spread a novel social technology. I would observe not only the number of adopters in each network but also how fast the innovation spread in each case.

It was exciting to think about. But not very easy to do.

I took solace in the fact that Stanley Milgram's idea had been even more ambitious. He had somehow persuaded random people in the Midwest to mail postcards to their friends with the ultimate goal of reaching an unknown stockbroker in Massachusetts. At the time of his study, most people did not even know what a social network was, let alone what it meant to measure one. Yet he was able to convince people to participate — and Harvard to fund it.

And I had one modern advantage: the internet. By 2007, when I started this experiment, people were using the internet to make all kinds of connections—sometimes to people they already knew, but often to people they did not. All I needed to do was find a way to entice thousands of people to want to be connected to one another. Crucially, I would need to be able to configure the connections among them any way I wanted to. And they would need to genuinely care about their contacts in the network so that they would influence one another's behavior.

It was a big ask.

But I had an idea.

The Health-Buddy Experiment

In 2007, I received funding from Harvard University to design my own Milgram experiment on social networks. I considered dozens of approaches to studying the spread of innovations using internet-based communities. I looked into everything from investment communities to dating websites. But the idea of *health communities* kept drawing me back.

The thing that impressed me the most about health communities was how engaged their members were. On Patients Like Me—a medical community for patients with ALS (also known as Lou Gehrig's disease) —people talked to strangers about their illness. One of the main problems with a rare and debilitating disease such as ALS is that the people who suffer from it never get to talk to anyone else who has it. Even though thousands of people with the disease are out there somewhere, there's no easy way to find them. Patients Like Me offered a solution. But it turned out that it was not just people with rare diseases who were looking to connect; on Patients Like Me and hundreds of other new online health communities, millions of people a year interacted with anonymous peers. They freely shared their private health information and personal experiences, and gave each other medical advice. I was amazed by how deeply engaged people were with one another, despite being strangers. They were influencing one another's medical decisions despite never having met face-to-face.

As I explored these sites, I found myself stuck on one question: Were these connections strong ties or weak ties?

I wondered whether people's similar health interests made these communities work. Or was there something about the underlying geometry of their social networks that led these communities to be so effective at spreading social influence?

I decided to use these communities as the template for my study. I constructed a new online health community and advertised it on mainstream health websites such as Harvard's Center for Cancer Prevention, *Prevention* magazine, *Men's Health* and *Women's Health* magazines, *Self* magazine, and others.

People were surprisingly interested: more than fifteen hundred people signed up for the study.

In order to join, participants completed a simple questionnaire in which they chose a username and identified all of their health interests and concerns. Once you signed up, you were matched with a group of "health buddies," whose interests were similar to your own. You couldn't change your health buddies; the ones you were assigned were the only ones you got. If your health buddies had any new health recommendations to share, you would receive email notifications from them. You would also be able to share your recommendations with them.

Once I had my 1,528 volunteers signed up, I divided the population randomly in half.

That gave me 764 people in each group.

But two groups was not enough. The key to good science is replication.

So I divided each group into six communities, each ranging in size from 98 to 144 people.

In the first group, the six communities were arranged into fireworks networks. The second group was arranged into six fishing nets.

As in a medical trial, this would allow me to conduct six replications of the comparison between the fishing-net networks and the fireworks-display networks. This way, I could ensure the reliability of any results I found.

Once people were arranged into their networks, from my perspective the study looked like six fishing nets side by side with six fireworks displays, each one filled with people who were all connected to exactly the same number of health buddies—either six or eight, depending on the network.

To the participants, the experiment looked different. If you were in a fireworks network, when you logged in you would see that you had six health buddies, all with similar interests as you. You would see the same thing if you were a participant in a fishing-net network—six health buddies, all with interests matching yours. In fact, just by looking at your network of health buddies, you could not tell anything about the geometry of your community, nor even how big it was. As far as participants could tell, the communities were identical.

Even though the network geometries were invisible to the participants, would they nevertheless control people's behavior? That was the question I wanted to answer. But in order for the experiment to work, people would have to be influenced by their peers.

How do you think you would feel about your health buddies if you had joined this community? They would have the same health interests as you, so you would probably be paying attention to their recommendations. But you wouldn't feel a strong emotional bond with them. They would be strangers.

Normally, these contacts would be weak ties. The connections among them would resemble a fireworks display. Would connecting them into a fishing-net pattern—an unnatural geometry for weak ties—change the behavior of the entire community, significantly *increasing* the spread of an innovation?

My hypothesis was that it would. But the theory of weak ties said the opposite. According to that theory, *reach* is good and *redundancy* is bad.

It was time to find out.

For the purposes of the experiment, I built a fun, easy-to-use social technology that would enable participants to search a vast database of new health resources. They could share these resources with one another and rate each resource. But to access this technology, they would first need to visit a website and complete a registration form.

The innovation I built was designed to be useful—but also to meet resistance. Like all social technologies, it was a complex contagion. There were two barriers to adoption: credibility and coordination. First, if you were considering adopting it, you would want to know whether this social technology was useful enough to merit the time it took to register for it. Second, the value of the technology depended on the number of fellow adopters. The more of your health buddies who joined, the more recommendations you would get. You were likely to adopt this new technology only if you thought others were adopting it too.

To start the study, I followed the same process as Milgram. I "seeded" the experiment by giving the innovation to one person in each network. This person was my initial adopter, or "change agent." Each new adopter would trigger a message to their contacts, letting these contacts know that one of their health buddies had adopted the innovation, and inviting them to adopt it as well.

Then I watched something amazing happen.

In the fireworks networks, information spread out at light speed. Each person who adopted the innovation triggered an explosion of notifications across the network. If any of their neighbors then adopted, a new blast of messages went out in all directions.

The spread of information looked exactly like a cascading sequence of fireworks. It was viral diffusion at its best. But although each new explosion of signals reached a lot of people in different parts of the network, it did not trigger many new adopters. Despite all the people who had been made aware of the innovation, actual uptake was lagging.

By contrast, the fishing-net communities were painfully slow at first. Each new adopter sent notifications back to the same cluster of people who had just heard about the innovation from a previous adopter. If any of those people adopted, most of their notifications likewise went back to that same cluster of contacts. People would hear about the technology from two, three, or even four health buddies before word of the innovation finally spread to a new social cluster.

Granovetter was clearly right about one thing: information was spreading much faster in the fireworks networks.

But actual *adoption* of the innovation—people completing the registration form, then logging in to use the social technology—showed the opposite. Although redundancy in the fishing nets was slowing down the spread of information, it was *speeding up* the spread of adoption.

People who received reinforcing messages from several peers were much more likely to adopt the innovation. And once they did, their signals added to the chorus of reinforcing messages for their neighbors, resulting in still more adoption.

I found the same results in all six pairs of networks. Although information spread faster in the fireworks networks, significantly more people adopted the innovation in the fishing nets. Social redundancy *wasn't* wasteful; it was doing the crucial work of strengthening social coordination on the new behavior.

In the fireworks networks, the "early adopters" (those who adopted the innovation after seeing a single message) typically used the technology once but never logged on again. In the fishing nets, people who required social confirmation from multiple health buddies in order to sign up (the so-called "laggards") were significantly more likely afterward to keep logging on and using the technology to find and share new health recommendations. In fact, the laggards were more than *three hundred times* as likely to keep using the health technology as the early adopters. Even months after the experiment had ended, these people kept logging on and using it.

Why?

Network redundancy was doing double duty. Initially, reinforcing messages from multiple health buddies showed the coordination value and credibility of the innovation. That led to adoption.

But, just like the telephone or Twitter, the reasons for adopting a social technology were also the reasons to keep using it. More neighbors who adopted meant more recommendations, which meant more value. Even among strangers, the geometry of reinforcing networks kept people coming back.

CHAPTER 5

Complex Contagion in Action: Memes, Bots, and Political Change

In the fall of 2012, the US presidential contest between Republican challenger Mitt Romney and Democratic incumbent Barack Obama was heating up. During a highly watched debate, Romney accused the Democrats of spending frivolously. In a spontaneous ad lib, he called for an end to government support for the Public Broadcasting System, a federally funded TV network perhaps most famous for its innovative educational programming for children. All it took was Romney's offhand mention of canceling the beloved children's program *Sesame Street* for the Twittersphere to explode. Within minutes, #SupportBigBird had been tweeted thousands of times and a new meme was off and running. Was it simple or complex?

The Speed of a Hashtag

A year before Mitt Romney's Big Bird comment lit up the Twittersphere, a team of computer scientists at Cornell University, led by renowned scientist Jon Kleinberg, set out to solve the mystery of why some hashtags spread across Twitter much faster than others.

Kleinberg—a wiry polymath with a friendly disposition and a penetrating mind—reasoned that the distinction between simple and complex contagions might be helpful in understanding this mystery. The real puzzle, he believed, was to figure out why something as simple as a hashtag would have any complexity at all. Literally all that is required to propagate a meme is to copy and paste a viral tag (such as #SupportBigBird) into your next tweet. Or, more simply still, to hit the Retweet button.

At twenty-five, Kleinberg was already a luminary. After finishing his undergraduate degree at Cornell, he completed his PhD at MIT, at which point he was aggressively recruited to return to Cornell as an assistant professor. Following in the footsteps of physicist Richard Feynman, Kleinberg started teaching as a professor at Cornell while he was still younger than many of his own graduate students. As if to dispel any concerns people might have about his early advancement, Kleinberg soon won a prestigious MacArthur Foundation grant—the so-called "genius award"—for his work on social networks. Kleinberg's impressive reputation as an innovative and rigorous thinker was now cemented. From that day on, he could work on any topic that struck his fancy. And what had caught his attention was the problem of understanding how hashtags travel across Twitter.

Kleinberg and his coauthors, Daniel Romero and Brendan Meeder, examined the differences among several different kinds of hashtags popular on Twitter that year. Looking at the patterns of adoption of these hashtags, Kleinberg's team found something striking: a clear divide between what they called "idiom hashtags" (such as #dontyouhate or #musicmonday) and political hashtags (such as #tcot and #hcr—"Top Conservatives on Twitter" and "Health Care Reform"). For the idiom hashtags, the story of viral diffusion worked. Users would start to deploy them after seeing them just once. These hashtags spread effectively from person to person with only a single contact. They were simple contagions.

The political hashtags were a different story. As Kleinberg's team put it, political hashtags were "riskier to use than conversational idioms...since they involve publicly aligning yourself with a position that might alienate you from others in your social circle." Twitter users would typically wait until they received the same hashtag from several people in their social circle before adopting it themselves. Political hashtags were therefore complex contagions.

The Speed of an Equal Sign

On March 25, 2013, the civil-rights organization Human Rights Campaign (HRC) initiated one of the largest social movements in online history. That week, the US Supreme Court was hearing two cases that would decide the fate of same-sex marriage in the country. To accompany this landmark event, the HRC urged people to change their Facebook profile pictures and avatars to the image of an equal sign to show support for marriage equality. Until that point, the HRC logo had been a bright-yellow equal sign on a blue background. The logo was now recolorized into a red-on-pink equal sign. The red and pink symbolized love.

Within a week, nearly three million people had changed their profile pages to include the new logo. It was an unprecedented nationwide show of support for marriage equality.

If we look at the incredible growth of the HRC initiative, it might seem reasonable to conclude that it is a textbook example of social activism gone viral—a simple contagion, helped perhaps by a "sticky" new logo. However, two researchers at

Facebook, including physicist Lada Adamic—who conducted the Second Life study discussed in chapter 1—decided to take a closer look.

One of the many attractions of working at Facebook, in addition to unlimited free ice cream and the edgy industrial architecture, is the unprecedented access to data. Although lots of people speculated about what gave rise to the massive spread of the equality symbol on Facebook, Adamic and her colleague Bogdan State were in the enviable position of being able to study it scientifically.

Tracing back through many millions of shares, comments, and likes, the scientists analyzed the spread of not just the equality symbol but dozens of other, unrelated social memes that had become popular on Facebook in the previous year. These ranged from photos that were widely shared and liked to popular behaviors such as posting themed messages about the meaning of Easter and other holidays. What Adamic and State found resonated with Kleinberg's findings on Twitter: photo sharing was a simple contagion. Photos spread quickly—on average, jumping from person to person after only a single contact. But the equal sign required reinforcement from more contacts in order for people to adopt it. Why was that? What was the difference between sharing a popular photo and adopting a popular profile change?

Adamic and State concluded that Facebook users needed social proof—approval from their peers—before they believed that the equal-sign movement was legitimate and widely accepted enough for them to support it. As the researchers put it, "it is easy to see why social proof obtained from multiple sources would be necessary for many individuals to show their support for a cause they believe in. Engaging in a behavior that challenges the status quo carries inherent risks." These risks, they explained, ranged from the local and personal ("a quarrel with one's otherwise-thinking friends") to "the life-threatening, as experienced by activists in a political movement challenging a repressive regime."

The equal-sign movement gained steam through reinforcing ties—groups of contacts that are densely interconnected. It was not viral. It was a complex contagion. And it spread only because adopters received enough social confirmation to overcome their sense of risk. The big takeaway from both Adamic's and Kleinberg's research is that any potentially contentious idea requires networks that can provide redundant social confirmation—even on Twitter and Facebook.

Of Ice Buckets and Other Memes

The Ice Bucket Challenge is one of those bizarre social-media contagions that remains hard to explain years after it happened. Like any fad, it would have been impossible to predict ahead of time. Or so we thought.

The Ice Bucket Challenge took hold in the summer of 2014, when millions of people from around the US—and then around the world—voluntarily recorded themselves dumping a bucket of ice-cold water over their heads. These videos were uploaded, watched, forwarded, and then imitated. And they were big. Governors, professional sports stars, movie stars, and television personalities all joined in.

A college baseball player named Pete Frates launched the Ice Bucket Challenge in 2014 to raise awareness for ALS. But it grew into something much larger, not only raising awareness about the disease on an unprecedented scale but generating an avalanche of donations for ALS charities.

From June 1 to August 13 of that year, more than 1.2 million videos were shared, generating more than 2.2 million mentions on Twitter. In the stretch from July 29 to August 17, the social-media campaign raised more than $41.8 million in donations for ALS charities—significantly more than had been raised in the entire previous year. The Ice Bucket Challenge became the embodiment of the viral video. Scientists and marketers spent years trying to figure out which key features made this video so special. Why did it take off when so many others didn't? What was the secret to its viral success?

In 2014, British mathematicians Daniel Sprague and Thomas House set out to understand the mathematical principles behind the success of the Ice Bucket Challenge—and of every viral video out there. They examined the top twenty-six memes from 2014, ranging from "planking" (holding a particular stiff-limbed yoga pose in a public place) to pretending to eat large-denomination bills. No common theme, feature, or trigger linked all of these successes together. Some had emotional triggers, but others did not; some had social currency, while others lacked it; some had practical value, others none. Statistically, there were no systematic differences between the features of the successes and failures. In fact, the only mathematical distinction was that in almost every case the successes had benefited from networks of social reinforcement. They were complex contagions.

Sprague and House then did something remarkable. They made a prediction. Could the model of complex contagion allow these mathematicians to see what meme would take off next? Sprague and House bravely put their findings to the test.

In early summer 2014, the Ice Bucket Challenge was just getting going. Though it was clearly catching on, no one knew how far it would go. Would it keep growing? Or—like most fads—fizzle out? Sprague and House analyzed the available data;

using the complex-contagion model, they calculated how likely it would be that clusters of social reinforcement would form in the Twitter network, giving rise to the popular spread of this new social meme. They predicted it wouldn't happen immediately. It would take a few weeks for social reinforcement to build up within the online networks. But once it did, the contagion would hit a critical mass and become extremely popular.

Sprague and House predicted that the popularity of the Ice Bucket Challenge would increase 1,000 percent in a matter of weeks, exploding across the internet by mid-August. But they also forecast its decline: once it had saturated these networks, they said, it would rapidly disappear. By the end of August, they speculated, the Ice Bucket Challenge would pass its peak of popularity and return to its early-summer levels.

In chapter 1, you saw that influencers didn't cause Twitter to take off. That was also true for the Ice Bucket Challenge. Like Oprah adopting Twitter, the host of NBC's *Today* show, Matt Lauer, performed the Ice Bucket Challenge on air to everyone's enjoyment and approval. His performance certainly contributed to the meme's growth, but by that point the meme had already entered its rapid-growth stage. Just as with Oprah and Twitter, the real question behind a social contagion's success is not *How did they get a celebrity to endorse this idea?* but rather *How did this idea grow so effectively that celebrities wanted to be associated with it?*

Sprague and House's prediction about the future of the Ice Bucket Challenge was based not on celebrity endorsements but on the mathematics of complex contagion. And the two were right: they successfully anticipated the timing of the rapid upswing, the peak activity, and the steep decay. In the process, they created a model that was able to accurately predict the growth, peak, and decay of other (perhaps less notable) memes.

Sprague and House's remarkable findings change how we think about spreading on social media. Whereas viral memes achieve their rapid expansion by spreading across weak ties, complex contagions can also grow rapidly. But they require social redundancy in order to do so. This insight is useful not only for understanding past successes but also for predicting future ones.

Bots for Social Good

In 2014, Danish computer scientist Sune Lehmann and three colleagues—Bjarke Mønsted, Piotr Sapiezynski, and Emilio Ferrara—took this idea one step further. Instead of simply observing contagions that happened to spread across Twitter, Lehmann and his team wanted to see if they could use the scientific principles of complex contagion to spread their *own* Twitter memes.

Being computer scientists, they wanted to automate the process. Their idea was to use "bots"—automated message-sending programs—to spread their Twitter messages. What's more, their goal was not just to spread random messages but to spread messages that would promote social cooperation and positive feelings. They wanted to use their bots to do some social good.

In 2014, bots had been in the news a lot—and not for good reasons. They had been increasingly used by political candidates to artificially bolster the appearance of grassroots support for their campaigns (a technique referred to as *astroturfing*, as in fake grass that looks real). Lehmann and his team knew about the serious concerns raised by the proliferation of bots on social media, but they wanted to turn the problem of bots on its head. Instead of studying how to prevent bots from doing mischief, they wanted to find out how bots might be used to promote civility and social engagement.

The core question they set out to answer was whether positive memes were simple contagions or complex contagions. What would be the best bot-strategies for spreading them?

A month after the Ice Bucket Challenge had run its course, Lehmann and his team deployed a small group of thirty-nine cleverly designed bots on Twitter. For a period of six weeks—from September 2014 through November 2014—the bots posted away, growing a connected network in excess of 25,000 human followers (you may have been among them).

Then the Lehmann bots connected to one another. The idea of connecting bots to bots seems ridiculous. From a viral-marketing perspective, it looks like an embarrassing waste of resources, like having telemarketers call each other: what's the point?

But this idea was one of the more ingenious features of the study. This network of bots (or *botnet*) created two kinds of social reinforcement. The obvious kind came from the bots' followers receiving the same message from multiple bots. But the less obvious kind came from people observing the bots' interactions with one another. It created a third-party effect in which the bots' forwarding and liking of messages by other bots created more legitimacy for those messages. Bots' interactions with one another offered a visible indicator of social approval that helped to strengthen the illusion that the bots were real—and that they had interesting things to say.

After the bots had established their networks of human and bot followers, the next step was to spread social good. From November 2014 through December 2014, Lehmann's bots sent novel memes into the world.

Much like Milgram's message-sending experiment, Lehmann

and his team used the bots as initial seeds to spread new memes. But their goal was not to reach a single target in Massachusetts. Their goal was to spread their social memes to everyone. There were eight in all, and you may have seen some of them, such as #getyourflushot, #highfiveastranger, #HowManyPushups, #somethinggood, or #SFThanks.

For instance, #getyourflushot does exactly what it sounds like; it encourages people to get an annual flu shot, then post a celebratory tweet about it. Similarly, #highfiveastranger encouraged people to give a high-five to a random person on the street, then post about the experience. These were not terribly profound memes, yet each one offered a positive social message.

They were surprisingly successful. Lehmann's memes spread far and wide. And every one of them was a complex contagion, traveling through redundant social ties. Social reinforcement was the key to their success.

Just like my innovation-spreading experiment we explored in chapter 4, Lehmann found that sending repeated messages from a single source did not work. The crucial factor for the spread of these memes was not whether people received the same message multiple *times,* but whether they received the message from multiple *sources.* People who received reinforcing signals from the same bot were actually less likely to adopt the meme than people who received only one signal. However, redundant signals from multiple bots accelerated the rate of adoption. In fact, the more reinforcing signals the better: adoption rates soared as more bots offered social confirmation for the same meme.

Nearly a decade before Lehmann's study, Twitter itself had used reinforcing networks among neighbors and friends to spread across the country. It turns out that memes traveled the same way, following pathways through Twitter that provided a geometry of social reinforcement. The novel insight from Lehmann's team was that this social process was not only predictable but automatable. And it took only a small number of bots to get it going.

For many years, we have been told that emotional triggers and sticky messages are the essential ingredients for contagious spreading. Lehmann's thirty-nine bots showed something else. Even messages that encourage vaccination can be contagious. The key to their success was to have their messages take root in the social network in the right way—within clusters of redundant ties. More important than the stickiness of the message is the social reinforcement it gets.

CHAPTER 6

Contagion Infrastructure: The Importance of Wide Bridges

Ever since Mark Granovetter's pioneering work on social networks in the 1970s, the connections between people located in different social clusters have been called *bridges*. These bridges were synonymous with weak ties; they were tenuous social connections linking people whose social groups were far apart. Early network scientists often gauged the value of bridges by their length, meaning the social distance they spanned—what I call *reach*. Even today, the prevailing assumption—among not just social scientists but most people in industry and advocacy— is that *reach* is the key to success.

But there is another way to think about bridges, and that is in terms not of length but of *width*—by which I mean the *number* of ties they contain. A weak tie is a *narrow bridge*. Within an organization, a narrow bridge might consist of a single tie between a person in one division, such as the engineering group, and someone in another part of the organization, such as sales. In a company where the members of the engineering group almost never meet the members of the sales group, a weak tie between, say, Isabella the engineer and Celine the sales manager establishes a narrow bridge across the organizational

Narrow Bridges   **Wide Bridges**

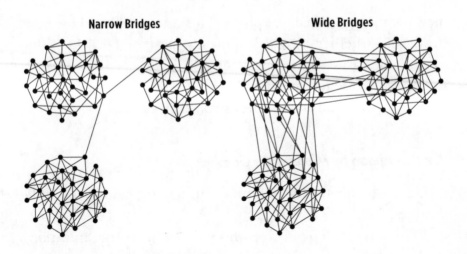

network. It offers a rare opportunity for useful information to spread between the two groups.

A *wide bridge,* by contrast, reflects a true collaboration: it involves a group of people from one division engaging with teams from another through multiple overlapping connections. Wide bridges are not about reach but *redundancy.* They allow people on both sides of the bridge to hear the opinions and recommendations of multiple peers and colleagues, and to discuss and debate ideas with them. Wide bridges mean stronger ties.

The frequency of wide bridges across residential neighborhoods is the reason why complex contagions so often spread geographically. But geography is not the key to bridge width. Redundancy is. A perfect example of this comes from the history of Twitter. After expanding locally around San Francisco, Twitter made the leap to Cambridge, Massachusetts. It traveled across the country using a reinforcing network of strong ties — a wide bridge — that connected the two geographically distant cities. This wide bridge supported social coordination between these communities, establishing the credibility and value of the new technology. Whatever physical distance a wide bridge may traverse—whether it's geographically close or far—its influence comes from social reinforcement.

Narrow bridges speed information over weak ties. Wide bridges bear social change over strong ones.

Getting Ahead by Minding the Gaps

Which is better for an organization, narrow bridges or wide bridges?

The answer depends on who you are in an organization, and on what you want to achieve.

If your goal is simple information sharing, narrow bridges are the perfect solution.

Consider an organization composed of a series of unconnected silos. People in engineering never talk to people in sales. And the salespeople never talk to people in design. The ties within each group are connected in a fishing-net pattern. But there are gaps in the organizational network, and a lot of valuable opportunities are lost.

Suppose that Isabella the engineer has read a few business books on social networking. She's learned that gaps in the organizational network can be seen as strategic opportunities. If she can bridge those gaps, she can become a *broker* for the spread of information across different groups. She wants to get ahead, and she will use her social network to do it.

She knows that one of the groups farthest away from the engineers is the sales group. There are no occasions where people in either the engineering or sales group would be likely to meet one another—nor would they particularly want to.

Isabella takes it upon herself to establish a connection—a narrow bridge—from the engineering group to the sales group.

She runs into Celine the sales manager in the elevator and strikes up a conversation. They have a good rapport. She tells Celine about some work the engineers are doing that might be interesting to the sales group, and she learns about the sales group's plans for the coming year.

A while later, Isabella sees Aria from manufacturing at a regional conference and introduces herself. Aria tells her the issues that manufacturing is dealing with, and Isabella shares some of the news from the sales group that she heard from Celine. At the company holiday party, Isabella meets Jackie from human resources. They hit it off, and discuss some of the new diversity-and-inclusion initiatives that the organization is pioneering.

Every month or two, Isabella follows up casually with her weak ties. She checks in to see if there are any new developments, and shares her news from across the company.

The more people to whom Isabella is connected, the more well-known she becomes as the go-to person for learning about what's happening in the firm. The more people who see her that way, the easier it is for her to make new connections. And the more successful she is, the more her personal network of narrow bridges comes to resemble a fireworks explosion. Her weak ties reach out to every part of the organization.

It's *good* to be an information broker. The strategic benefits are enormous: Isabella has exclusive access to novel and sometimes closely guarded information. The diversity of her contacts increases her visibility in the organization, and her access to diverse sources of information makes her valuable to other people looking to establish new bridging connections.

And Isabella's network of narrow bridges doesn't benefit just her. The more expansive Isabella's network becomes, the more valuable she is to the company. As a result of Isabella's networking efforts, there is far greater information flow among groups than ever before.

Isabella's networking strategy seems like a textbook case of using your social networks to get ahead.

But you've read enough by now to suspect that narrow bridges can also cause problems.

The problems arise from the crucial difference between *information sharing* and *knowledge transfer.* Narrow bridges are great for simple information sharing. Isabella's weak ties allow her to aggregate lots of new facts from remote parts of the organization.

But what her network of narrow bridges *cannot* do is help her spread organizational change.

Why?

Because organizational change requires persuading *people* to change. People must learn new competencies, develop new routines, adapt to new procedures. Organizational change requires deep knowledge transfer across groups and divisions. Convincing people to work on a new research collaboration — or accept a new corporate-planning strategy, or adopt a new project-management technology — is not easy. People resist innovation because change is usually difficult, and almost always risky.

Isabella's network of narrow bridges enables her to learn a lot about what's happening in the organization. But if she wants to *implement* what she's learned, she needs social reinforcement in order to do so.

Suppose the engineering team has developed an exciting new spreadsheet technology for project management. It's easy to use, and the engineers predict that it can increase productivity across the organization. Management is excited by it, but internal politics are preventing other groups from accepting the innovation: everyone outside engineering sees the new technology as a geeky tool developed *by* the engineers *for* the engineers—not likely to be very useful for anyone else.

The intrepid Isabella wants to start a campaign to use her network of narrow bridges to spread the new technology across the firm. She starts by talking to Celine the sales manager. She proposes a collaboration agreement for transferring the new technology from the engineering group to the sales group. It's an enterprising idea. How will the sales group respond?

There are several barriers to overcome before they'll consider it.

The first is **trust.** This is a not matter of personality, but of position. Because of her advantaged position as a broker, Isabella has incentives to persuade both sides to participate in an exchange as a way of polishing her reputation. And both sides know it. Which makes it hard for them to trust her. This may not have any significant consequences for their willingness to share information, but it can be a big obstacle to convincing the sales group to form a collaboration agreement that commits them to adopting a new project-management technology. It is a problem of credibility.

Celine's colleagues do not know Isabella, and they don't know why she's so eager to persuade everyone to use the engineers' new product. True, they have no reason *not* to trust Isabella. But they have no reason to *trust* her, either. Convincing the sales group to invest the time and resources required to structure a collaboration agreement, then change their routines to integrate the new project-management technology, requires not just information but trust.

The second problem is **risk.** Suppose Isabella has good intentions. She truly believes in the new project-management technology. It's been a huge hit inside the engineering group.

She's seen a marked improvement in her team's productivity, and she feels certain that it can do the same for the rest of the company.

Celine is convinced. Her colleagues less so; the sales group thinks their current project-management tools work just fine. To them, the innovation would be an enormous disruption to their routines, likely affecting their ability to reach their quarterly sales quotas. Making the change would involve a big risk.

Not only that, but the members of the sales group do not know anything about the engineers. They don't know what kinds of tasks the engineers work on, nor what kinds of challenges they encounter. Even if Celine's coworkers trust Isabella and believe her innovation worked well for the engineers, they may still suspect that the engineering group is just too different to offer anything useful. (Privately, the salespeople also share a secret fear: what if this new technology is indeed better, but it's so sophisticated that they cannot use it effectively? Nobody wants to be exposed to that kind of humiliation.)

But the greatest obstacle to spreading organizational innovations is often not credibility or legitimacy; it's **coordination.**

For the new project-management technology to spread, everyone on the sales team must adopt it—or else no one can.

Celine cannot do it alone. Her coworkers need to learn how to use the technology and be willing to work together to integrate it into their daily routines. For the innovation to be viable, everyone on the sales team needs to coordinate on adopting a new way of managing their projects.

Even if Isabella's innovation is genuinely impressive and effective, her narrow bridge from engineering to sales is not enough to convince everyone in the sales group to take a risk on it. Isabella's tie to Celine cannot solve the coordination problem.

She needs a wider bridge.

To implement the change she wants to see, Isabella would need to take a new approach to managing her professional networks. She would need to build wide bridges rather than narrow ones.

How would she do that?

Suppose Isabella starts out as before. She meets Celine in the elevator, and they have a good rapport. But instead of moving on and forming additional narrow bridges, suppose she recruits Celine to help her build a wide one? Isabella arranges a lunch for Celine and her colleagues to meet some members of the engineering group. Celine, in turn, runs a short seminar on new technologies for improving sales performance, and invites Isabella and her friends from engineering to attend. Isabella then has another lunch where she introduces a few more engineers to the salespeople who attended Celine's seminar.

Soon, the network between engineering and sales is not just a single tie between Isabella and Celine but a fishing-net-style cluster of redundant ties—a wide bridge—between the two groups.

From Isabella's point of view, some of her "structural advantage" has been lost. She's given up the opportunity to be the sole information broker between engineering and sales. She is no longer at the center of a network of narrow bridges. However, the benefits are substantial. She is now in a much better position to spread the engineering group's exciting new technology to the sales group. The wide bridge she and Celine created between engineering and sales forms a channel for knowledge transfer. The more wide bridges Isabella can create, the more she can transform her organization's capacity for coordination, and therefore its responsiveness to innovation.

First, this is because a wide bridge increases trust. When

multiple ties exist between groups, there are more opportunities for people on both sides to observe one another. Careless or exploitive behavior by a bridging individual is more likely to be detected and is thus less likely to happen. Greater bridge width increases the trustworthiness of the information coming from other parts of an organization.

Second, along with increasing trust, a wide bridge decreases risk. Disruptive innovations are inherently risky. The members of the sales group would need to answer many questions in order to feel comfortable adopting a new project-management technology from the engineers: Has the new technology actually improved the bottom line for the engineering group? Are the engineers trying to solve the same kinds of problems that the salespeople often encounter? Is the new project-management technology a good fit for the skill set of the members of the sales group?

If there's only a narrow bridge between the groups, there is no way for the sales group to get satisfying answers. That creates a lot of uncertainty. Which creates resistance.

A wide bridge changes that.

If several members of the sales group share connections to engineering, they can independently observe how the new project-management technology works for the engineers. They can evaluate together whether it would also be right for them. A wide bridge between the groups enables the members of the sales team to compare their observations, then coordinate their efforts with the other members of their group to bring everyone on board if they decide that's a good idea.

But wide bridges are not just conduits for spreading innovation. They are a foundation for organizational stability. They sustain the continuity of knowledge transfer over the lifetime of an organization.

A *narrow* bridge is a *fragile* bridge. The power that an individual gains from being a broker is due in part to the costs an organization will incur if she leaves. A broker's departure from a firm threatens the collapse of vital communication channels and the loss of valuable information. Wide bridges, by contrast, reduce an individual broker's advantage and strengthen the organization's stability. They ensure that channels of communication and exchange remain intact even as individuals come and go.

The Era of Open Innovation

The crucial role of wide bridges in organizational change is not limited to social networks within an organization. Wide bridges are equally important for partnerships between organizations.

The wider the bridge between organizations, the more reliable and enduring these relationships are likely to be. Wide bridges enable organizations to coordinate not just on adopting new technologies but, crucially, on adopting new office cultures. Organizational learning begins with an infrastructure that can support the flow of innovation and coordination across organizational boundaries.

In fact, this is how one of the greatest scientific collaborations in history—the mapping of the human genome—managed to succeed.

In 1990, the US government launched the Human Genome Project, one of the most intensive scientific initiatives ever conceived. The project would require partnerships across twenty major research centers in the US, UK, Japan, France, Germany, and China.

The project promised new possibilities for treating an untold variety of diseases, from arthritis to cancer. It would yield applications for biofuels, virology, agriculture, archeology, and even forensic sciences. It would reveal the uses of stem cells, offering new hope to hundreds of thousands of people with lifelong illnesses. It would even offer new insight into the evolutionary history of humans, and the potential for genetic testing and early disease detection. It would be a quantum leap for medical science.

But to succeed, it would require solving some of the hardest problems in the field of social networks. How should these research centers be connected? Who should have authority over whom? Whose protocols and standards should be used? How would privacy be protected, and knowledge be transferred?

The most important biological initiative in human history hinged on a question of sociology—and more specifically of network science.

The US government had a good track record of managing world-changing research projects. In 1942, the United States had coordinated with the UK and Canada to oversee the Manhattan Project—the creation of the atomic bomb. Hidden away beneath the dusty sagebrush of Los Alamos, New Mexico, Robert Oppenheimer led a team of theoretical and applied physicists whose discoveries shook the world and ushered in the Atomic Age.

A generation later, in 1961, the US space administration, NASA, pioneered Project Apollo, John F. Kennedy's remarkable vision of landing a man on the Moon. It was the most ambitious undertaking of any government in history, and Kennedy had given his scientists a strict deadline: "by the end of this decade." Like the Manhattan Project before it, Project Apollo was organized under the central authority of a lead scientist, George Mueller, who oversaw the activities at all of the related sites, including the Manned Spacecraft Center, the Marshall Space Flight Center, and the Launch Operations Center. Within eight years, Kennedy's vision was fulfilled. Project Apollo was a stunning success. On July 20, 1969, the first human landed on the Moon. It was the crowning achievement of the Space Age.

The Human Genome Project was the successor to these monumental undertakings. But the organizational strategy used for the Manhattan Project and Project Apollo would not work this time. The Human Genome Project was not organized under the central authority of a US agency. Nor was one person running everything. Instead, it was a collaboration across competing nations and competing research centers. Each nation had its own laws regulating scientific procedures, and each research center had its own internal culture and organizational structure. Instrumentation and methods varied across research centers, as did reporting procedures and protocols for replication. Before any science could be attempted, these organizations needed to design an infrastructure that could support knowledge transfer across national and organizational boundaries. They needed an infrastructure for innovation.

The solution they developed was an archetype of wide bridges in action.

In the decades leading up to the Human Genome Project and beyond—from the late 1970s to the turn of the millennium—scholars noticed a remarkable change in the pattern of organizational-collaboration networks, not only among the organizations participating in the Human Genome Project but across their respective industries as well. It was the beginning of the era of open innovation.

For generations before, firms had worked to maintain rigid network boundaries. In a highly competitive industry such as biotech, each firm had only a few narrow bridges connecting it to industry partners, clients, and collaborators. The bulk of its networks were internally focused, and often hierarchically structured.

A new picture emerged during the 1980s, when firms needed to respond to growing technological complexity and the interdependence of increasingly competitive markets. No longer could a successful firm simply make a product and sell it. It needed financial, scientific, and even social ties with other firms with whom it could coordinate, innovate, and develop new markets.

The Japanese manufacturing and electronics industry started pioneering these new organizational patterns in the late 1970s. Major firms such as Toshiba, Mitsubishi, and Hitachi had previously viewed subcontractors as little more than part-time help for completing specialized tasks. But rapidly growing sophistication in the electronics industry turned these specialized subcontractors into increasingly valuable members of the emerging high-tech community. Toshiba and Mitsubishi created special teams within their organizations and tasked them with creating cooperative-exchange networks with their subcontractors. They worked to integrate people from outside the firm into the firm's research-and-development plans; external collaborators now helped to manage the firm's manufacturing teams, and to develop their timelines for production.

By the early 1980s, Japan's high-tech industry had been transformed into an infrastructure of wide bridges. It was an engine of innovation. The pace of knowledge transfer and novel product development among Japan's cooperating firms was far too great for individual US firms, even large ones, to keep up. It looked as though Japan would soon dwarf such US high-tech hubs as California's Silicon Valley and Boston's Route 128.

Following Japan's lead, industry networks in Silicon Valley were transformed. Wide bridges between firms were sustained through joint meetings and inter-firm working groups that enabled companies to draw on one another's expertise and excel in their respective markets. A host of rapid innovations emerged. Sun Microsystems' servers, Tandem's fail-safe infrastructure for secure online transactions, Silicon Graphics' high-performance workstations, and Pyramid Technology's miniaturized mainframe computers were all collaborative innovations. A remarkable level of reciprocity was established across organizational boundaries, creating trust and reducing risk.

The collaborative model of open innovation had become a new modality for tech and biotech innovation—for IBM, Sun Microsystems, Cisco, Genentech, Millennium Pharmaceuticals, Intel, and many others.

This was the network pattern that the Human Genome Project would need in order to succeed. Unlike most scientific projects, the Human Genome Project was not pursing a theoretical hypothesis. It was creating a transformative scientific innovation—the technical capacity to read the complete sequence of human DNA.

It was similar to the kind of research-and-development projects pioneered in Silicon Valley. But its goal was far more ambitious. To succeed, it would require sustained, often rigorous coordination among research centers. Each one would need to analyze and assemble vast amounts of genetic data, then work together to integrate the data into a meaningful pattern. It was history's biggest and most complicated jigsaw puzzle.

Over a dozen university laboratories and government research centers coordinated through a consortium arrangement, in which centers would share their findings for replication and evaluation by their peers. Regular conferences, reciprocal research-center tours and on-site meetings, shared research databases, and electronic peer-to-peer exchange networks (which corresponded with the dawn of the modern internet) enabled coordination among research laboratories.

Centers that had once jealously guarded their internal procedures now met regularly to discuss their progress and evaluate methods. They agreed on shared protocols for knowledge transfer, replication techniques, and peer evaluation. Centers even exchanged their sequenced data to see if they could replicate one another's processes for reassembling the genetic code.

It was a model of collaborative science. And it advanced at a breakneck pace.

By 2003, the entire human genome had been mapped. A new era of genetic research had begun.

The Case of the Hijacked Hashtag

For the Human Genome Project, the newly formed contagion infrastructure resulted from a conscious effort to design a new kind of collaboration network for the transfer of complex knowledge. But contagion infrastructures often develop spontaneously. In Silicon Valley, a contagion infrastructure emerged in response to growing technical complexity and competitive pressures. Each firm responded individually, but in the process a shared ecology of interconnected organizations took shape.

This can also happen among the diverse communities in society at large. A new pattern of wide bridges can form between geographically and socially distant communities through an unplanned series of historical and technological developments. Most recently, connective technologies such as email and social media have been able to forge wide bridges across previously disconnected communities. These rapid changes in the infrastructure of social ties can usher in a remarkable new potential for coordinated action and the explosive growth of social movements.

On April 22, 2014, the New York City Police Department launched a new public relations campaign on Twitter. @NYPD-News invited the public to share friendly photographs of officers in their neighborhoods, posted with the hashtag #myNYPD.

Within a few hours, dozens of posts showed New Yorkers with their arms around NYPD officers, giving high fives, and walking down the sidewalk together.

Then something happened that the NYPD did not expect.

An @OccupyWallStreet activist posted a photo of an NYPD officer mid-swing, baton in hand, attacking unarmed protesters. A group called @CopWatch followed up by posting a picture of a seventeen-year-old boy, Deion Fludd, in the hospital after he had been severely injured after running from the police. These activist posts were reinforced by others, and this new use of #myNYPD began to take off among their Twitter followers.

The contagion first took hold among the activists, but then it began to spread more widely through the network of New York City's Twitter users. Regular citizens started receiving message after message in their feeds. The contagion was gaining social reinforcement across different communities—activists, parents, students, and others.

From Brooklyn to Staten Island, Manhattan to the Bronx, regular people, using their personal Twitter accounts, started posting their own pictures of the NYPD.

A Black youth posted a picture of his friend outstretched on the hood of an NYPD cruiser, wincing in pain, as three officers in tactical gear bore down on him. The picture showed a sea of other officers in the background standing around calmly. The caption read sarcastically, "Sure thing! MT@NYPDnews: Do you have a photo w/ a member of the NYPD? Tweet us & tag it #myNYPD."

Another citizen posted a picture of six NYPD officers carrying a crying protester into a paddy wagon. The caption read in jest, "If you can't walk, don't worry, the NYPD will carry you. How helpful #myNYPD."

A growing number of posts and retweets spread across New York until they reached a *critical mass*. A spontaneous movement began to snowball, and it overtook the #myNYPD hashtag.

The snowball became an avalanche. Within forty-eight hours, more than a hundred thousand posts had flooded the #myNYPD hashtag, almost all reinforcing the same critical theme.

The NYPD had wanted to spread a social contagion. But not like this.

On April 24, 2014, two days after it launched, the NYPD shut down its Twitter campaign.

It was a minor victory for the activists. But not in most of the mainstream media. Reporting on the #myNYPD movement in the *New York Post* and the *New York Daily News* referred to it as a "hijacking" by "cop-haters" and "trolls"—something that was "gross, sloppy, and just plain wrong."

Just a few months later, another similarly spontaneous movement would erupt. This time, it would take over the nation. And then the world.

The Ferguson Revolution

The first tweet went out on August 9, 2014, at 12:48 p.m.

"Ferguson police just executed an unarmed 17 yr old boy that was walking to the store. Shot him 10 times smh." The teenager was Michael Brown.

This message was posted by a resident of Ferguson, Missouri, with the Twitter handle @AyoMissDarkSkin, who happened to be walking by the crime scene just after it happened. She was not an activist, nor was she a social star. She was not trying to start a revolution. But her tweet would trigger others, and together they would become part of one of the largest and most influential social movements in recent US history, Black Lives Matter. (The term *Black Lives Matter* means several different things. Here I am using the term to refer to the Black Lives Matter movement, an international anti–police brutality campaign that grew out of the events in Ferguson, also referred to as BLM. *Black Lives Matter* also refers to an organization founded by Alicia Garza, Patrisse Cullors, and Opal Tometi in 2013. The Black Lives Matter movement includes the Black Lives Matter organization, but it also includes other organizations.)

The hashtag #BlackLivesMatter dates back several years before Ferguson. In the spring of 2012, teenager Trayvon Martin was killed while walking home from a convenience store by George Zimmerman, a member of the local neighborhood watch. Public outrage was palpable, but nevertheless contained—at least during Zimmerman's trial. Everyone was waiting for Zimmerman to be found guilty.

But then Zimmerman was acquitted. During the public outcry afterward, the hashtag #BlackLivesMatter was created by Garza, Cullors, and Tometi. But it wasn't taken up by the mainstream public. And two years later, in June 2014, the hashtag #BlackLivesMatter had still been used only forty-eight times on social media. In July 2014, Eric Garner, a forty-three-year-old father of six, was killed by an NYPD officer during a routine arrest on Staten Island. The outrage over Garner's death was amplified by videos and pictures posted on social media. In the weeks following Garner's death, the hashtag #BlackLivesMatter spiked to about six hundred tweets. But it did not grow beyond that.

Each moment of public outrage stood alone.

Then came Ferguson.

Michael Brown was killed on August 9, 2014.

By September 1, the hashtag #BlackLivesMatter had been used fifty-two thousand times. Less than a year later, it had been used four million times. By May 2015, the number of tweets using #BlackLivesMatter along with related keywords (such as #Ferguson) had reached more than forty million messages.

A social movement had taken off.

But why then?

In retrospect, we can call Ferguson a "tipping point." But *why* was it a tipping point? What was different?

It was not the media, which had covered each of the earlier stories from the previous two years. Nor the involvement of celebrities, who had tweeted and commented about Martin's and Garner's killings. Nor was it the hashtag #BlackLivesMatter, which had been around since 2012. None of these obvious factors explain why the movement took off in Ferguson.

Deen Freelon is a charismatic activist and communication scholar at the University of North Carolina, Chapel Hill. He is one of the pioneering researchers in the field of Twitter networks and activism. In a strikingly lucid account of how Twitter networks propelled the growth of Black Lives Matter, Freelon showed the changing pattern of connections among citizens, activists, and mainstream media outlets over the course of the months leading up to, during, and after Ferguson. The transformation that occurred during the Ferguson protests involved a rapid coalescence of relatively disconnected Twitter communities into a new social infrastructure linked by wide bridges.

In July 2014, a month before Ferguson, the network of Twitter conversations about civil rights, Black activism, and police violence was composed of several independent communities, or "groups," with narrow bridges between them. There were communities of activists posting news and reports about Eric Garner's death. Mainstream media outlets were posting their own reporting. A separate set of communities, composed mostly of African American youths, were having their own conversations, almost entirely distinct from the conversations among activist groups and those among media outlets.

The network pattern among these communities resembled the network pattern among firms before the era of open innovation. Each Twitter community was largely a self-contained conversation. Internally, each conversation was a densely woven network of connections. Externally, posts were occasionally commented on and retweeted across conversation bubbles. But these were narrow bridges. The vast majority of interactions were internal to each group.

A month later, these networks looked very different.

Remember the earthquake that shook San Francisco in 2006 and awoke Twitter's founders to the value of their technology? As the first tremors hit, diverse Twitter communities suddenly became relevant to one another. Across the city, widening bridges of contact across these communities enabled people to find out in real time where the aftershocks were hitting, and how others were responding. A social infrastructure for coordination and empathy spontaneously emerged.

Ferguson was a much larger earthquake.

Events erupted quickly. Michael Brown was killed on August 9. By August 10, citizens had organized to protest his death. The police responded with a militarized stance, arriving in body armor with attack dogs. Citizens responded in person and online.

It wasn't media activists who led the charge. Regular residents of Ferguson uploaded posts using their personal accounts, reporting on the minute-by-minute activity around them. In much the same way that the #jan25 hashtag had helped galvanize the Arab Spring revolution in Egypt, citizens in Missouri organized using the hashtags #Ferguson and #BlackLivesMatter, not only as symbols of emotional solidarity but also as tools for strategic coordination.

The most retweeted members of the Twitter community during the first few days were Ferguson residents. One citizen, using the Twitter handle @natedrug, posted continuous tweets from within the protests. Another was a college student with the handle @Nettaaaaaaa. As the volume of posts about Ferguson ballooned, the members of the network periphery were among the most influential actors in the conversation.

By August 12, a contagion infrastructure was taking shape on Twitter. There was a large cluster of Ferguson activists in one conversation. International activists and commenters were in another group. Celebrities and mainstream news outlets formed another group. There was a well-defined network composed primarily of white liberals. There were also multiracial and primarily Black groups. And for the first time, these groups were in conversation with one another. Wide bridges were forming between them.

People in the multiracial conversation were also part of the international-solidarity conversation. People in the primarily white-liberal conversation were also part of the multiracial and primarily Black conversations. People in each of these groups were connected to radical activist groups such as Anonymous, as well as to groups dominated by mainstream media.

The Black Lives Matter movement would take many months to reach its full scale, but it was already becoming an influential vehicle for coordination across the groups. The widening network of interactions established a shared language among

Black youth, activists, Ferguson citizens, and the mainstream media. The major unifying themes of Black Lives Matter began to take hold across communities: excessive police violence; racially targeted police action; civil-rights violations.

By August 13, reporters from national news outlets had arrived to cover the protests and the increasingly militarized response of the local police. Just two days later, the National Guard would be mobilized. The presence of national media increased the activity on Twitter. The dialogue among citizens, police, and media was unfolding both in the streets and online. Surprisingly, the online exchanges were being dominated by citizen posts, which garnered more attention than prominent news outlets such as @CNN. A previously unknown citizen activist, DeRay McKesson, accrued more than a million retweets and mentions during the week. His reports from the streets of Ferguson helped to frame Americans' views of the shooting, the protests, and the police escalation.

People far away from Ferguson began to feel their connection to what was happening in the small Missouri town. Solidarity grew among citizens from different parts of the country. The significance of the burgeoning Black Lives Matter movement was coming into focus. Meanwhile, tension was building between mainstream media accounts of Ferguson and citizens' own accounts of the events taking place there.

During the impromptu #myNYPD movement, wide bridges never formed between activists and the media. These conversations never converged. Mainstream media developed one vocabulary to describe the movement; activists developed another. Mainstream media won that battle. To most outside observers, the activists indeed looked like hijackers.

This time, though, something different happened. Widening bridges among networks of citizens, activists, and mainstream media enabled citizens to both engage and influence the language used by the media.

On August 9, the very first media report about Michael Brown's death — a tweet by the *St. Louis Post Dispatch*, @stltoday — read: "Fatal shooting by Ferguson police prompts mob reaction."

Local alderman Antonio French was among the first to respond. " 'Mob'? You could also use the world 'community.' " Echoing this sentiment, Ferguson-born author Andrea Taylor posted retweets that changed "mob" to "crowd." She also corrected other news reports that referred to Michael Brown as a "man" (he had graduated from high school only a few months before his death).

As Twitter activity soared and mainstream media flocked to Missouri, the expanding online dialogue between media reports and citizens' firsthand accounts invited people from around the country to engage in the conversation. A Twitter follower from the Midwest tweeted, "PAY ATTENTION as 'teen' becomes 'man,' 'community' becomes 'mob,' and 'murder' becomes 'alleged shooting.' #Ferguson #medialiteracy." Members of Anonymous, the activist collective, likewise expanded their conversation networks to include posts from mainstream media outlets. The surprising fruit of these widening pathways was that activists and citizens forged a coordinated narrative alongside mainstream news sources such as the *Washington Post*, the *New York Times*, *Huffington Post*, and *USA Today*. Citizens' efforts to reframe the Ferguson protests were successful. Mainstream media outlets began referring to protestors in Ferguson with terms such as *citizens* and *community* rather than *mob*.

By the end of the month, Black Lives Matter had already begun to show its influence. In September 2014, the US Justice Department initiated a civil-rights investigation into the practices of the Ferguson Police Department, which included an in-depth review of the department's use of force over the previous four years.

Several months later, the movement would take hold nationally.

On November 24, 2014, the acquittal of Ferguson officer Darren Wilson reignited the Ferguson protests, this time across the nation. A vast contagion infrastructure had taken form. Citizens and activists across the country organized their responses to Wilson's acquittal by coordinating on the core message of the Black Lives Matter movement. A week later, on December 2, the acquittal of NYPD officer Daniel Pantaleo in the case of Eric Garner unified those who were outraged under the motto BLACK LIVES MATTER. Geographically distant and culturally distinct communities, such as New York City and small-town Missouri, were now part of the same movement. During that time, twelve-year-old Tamir Rice was shot and killed by a police officer in Cleveland, Ohio, and Akai Gurley was killed by a New York City police officer. Public responses to these deaths were now indelibly connected to Black Lives Matter as well.

On Twitter, Black Lives Matter groups, Black youth, activists, journalists, pop-culture groups, and entertainers were all connected through wide bridges that coordinated them in their responses to these events. Even conservative groups were connected to the Black Lives Matter conversation. Remarkably, Black Lives Matter had gained sufficient legitimacy at this point that these groups were no longer staunchly oppositional in their engagement with the movement.

Months later, Walter Scott was shot in the back and killed in Charleston, South Carolina; Eric Harris was killed in Tulsa, Oklahoma; Sandra Bland died in police custody in Waller County, Texas; and Freddie Gray was killed while in police custody in Baltimore, Maryland. Activists and local citizens were no longer the only ones interpreting these events through the lens of the Black Lives Matter movement. National news media and government officials were all coordinated on the message of Black Lives Matter. Within less than a year, the movement had forged a national and international conversation that engaged the White House, the US Justice Department, and the mainstream media.

Ferguson, Missouri, is an unlikely place for an international movement to begin. It is not nearly as connected to the world as New York City. Michael Brown's death was not recorded with photographs or videos. Nor was Michael Brown the youngest or most civically engaged person to be killed during those years. Yet the response to his death changed the national conversation about police violence.

An important reason why the outcry was heard this time is that people like @AyoMissDarkSkin, @natedrug, @Nettaaaaaaa, and all the citizens in Ferguson and elsewhere in the network periphery helped to form and sustain a contagion infrastructure. Like the San Francisco earthquake in 2006 and the #myNYPD movement a few months before Ferguson, these networks emerged spontaneously. The pattern of wide bridges that took shape over those weeks and months marshaled an unprecedented number of communities in a single, organized conversation, enabling them to coordinate around a shared idea: Black Lives Matter.

For the Black Lives Matter movement, the victories came slowly at first. But they did come, and they have continued. The investigation of the Ferguson Police Department initiated in September 2014 was published in March 2015. The findings were conclusive. The report detailed a discomforting laundry list of constitutional violations, including a racially targeted municipal code that governed the "manner of walking along the roadway." Within the month, the chief of police resigned, and five city officials and police officers were fired.

On May 9, 2016, Delrish Moss was sworn in as the first permanent Black police chief in Ferguson's history. Moss has since retired, but Ferguson has had a Black police chief ever since. Beyond Ferguson, Black Lives Matter brought attention to the issue of abuses against African American citizens across the country.

Over the following years, the boundaries that defined the key Twitter communities supporting the Black Lives Matter movement have changed. The intensity of activity has grown in some groups and shrunk in others. New groups composed of international activists, Black media figures, and entertainers have emerged, and other groups, such as isolated Black youths, have been incorporated into larger conversations. Although these online communities and the bridges among them are fluid, the conversation itself has continued to grow. According to a 2019 study by the Pew Research Center, the #BlackLivesMatter hashtag had been used approximately thirty million times since 2014—an average of more than 17,000 times per day.

And in May 2020, when a shocking video emerged showing a forty-six-year-old Black man in Minneapolis, George Floyd, being slowly choked to death by a white policeman, the expansive network of wide bridges that began forming in 2014 was ready to spread public outrage and transform it into first a national and then a global movement for change.

Within days of the video's release, Black Lives Matter protests spread to New York, Philadelphia, Atlanta, Washington, Detroit, San Francisco, and hundreds of other American cities and towns. Within a week, solidarity protests spread to Europe, Asia, Africa, Australia, and the Americas. The Black Lives Matter protests had become the most widespread solidarity campaign in history.

Back in 2014, shocking videos of Eric Garner's death in New

York City led to small-scale protests and a slight increase in the use of the #BlackLivesMatter hashtag. The officer was not charged with a crime. And more than half of American voters believed that the ensuing protests against police violence were not justified.

In June 2020, the police officer responsible for the death of George Floyd was charged with murder, and felony charges were brought against the other attending officers. A poll taken in the following weeks showed that 78 percent of Americans believed that the Black Lives Matter protests were justified, prompting Congress for the first time to draft federal legislation targeting racial bias in local policing.

What made the difference was the wide bridges that enabled the spread of solidarity and coordinated action across diverse communities in the United States and abroad. The contagion infrastructure created by Black Lives Matter transformed isolated communities suffering from local police violence into a coordinated international movement that reshaped citizens' ability to spread change.

How broadly might these insights from Black Lives Matter be applied? What do they mean for other kinds of social-change initiatives, among them the #MeToo campaign, the equal-pay movement, or efforts to change the culture of gender relations within organizations?

The next chapter will expand on the idea of wide bridges by introducing you to the concept of *relevance,* the other crucial element of a robust contagion infrastructure. You will see how reinforcement from our peers—both those who are like us and those who are unlike us—can make a crucial difference to the success of a change campaign.

CHAPTER 7

The Principle of Relevance: The Power of People Like Us and Unlike Us

If you spend any length of time channel surfing on your TV, you'll inevitably land on an infomercial. And you'll quickly notice that fitness and weight-loss programs are huge. The format is formulaic: a bronzed, buff, celebrity trainer such as Jillian Michaels (*The Biggest Loser*), Autumn Calabrese (*21 Day Fix*), or Billy Blanks (*Tae Bo*) inspires you to start and complete your journey to physical health and strength through their proven solution.

Interspersed with all this "trusted" guidance are the allegedly true confessions of people who have used the program to achieve weight-loss success. They share their emotional struggles. They show compelling before-and-after photos. Some have lost massive amounts of weight, while others have realized more modest changes. Some are white and some are people of color. There are stories of millennials who have fought the good fight most of their lives, young mothers struggling to lose that postpartum weight, middle-aged men who have grown paunchy, and a sprinkling of women in their fifties and sixties who want to reverse the saggy ravages of time.

So who are the most influential—and most trusted—sources in your decision to embrace a new weight-loss program or adopt more healthful eating and exercise behaviors? Is it the person you aspire to be? Or the person who is just like you now?

I studied this question in 2009, and the answer, I found out, comes down to *relevance*. Who is most relevant for you? Is it always the same person (or the same kind of person)? Or does it change depending on the circumstances? And, if so, how and why? *Relevance* is key to understanding how the right contagion infrastructure helps to spread behavior change.

Fit (Or Not) Like Me

In 2009, I took on the task of building another social media–based "health buddy" community. This one was freely available to members of the MIT fitness program. (I had joined the faculty at MIT the previous year.) The program included thousands of students, faculty, and affiliated members who volunteered to participate. My goal was to promote the spread of a new health technology among members of the community.

This technology was called the "diet diary"—a diet-management tool that provided users with detailed information on the quality and quantity of their daily food intake. It was designed to promote healthy eating and, in conjunction with daily exercise logs, it could be used to significantly improve users' ability to achieve and sustain a healthy weight. If one person—let's call her Sally—adopted the innovation, then her neighbors in the community, Jesse and Sarah, could see that fact on their profile pages. Of course, once they saw Sally's new tool, they could likewise sign up for it and start using it themselves. From there, the technology could spread to others.

I was less interested in the technology itself than in finding out what would make it spread. Which participants would be most influential in convincing other members of the community to adopt the new dieting tool? What I discovered was that people were far more likely to adopt the innovation when they received notifications from people whose fitness profiles were like theirs—in fact, *a whopping 200 percent more likely.*

Healthy people were more likely to adopt the innovation when they were connected to other healthy people. That makes sense. But what about the group on the other side of the spectrum—the less fit ones with pounds to lose, breath to catch, and health issues to resolve? You might think they would be most influenced by those who had found success—aspirational role models who embodied their goals. But, strikingly, the opposite was true: less-fit people were more likely to adopt the new health technology when they heard about it from *other* less fit people. Even though all the community members were equally motivated to take advantage of the health technology, the chances that they would register for and use the innovation could be doubled if they heard about it from people they perceived to be more like them.

The Three Rules of Relevance

When we think about people our own age and gender, with similar educational and cultural backgrounds and jobs and family situations, seeing life through their eyes—otherwise known as *perspective-taking*—feels effortless. We intuitively understand their decisions because we understand—and likely share— their core beliefs and values. The more that people are like us, the more easily we can empathize with them, and the more inclined we are to take their choices seriously. Conversely, the more someone differs from us—the less similar their core commitments, concerns, circumstances, and so on are to our own—the more difficult it can be to understand why they do what they do.

It doesn't take a network scientist to realize that the principle of relevance extends far beyond dieting. It holds true when it comes to thinking about all sorts of important life changes, such as moving to a new neighborhood or switching career paths or joining a political campaign. Our lives are filled with considerations based on time, physical proximity, and financial responsibility, all of which can make it difficult to change our familiar behaviors. To overcome these inertial forces, we need to be convinced that change makes sense for *people like us.*

Pretty simple, you may be thinking. Experts talk about our tendency to see and hang out with similar others as *homophily*— "birds of a feather" and all that.

In fact, it's not simple at all. As we dive deeper, you will see that putting the principle of relevance into action is more nuanced than we might think: sure, "people like us"—but like us *in what way?*

It turns out that only certain forms of similarity create relevance—and they vary. Your spouse is relevant for some decisions, but not for others. The same holds true of your college classmates, your professional colleagues, your workout buddies, your fellow hobby enthusiasts, and the people who live on your block.

The key is context. Whether or not a contact is seen as relevant for you is largely determined by the situation. For a patient looking for help with their asthma, finding people with the same ailment is a much stronger basis for social influence than simply finding people of the same race or gender.

There is no magic bullet for establishing relevance, no

single defining trait—gender, race, fitness, status, age, income, or political ideology—that is always influential. However, there are three key principles for understanding how relevance gets established from one context to another:

Principle 1: When people need *social proof* that a particular innovation will be *useful for them,* then *similarity* with earlier adopters is a key factor for creating relevance. People become convinced about the usefulness of a new diet, an exercise program, or a cosmetic treatment only when they see people similar to themselves adopting it.

Principle 2: When behavior change requires a degree of *emotional excitement,* or *feelings of loyalty* and *solidarity,* then—once again—*similarity* among the sources of reinforcement will help to inspire behavior change. For instance, the Pals Battalions campaign in World War I mobilized citizens to action through emphasizing people's sense of solidarity with recruits from the same hometown as them.

Principle 3: When behavior change is based on *legitimacy*— that is, believing that the behavior is widely accepted— then the *opposite* is true: *diversity* among reinforcing sources of adoption is key for spreading the innovation. For instance, people's willingness to join the equal-sign campaign on Facebook depended on seeing it adopted by peers from diverse social circles, who could establish the movement's broad legitimacy.

The important idea for building a successful contagion infrastructure is not similarity, but *relevance.* There are some situations in which the diversity of adopters, rather than their similarity, is actually more important for determining their relevance. It all depends on the context. Fortunately, these three principles can help us determine who will be the most relevant sources of social influence as contexts change.

Principle 1: Credible Sources

Should doctors be role models for the healthy lifestyles they advocate? Nobody wants to get dieting advice from an obese physician, right?

Actually, it depends on the patient.

In 2017, two social scientists from Stanford University, Lauren Howe and Benoit Monin, wanted to find out how to make health messages from physicians more effective. For decades, marketing firms have relied on the popular idea that medical experts are the most influential people for spreading health-and-lifestyle changes. If a physician wants you to try a new diet, they would be most convincing if they were to model that behavior themselves.

But for an obese patient, a healthy physician who advertises the merits of exercise by discussing their personal routine is not in fact likely to be an effective source of influence. In fact, this role-model strategy can backfire: Howe and Monin found that less healthy patients feel judged—even devalued—by physicians who advertise their own healthy lifestyles. The unintended effect is to make patients less receptive to medical advice regarding changes to their diets and exercise habits.

When people need to be convinced that a new behavior or technology will be useful for them, the most influential contacts are typically people who resemble them. In the diet-diary study, for example, obese participants were far more likely to adopt the innovation when they learned about it from similarly overweight peers. For them, less healthy people were more relevant sources of influence than highly fit ones.

I once attended a lecture by a world expert on the topic of obesity. He presented a chart of height-to-weight ratios and asked the audience to find themselves on that chart. He then proceeded to lecture them on the problem of obesity in the United States, and the changes that most Americans needed to make to their diets.

Afterward, my colleagues and I stood silently in the lobby. Finally, someone spoke. "I've never felt so defensive in my entire life," he said. "All I could think about was how skinny that lecturer was." We burst into a chorus of agreement.

My colleagues and I were all recent PhDs. All of us were young, athletic, and fit. In fact, my colleague who spoke up was a runner who had been a competitive athlete all through college and graduate school.

It didn't matter. Nor did it matter that we were all working on health-policy research at the time; somehow the lecturer had made us all feel self-consciously different from him. None of us could even remember the main points of the lecture. All we could think about was how offensive it was. (And how much we suddenly felt a craving for junk food.)

So how can physicians more successfully influence their patients?

Their ability to persuade their patients to try something new may come not from their medical authority but from their perceived similarities with the patients. For instance, pediatricians are often more influential in giving advice to parents when they supplement medical information with anecdotes about their experiences with their own children. Their influence comes as much from being parents as from being doctors.

A particularly well-known example in the medical community is vaccination. For new parents trying to determine the credibility and safety of vaccines, the opinions of other parents are often seen as more relevant than the opinions of expert epidemiologists. It's not surprising that physicians' advice about vaccination is often more influential when they share stories about vaccinating their own children.

The same principle powers the success of the online patient community Patients Like Me. People with rare illnesses are receptive to advice coming from others who have the same condition. For patients considering the use of a new medical device or weighing whether to join a randomized controlled trial, advice from peers who have faced similar challenges is often viewed as more credible than advice from medical professionals.

It's not just in medicine. In any situation in which the costs are high and people want to mitigate their personal risk, they seek confirmation from similar peers. Take corporate-governance decisions. Corporate boards make decisions about policies that will affect the stability and profitability of their company. There are always risks with a new strategy, and the stakes are high. The credibility of a new idea often comes from examining the decisions made by the board members of "peer institutions"— organizations that have the same size, capital structure, and general makeup as their own. Research findings show that corporate board members are far more likely to follow the lead of similar corporations than the lead of highly successful—but not very similar—ones.

In the 1980s hostile takeovers were becoming increasingly common. Boards needed to devise strategies that would simultaneously discourage predatory firms from making a hostile takeover bid while encouraging top executives to increase the company's value (which would inevitably make the organization more attractive for a hostile takeover). The "poison pill" was a corporate innovation designed to solve this problem. It promised key shareholders the ability to buy the firm's shares at just 50 percent of their value if a hostile agent succeeded in gaining a significant percentage of the firm's stock. The effect would be to dramatically dilute the value of the company's stock, raising the cost of pursuing a takeover.

After it was introduced in 1982, the poison pill was slow to take off. There was strong initial resistance because board members feared that adopting the poison pill would be seen as creating a self-destruct button in the event of a hostile takeover. Boards were worried that adopting the poison pill would lead analysts to preemptively devalue their company. These perceived risks prevented the innovation from gaining much traction among Fortune 500 firms in the early 1980s.

But that all changed in 1985.

As the climate of hostile takeovers worsened, boards of directors took special interest in the preventive measures adopted by firms in their same sector (for example, heavy manufacturing, textiles, software, and so on). All it took was for a few early-adopting firms to embrace the poison pill for their peer institutions to quickly see the innovation as a credible option for them too.

Once a company's peer institutions adopted an innovation, it lowered its own risks associated with adopting it. If *all the firms* in the same sector embraced the poison pill, analysts would not be able to devalue one firm without devaluing all of them. The more firms in the same sector that adopted it, the lower the risk for everyone else. There was safety in following the herd.

And there was danger in *not* following: any organization that failed to adopt the same measures as their peers for preventing hostile takeovers would look more vulnerable than the

rest of the firms in their sector—and therefore more susceptible to takeover. Once the poison pill started to catch on within
a sector, peer institutions could not afford to wait. The innovation took off.

From 1985 to 1989, the poison pill jumped from less than 5
percent adoption among Fortune 500 firms to being adopted
by a majority of them. An essential factor in the successful
spread of the new corporate-governance strategy was its transmission between peer institutions within the same industry sector and with a similar capital structure. By 1990, the poison pill
had rapidly propagated through the interlocking social networks among boards of directors to become the most widely
adopted strategy for preventing hostile takeovers.

Whether an innovation is a health technology or a new
corporate-governance strategy, its credibility is established most
easily through networks of similar peers.

Principle 2: Creating Solidarity

The second principle is not about establishing the credibility of
an innovation, but instead about triggering emotional engagement.

Emotional contagions spread most effectively through social
networks that activate people's identity as members of a particular region, cause, or religious group. In sports, collective
excitement often grows through regional antagonism toward
an out-group, which strengthens people's loyalty to the in-group.
Boston Red Sox fans, for instance, strengthen their feelings of
solidarity through shared animosity toward the New York
Yankees.

Political rallies are remarkably similar. Speakers spread
excitement about a cause by emphasizing the ideological, racial,

or economic similarities among supporters, and by stressing the differences between supporters and opponents. From political gatherings to sporting events, the emotional power of similarity, and its effectiveness for spreading excitement, is a pervasive feature of how emotional contagions expand.

But similarity itself is often defined by the social context. Precisely *who* is seen as similar to us can easily change.

In the 1980s, an epidemic of injection drug use was ravaging inner-city America, and so was HIV/AIDS. One of the main sources of disease transmission was HIV-infected drug users sharing their needles with fellow users. Late in the decade, a nationwide public-health campaign was initiated in the US to address the HIV/AIDS epidemic. The goal was not to stop drug use. It was to stop drug users from sharing their infected needles. Millions of dollars were spent on safer-injection programs, which were designed to persuade drug users to take precautions, such as cleaning their needles with bleach and water before sharing them.

The problem was that injection drug users were not listening to public-health messages. They knew they were viewed as addicts and criminals. They lived separate lives from most Americans. They were alienated from standard medical care. They were immune to advice from health-care providers and aid workers.

Most of the safer-injection programs did not fare well early on. But there were a few unlikely successes, including a series of experimental outreach efforts in small Connecticut cities such as New London and Middletown.

How did they succeed where other cities failed?

The credit goes to a group of innovative sociologists and public-health scholars, including the sociologists Doug Heckathorn and Robert Broadhead. Their idea was to use the principle of similarity to activate a contagion of safer-injection practices within the drug users' social networks. It was an unusual idea at the time, because no one was thinking about public-health behaviors as social contagions.

But it was clear that a new approach was needed. By the 1990s, sociologists had given up on the idea of using informational campaigns to promote public health.

They realized that although injection drug users were concerned about the risks of HIV, they were not interested in advice from mainstream health-care providers.

Heckathorn's new idea was to make the safer-injection program an emotional contagion. Instead of trying to work around drug users' alienation from mainstream medical care, he and his colleagues would instead turn it into a rallying point for social solidarity.

His clever twist on the traditional approach to a public-health campaign was to change the stigma of *drug user* from an obstacle into a resource. He would use drug users' sense of similarity with one another as the primary way to spread support for the intervention among this hard-to-reach population.

Heckathorn and other sociologists worked with these cities to develop outreach efforts that mobilized strong feelings of solidarity among drug users in their community. Remarkably, they asked the drug users themselves to help "recruit" their peers to come in for HIV testing, and to advocate for safer injection. New recruits who arrived at the outreach centers for testing and treatment were then invited to become the next line of "recruiters" to bring in new peers, and so on. It was astonishingly effective. Drug users wouldn't listen to traditional authority figures such as public-health officials, but they *would* listen to other drug users.

Initial outreach efforts expanded into chains of previously

undocumented drug users, who were persuaded to participate in HIV testing and peer education about safer-injection practices. The more people who were recruited, the greater the social reinforcement for others, and the wider the influence of the safer-injection program. The surprising effectiveness of the campaign stemmed from Heckathorn's strategy, which turned a stigma into a source of social solidarity. In doing so, the safer-injection program gathered unlikely traction within a vast and largely invisible community of drug users.

From regional sports affiliations to injection drug users, perceived similarity can emerge in a variety of ways. Regardless of how perceptions of similarity take shape, they have remarkable power to spread feelings of solidarity.

The earliest demonstration of this power comes from an unorthodox study conducted in 1954. In a remote boys' summer camp in Oklahoma, the renowned social psychologists Muzafer Sherif and Carolyn Sherif recruited a group of middle-class American boys, all about twelve years old, who were from identical social, economic, and religious backgrounds.

The boys were arbitrarily divided into two teams, called the Rattlers and the Eagles. The team identities were meaningless. No team was given extra privileges or special treatment. They were then pitted against each other in a series of competitions.

Before revealing the disturbing results of the camp study, it's important to tell you that it was not conducted under what we now consider to be proper experimental or ethical protocols. It would not be allowed today. But it highlights one finding that has been shown repeatedly since. Feelings of solidarity can be effectively spread among strangers simply by assigning them fictitious group identities.

The Sherifs' manipulations of the boys triggered strong feelings of loyalty within each of the teams, leading to dramatic changes in the boys' behaviors—even resulting in spontaneous, collective acts of violence by each team against the other. Despite the fact that the boys were otherwise identical across the teams, their newfound similarity as Rattlers or Eagles triggered sustained emotional support for attacks against the out-group.

A replication of this study in the Middle East randomly assigned Muslim and Christian boys to two teams, the Blue Ghosts and the Red Genies. Within days, growing feelings of team loyalty led to coordinated violence inflicted by one team on the other. The boundaries of solidarity and violence were not Muslims versus Christians, but Blue Ghosts versus Red Genies. The artificial team distinctions trumped elements of identity that were rooted in centuries of historical conflict.

This capacity for tribalism is reminiscent of recent political campaigns in the US and elsewhere. Emotional excitement is often effective for mobilizing the true believers. But doesn't that lock us into echo chambers? Doesn't this tendency to be more emotionally engaged with similar peers prevent people from achieving solidarity beyond traditional lines of similarity and difference?

In the previous chapter, we saw how wide bridges can coordinate people's language and transfer knowledge across group boundaries. They can also spread *emotional* contagions. And not just contagions that reinforce existing beliefs and loyalties. Remarkably, wide bridges can also be used to influence people's perceptions about which peers are similar, and how they experience feelings of group solidarity.

In 2017, Yale University social scientist Aharon Levy and his colleagues published a remarkable series of studies that applied the idea of wide bridges to the herculean task of spreading emotional solidarity to oppositional groups, for instance between

Israelis and Palestinians. The key to their strategy was to create *bridging groups*. The members of bridging groups had similarities to both sides. For instance, Arab citizens of Israel—ethnically Arab individuals who were Israeli citizens—had sympathies with both groups, and could act as a bridge between them.

A single individual cannot do this alone. There need to be wide bridges from each of the respective groups to the bridging group that sits between them. To study this process experimentally, the researchers went back to the idea of Reds and Blues. They recruited groups of Jewish Israeli students to play a game in which everyone was randomly assigned to be on a team in which they were either a Red, a Blue, or a Red/Blue (the bridging group in between). The participants were given some money (say, $10) and told that they could donate it to people in either the Red group or the Blue group. The control condition for this experiment had just two groups, Reds and Blues. But the experimental condition included the third group: the Red/Blues.

The results from the control condition were just as expected. As the Sherifs and many other researchers had already discovered, people were loyal only to their own groups. Reds gave to Reds, and Blues to Blues.

But in the experimental condition, people became significantly more likely to share their newfound wealth with the other groups. It was like the Sherifs' findings, but in reverse. Reds gave to Blues, and vice versa. Simply through the presence of the bridging group, people's sense of who was similar to whom had changed. The result was that both Reds and Blues were more generous toward outsiders.

How well would this idea work for Israelis and Palestinians?

In a follow-up study, the researchers ran a simple experiment in which they interviewed Jewish Israelis about whether they supported military policies toward Palestine, and whether they would support financial and medical aid to Palestinians. In the control condition, participants responded that they favored military policies, and did not favor aid. In the experimental condition, participants first read an article about Arab citizens of Israel who identified with both Palestine and Israel, then responded to the policy questions. This intervention was so slight that it seemed unlikely to have any effect at all. But, in fact, it did—much more than the researchers expected. Participants in the experimental condition were significantly less likely to support aggressive military policies against Palestine, and significantly more likely to favor the allocation of Israeli resources for Palestinian aid. Strikingly, participants in the experimental group reported greater feelings of personal identification with Palestinians, and significantly less anger toward them. The mere *existence* of a bridging group changed their feelings toward the out-group.

Emotional contagion is amplified by perceived similarity. The social context will often determine which people are seen as similar and how group solidarity is defined. Groups that do not have any contact, or only glancing contact, are more easily agitated by one another. Bridging groups can redraw the lines of similarity and change the way emotional contagions spread.

Principle 3: Establishing Legitimacy

In contrast to Principle 1 and Principle 2, which identify the importance of similarity, Principle 3 identifies contexts where diversity is essential. When the *legitimacy* of a movement or innovation is the crucial factor for its diffusion, diversity—not similarity—will be the primary principle for triggering adoption.

To understand the vital role diversity can play in the success of a change initiative, it's worth looking back at the success of the Human Rights Campaign's initiative to spread the red-and-pink equal-sign logo in a show of support for same-sex marriage. When researchers Lada Adamic and Bogdan State were studying how the logo spread to nearly three million Facebook users, they uncovered novel findings about this complex contagion: it mattered not only *how many* contacts adopted the change, but also *which* contacts they were.

Within the activist community, support for the equal-sign movement was mobilized by feelings of emotional excitement, pride, and solidarity. As you would expect, it spread quickly through reinforcing ties that were based on people's similarities. However, to reach three million people, the movement needed to achieve legitimacy among a much wider community. This is where the diversity of social contacts came into play.

Think for a moment about your own social-media network. Your community of contacts might be composed of your high-school friends, college friends, work friends, and family members, among other friends and acquaintances. Suppose a few of your college friends are part of the LGBTQ community, and they change their profiles to show support for same-sex marriage. Their decision does not necessarily mean that the movement is widely supported among your other friends and contacts. If you're straight, you might wonder if this new trend is really relevant to you. Indeed, the more similar the adopters are to one another, the more conspicuous it is that they are different from everyone else—namely, all the non-adopters. You already know the problem (you saw it with Google Glass, and with the Aerosmith gesture); it's the problem of *countervailing influences*.

Strong similarity among the adopters actually strengthens the countervailing influences coming from the diverse crowd of non-adopters in your network. These diverse countervailing influences are enough to give pause to anyone but a diehard supporter of the cause.

But what would happen if instead you saw people from different parts of your social-media community—that is, your family members, neighbors, college friends, and work colleagues—all changing their profile photos to support same-sex marriage? Instead of seeming like a niche initiative, the equal-sign movement would now appear to have much greater legitimacy. And Adamic and State showed that it wouldn't take hundreds of your contacts to persuade you of this. Just ten contacts, drawn from diverse segments of your social community, typically sufficed to convince people that the movement was broadly accepted. Once that threshold had been triggered, users perceived there would be minimal social risks associated with showing their support.

The power of diversity generalizes to a surprising variety of situations where *legitimacy* is the primary consideration for potential adopters. A 2016 study of political-campaign contributions showed that political donations were the same kind of complex contagion as the equal-sign movement. Campaign contributions spread through donors' networks by the power of social reinforcement. When there was enough early support for a candidate, campaign donations snowballed into a wealth of future contributions and widespread endorsements. But the *source* of early support was crucial.

Diversity was the key to success.

That seems oddly counterintuitive. An old saw in politics is the importance of "mobilizing the base." And indeed, that is a necessary step along the way to success. But early on in a political campaign, strategies that focus too narrowly on mobilizing the base can unintentionally backfire. Again: countervailing influences.

If the only support for a candidate comes from a homogeneous community, it sends an implicit but clear signal to everyone else: *this candidate represents a specialized group.* It's the same kind of signal that people would receive on Facebook if only members of the LGBTQ community were supporting the equal-sign movement. Too much similarity among the adopters indicates there's only niche support. By the same token, too much similarity among early donors can signal that the candidate is not widely accepted, nor representative of broader interests. Not only can this reduce a candidate's future campaign donations, it can directly increase potential donors' support for the *opposition* candidate.

The key to mobilizing support for a new candidate is to court diversity. Early fundraising from diverse sources provides a strong signal that a candidate has broad appeal. Just like the equal-sign movement, the numbers do not need to be overwhelming. The *quality* of early support can be more important than the quantity.

This lesson is particularly salient for political newcomers. The question on every donor's mind is whether the candidate is viable. The broader the perceived acceptance of the candidate, the more viable they appear. Viability becomes a self-fulfilling prophecy: establishing the broad appeal of a candidate early on can effectively trigger a contagion of additional campaign donations, further increasing the candidate's viability. The key to success is to get started in the right way. At the beginning of a campaign, donations from diverse sectors signal the candidate's appeal to a wide audience of donors, which in turn leads to substantial gains in the likelihood of political success.

The importance of diversity applies not only to social movements and political campaigns, but also to the acceptance of innovative products. In particular, the appeal of social technologies is often based on how widely accepted they are. In an insightful 2012 study, computer-science luminary Jon Kleinberg, along with a team of colleagues from Cornell University and Facebook, identified the key social-network principles behind Facebook's remarkable success. Not only was the spread of Facebook a complex contagion, but its explosive growth was driven by diversity in people's recruitment networks.

To identify how Facebook achieved its growth so efficiently, the researchers examined a collection of fifty-four million emails sent from Facebook users inviting non-users to join the site. Surprisingly, reinforcing messages from multiple peers who were from the same social group were not a major factor in the spread of Facebook. However, reinforcing invitations from people who belonged to diverse social groups directly predicted new users' adoption rates.

Going a step further, the researchers identified the principle underlying people's continued engagement with Facebook after they joined. The results were the same. Whether new adopters would continue to use Facebook or abandon it could be predicted by the diversity of their active contacts. Surprisingly, the diversity of a person's active network was more important than its overall size.

The takeaway?

The strategy for effective social reinforcement depends upon the context. In cases where establishing legitimacy or mass appeal is critical for further growth, courting diversity is key. As we saw with the equal-sign movement, the numbers need not be overwhelming. *Who* is adopting is just as important as *how many* are adopting. The perceived legitimacy of a social movement, a social technology, or a political candidate is significantly strengthened by reinforcement from diverse social circles.

* * *

The foregoing chapters identified the two essential elements—*wide bridges* and *relevance*—for building a contagion infrastructure. Wide bridges are necessary for carrying reinforcing signals across a population. The principle of relevance helps you figure out *which* reinforcing signals are most influential.

You saw that context is king when it comes to putting the principle of relevance into action. To decide whether the key factor is similarity (and what kind of similarity) or diversity (and what kind of diversity), you need to get specific. In chapter 4, I showed you that there are several possible sources of complexity for a social contagion—including the need for credibility, emotional excitement, and legitimacy. Identifying the specific source of complexity in a given social context will help you determine the relevant factors for social influence, from one change campaign to another.

The next part of the book moves from the essential elements of a contagion infrastructure to the crucial question of how to light the match that will get your initiative going. Where should you concentrate your resources to jump-start change? What's the size of the critical mass you will need to make your campaign take off?

Part III answers these questions, along with the hardest question of all: How can you overturn a social norm that has already taken hold?

PART III

THE 25 PERCENT TIPPING POINT

CHAPTER 8

In Search of a New Normal

At 5:50 a.m. on September 3, 1967, the Swedish people waited nervously. The highways were empty. The streets were silent. There was an eerie, almost postapocalyptic stillness across the nation. It was Dagen H—or "H-Day," as it would later be called.

Overnight, the Swedish government had switched the entire country from left-lane driving to right-lane driving. For four years, the government had been preparing the Swedes for this day. Daily television and radio commercials, billboards, and widely marketed H-Day underwear were ever-present reminders that H-Day was approaching. The government even held a national competition for a pop song to celebrate H-Day. A local journalist won the contest and had his song broadcast nationally for the better part of a year.

At 12:59 a.m. on September 3, all traffic was stopped in Sweden. For the next five hours, driving was illegal. From 1 a.m. to 6 a.m., the streets were repainted, the road signs replaced, the traffic lights adjusted. *Nationwide.* Only a small, wealthy, well-organized country could pull off such a feat.

Then at 6 a.m. the roads were opened, and Sweden was reborn. It was now a right-lane-driving nation. The official reports from the Swedish government indicate that the outcome was a big success. There were only 137 car accidents the first day, only 11 of which resulted in injuries.

But firsthand accounts of that day from Swedish residents are more telling.

People who remember H-Day recall chaos. For each of the 137 reported accidents, there were hundreds of unreported near-accidents throughout small towns and major cities. Bjorn Sylven, a Stockholm resident, recalled the streets that day as a dangerous tumult of cars and people. "Outside my school," Sylven told an interviewer, "I saw about three times that cars veered on the wrong side, and came very close to hitting the other schoolchildren."

The problem was not that people did not know what to do. Everyone knew that it was H-Day. The problem was that people did not know what *other* people were going to do.

Imagine driving down a country road outside Stockholm at 6:30 a.m. on H-Day. You are in the right-hand lane, as you expect everyone else to be. A pair of headlights rises over a hill on the horizon, coming toward you. You cannot tell from a distance which side of the road they're on. As the headlights approach, they appear to be closer to your side of the road than they should be. Should you stay on the right? You know what the law says. But perhaps this driver coming toward you is tired, or distracted, or simply does not like the new rule, as they appear to be moving toward your lane. What should you do? Accommodate the other driver and move to the left, or stick to your guns and stay on the right?

Sociologists call this a *coordination dilemma.* In a coordination dilemma, laws don't help us. Even television and radio and newspaper ads don't necessarily help us. Regardless of what the law says, and regardless of what people are told to do in Stockholm or in any part of the country, the only thing you care about on that country road at 6:30 a.m. is what that other driver is going to do.

Solving a coordination dilemma requires an everyday kind of mind reading. As you see headlights nearing you on the country road, you believe that you understand the other driver's intentions and can anticipate what they will do. You also believe that they know your intentions and can anticipate what *you* will do. You both believe that you can read each other's minds. Otherwise, driving at speed toward an oncoming set of headlights would be a very dangerous prospect.

If you hit a pothole and swerve into the left lane, the other driver must make a quick judgment about you—are you moving to the left out of habit, or did you simply lose control of your car for a moment and do you now intend to move back to the right? If they respond by moving to their left, now you must determine what *they* are thinking. Are they moving to the left because they have forgotten about H-Day, or are they doing it in response to you? These calculations take only milliseconds, but they are crucial.

When you have no idea what people will do, you cannot coordinate with them.

This is exactly what happened in Sweden. Cars swerved and veered and skidded off the road. Traffic came to a standstill. By the end of the day, the streets were littered with abandoned vehicles. The problem was not that no one knew the rules. Everyone knew the rules. The problem was that people couldn't read one another's minds.

These kinds of coordination dilemmas are more common than you might think. You can probably recall a moment when you accidentally bumped into someone in a hallway. Once you both regained your composure, each of you tried to carry on. But, by accident, you both moved in the same direction, and in a blink you wound up back in front of each other. The normal thing to do is laugh and shrug, acknowledging that you both feel the absurdity of the situation—as if two adults cannot figure out how to walk down a hallway without running into each other. But if this keeps happening, it quickly goes from funny to annoying.

We encounter these kinds of coordination dilemmas every day. Intuitively, we all know how to solve them—by using social norms. In the US, we usually each move to our right and continue on our way. But what happens when social norms change?

In 2014, *Business Insider* reported on the strange case of Chris Padgett, an executive coach living in Ohio. Chris is in his late thirties, with sandy blond hair and a welcoming smile. As an executive coach, his job is to have monthly meetings with top-level executives and provide guidance on strategies for negotiations, best practices for management, and tips for professional relations. If anyone knows the proper way to interact in a business setting, it's Chris.

But even Chris found himself appreciating how complicated social norms can be. A few months before, he had met a new client who was a C-suite executive. Chris noticed that the meeting did not begin with the customary handshake; instead his client sat down with him and got right to work. Chris thought it was strange. "Weird," he thought. "Maybe he just forgot."

The meeting was productive, and everyone felt satisfied. As they all stood up from their chairs, the pleased executive looked at Chris and smiled. Then he thrust his fist toward Chris. "It threw me," he recalled. "At that level there's more formality, and this guy in his mid-fifties was like, 'Nope.'"

Their knuckles met in midair. Chris's executive fist bump was complete.

It was a revelation for Chris. Reflecting on recent meetings, he realized he had noticed other highly respected senior people forgoing the age-old tradition of shaking hands for the hipper, germ-friendly fist bump. The handshake is a tried-and-true business tradition. How could the fist bump replace it? Chris was a professional expert in business etiquette, and he hadn't seen this coming. But now he had to think about it. He had new clients arriving the following day. How should he greet them?

It wasn't just Chris. The increasing acceptance of the fist bump among executives caught the world by surprise. In 2012 and 2013, top news outlets such as the *New York Times* and the *Chicago Tribune* ran stories about whether the fist bump might permanently replace the handshake. By 2014, *Adweek, Business Insider, Fast Company,* and *Forbes* were running stories about this etiquette crisis, offering advice for executives trying to figure out whether to shake hands or bump fists.

For Chris, it was like the chaos on Sweden's roadways. He didn't know what other people were going to do. No one did. And none of the professional journals could help him solve his coordination dilemma. When Chris meets a new client for the first time, he doesn't know which articles they've read or not read. He doesn't know what trends they've seen or not seen. Will they think the fist bump is tacky? Or that the handshake is too retro? Chris doesn't actually care whether they shake hands or bump fists. All he cares about is making his new clients feel comfortable, and establishing a good rapport. Figuring out whether to shake hands or bump fists might seem like a small coordination dilemma, but it has big consequences. For anyone in business, your greeting is your first impression. You need to get it right.

The Power of a Witch Hunt

The famous twentieth-century philosopher David Lewis wrote, "It is the profession of philosophers to question platitudes that others accept without thinking twice." In fact, Lewis was talking about social norms—like driving on the right or shaking hands—that make our world feel orderly and normal. We often forget how important they are. Only when they break down, or when they start to change, can we begin to see how much they matter.

Consider this simple example. Two neighbors sit in a rowboat in the middle of a river. Each has one oar, and they must figure out how to row to shore. One person can work hard while the other lazes in the sun. But then the boat will go in circles, and they will both be no closer to land. Alternatively, they can each work diligently. But unless they coordinate their efforts, they may row in opposite directions, and again they will go nowhere.

To succeed, they must work together. Most importantly, each must anticipate what the other will do—and trust that the other will anticipate what *they* will do. They must solve the coordination dilemma by coming to a shared understanding of what is normal.

This simple idea dates back to 1740, when philosopher David Hume used it as an analogy for a well-functioning democracy. Neither person can row the boat alone. But they can both succeed if they reach an agreement that allows them to pull together, which gets each of them where they want to be.

That's the sunny side of social norms. But norms also have a dark side.

On June 21, 1956, American playwright Arthur Miller appeared before the House Committee on Un-American Activities. It was less than a month before his wedding to movie star Marilyn Monroe, but he had other things on his mind. He had been compelled by a federal subpoena to come to Washington, DC, and answer the committee's questions. The interrogation took hours, but in the end there was only one question that truly mattered: "Do you now know, and will you please provide the names of, any Communist sympathizers?"

For anyone called before the committee, the best way to protect themselves from the social and professional consequences of failing to support the anti-Communist norm was to become an enforcer of that norm. The accused became the accusers. Each additional citizen who protected themselves by levying accusations against their peers inadvertently increased the legitimacy of the anti-Communist norm.

Industry leaders, Hollywood stars, and even President Harry Truman conceded to the power of the rising tide of anti-Communist sentiment. The cleverness of the committee's tactic was that it took aim not at people but at their social networks. By turning peers into informants against one another, this strategy dismantled the reinforcing networks of trust and support that might have mobilized dissent. Collective suspicion weakened the social bonds within American communities, eliminated trust within friendships, and disrupted the infrastructure that would be needed to mount an opposition.

A few years before Miller was called before the committee, he had written a play that would come to be regarded as one of the greatest works of twentieth-century American theater. It was called *The Crucible*. It was a story about a trial very much like the one he would soon face.

The Crucible recounts the Salem Witch Trials of 1692, drawing out the uncanny parallels with McCarthyism and its bare-fanged hunt for so-called un-American activities. Miller recalled,

"*The Crucible* was an act of desperation....I was motivated in some great part by the paralysis that had set in among many liberals who, despite their discomfort with inquisitors' violations of civil rights, were fearful, and with good reason, of being identified as Communists if they should protest too strongly....The more I read into the Salem panic, the more it touched off corresponding images of common experiences in the fifties: the old friend of a blacklisted person crossing the street to avoid being seen talking to him; the overnight conversions of former leftists into born-again patriots; and so on."

The twentieth century is replete with examples of oppressive social norms. In Nazi Germany, anti-Nazi citizens not only failed to protest as their Jewish neighbors were arrested, they voluntarily identified other neighbors who were harboring Jews. They did this not because they supported the regime, but because, as Miller recounts, "the best proof of the sincerity of your confession was your naming others whom you had seen in the Devil's company." In postwar Russia, Stalin's brutal and unpopular regime was inadvertently strengthened by terrified citizens who outed the dissenters in their neighborhoods. Similar stories emerged from Pinochet's Chile and Mao's China. In all corners of the world, destructive yet somehow self-enforced social norms had overtaken entire societies.

The social power of a witch hunt comes from the fact that the only way for citizens to protect themselves is to conceal their distaste for the ascendant social norm. The result is that people lose the ability to read each other's minds. Their best guesses about what they should expect from others, and what others will expect of them, becomes based on the shared illusion that everyone supports the norm. The more people conceal what they truly believe, the more reason everyone has to enforce the social norm for fear of being seen as a deviant.

These chilling stories remind us of a dangerous past. But is this past entirely behind us? Racist policing policies, gender discrimination in the workplace and on college campuses, and biased medical practices have been illegal for years in the United States. But in the last decade, the explosion of protests on social media, including #BlackLivesMatter and #MeToo, revealed hidden, widespread American conformity with racist and sexist social norms that, despite progressive laws, have endured for decades.

From ruinous norms such as anti-Communist witch hunts and long-entrenched patterns of discrimination, to harmless norms such as greeting strangers with a handshake, why is it so difficult for these seemingly permanent features of our society to be transformed into something new?

Copernicus Shifts the Paradigm

The challenge of dislodging social norms is that we conform to them without realizing it—which means we rarely consider alternatives. Let's start with something easy. Think back to the last time you boarded an elevator. (If you're reading this during the COVID-19 pandemic, it may be a distant memory.) I'm sure that you, like me and everyone else, faced front, toward the elevator doors, without a millisecond's thought. But why didn't you face the back? Or think about the last time you approached a ticket window where lots of people were waiting in line. Did you walk to the front and try to elbow your way to the window? Or did you walk to the back and wait your turn?

Normally, our decisions about how to stand in an elevator or join a ticket line aren't really decisions. They are more like reflexes. We do them "naturally." Not only do we all follow these norms, but we have a visceral sense that people would feel uncomfortable if we flouted such conventions. *We* would feel uncomfortable, too—even though we may realize, rationally, that these norms are arbitrary and vary from community to community, country to country. Often we don't notice our norms until we travel to a new place where the norms differ. In parts of Italy, for instance, it would be odd for someone to walk to the back of the line and wait, rather than just crowd in near the front. In Africa and the Middle East, it is common for men to hold hands as a sign of heterosexual friendship.

But norms serve an important purpose. They make our lives feel orderly and, well, normal. Which is part of why it was so disconcerting during the early days of the pandemic when many of these norms suddenly shifted. People were forced to question their most basic behaviors. The prospect of riding in an elevator or joining a ticket line or encountering a stranger on the sidewalk could now trigger paralyzing anxiety. We no longer had a natural sense of where to stand or how to interact with others. Once-automatic behaviors became coordination dilemmas that everyone was suddenly struggling to solve.

It's good that every aspect of our daily routines is not like this. Our existence would be unbearable—and our brains would likely short-circuit—if we had to deliberate about each of our everyday behaviors. So we take mental shortcuts.

But here's the catch. These mental shortcuts can quickly become problematic. People choose behaviors and make decisions that feel "right"—just as it feels "right" for an American traveler to walk to the back of the ticket line, instead of trying to wedge in near the front. In the mid-twentieth century, it felt "right" for Americans of different races to use different water fountains. And as the #MeToo movement has shown, for many men in the workplace it feels right and "normal" to make sexual comments or advances to female employees. Some of the most heated and vexing ethical and political debates of recent years turn on the question of how to evaluate past behaviors that were once "normal" but are now widely understood to be transgressive. Just because something *feels* right does not mean that it is.

The reason that changing a social norm is difficult is the same reason that learning a new language is difficult: it requires breaking something that works. It requires replacing something familiar and natural with something new and foreign. During a time of social change, our native language fails us. Our mutual efforts to row the boat are flummoxed. We are suddenly transformed from experts into novices—novices who have no idea how to communicate with one another, nor how to figure out what the other person is thinking.

One of the best descriptions of the disorientation that people feel in times of social change comes from physicist Thomas Kuhn, who coined the phrase *paradigm shift*. Kuhn became famous in the 1960s for demonstrating that every major scientific breakthrough—in physics, chemistry, and biology—is accompanied by a period of social bewilderment. These periods reflect changes in social norms. Kuhn's idea of paradigm shifts extends far beyond its implications for social norms, but it is these implications that are most surprising. During paradigm shifts, scientists who had been regarded as world leaders suddenly felt incompetent and irrelevant. In fact, Kuhn described this process of scientific change as nothing short of a "revolution."

There are dozens of examples of these revolutions across every scientific field, but perhaps the most famous is the Copernican revolution. It is a perfect illustration of how a change in social norms can leave people feeling as though they've lost their footing in the world. In a paradigm shift, even expert scientists can come to feel that they are no longer competent professionals. Simply as a result of one new idea.

In Copernicus's day, physicists believed that the Sun revolved around Earth. This seemed true for the obvious reason that it is exactly how it appears in the sky. The Sun moves across our sky, just like the Moon. Obviously, they both circle around us. That seemed to make sense.

The problem was the planets.

If you watch the night sky over time, you will notice that each night Mars moves a little to the left. Night after night it dutifully marches leftward, ever so slowly. It moves at a much slower pace than the Sun and the Moon, but it moves across our sky in the same basic way that they do. However, if you keep watching, you will notice something strange. One night, without warning, Mars will stop moving to the left. A few nights later, it will unexpectedly start moving to the right. The next night, it will move to the right some more.

This doesn't seem normal. But if you wait a few more nights, you can give a thankful sigh of relief as Mars once again begins to make its way back across the sky toward the left. The universe is again on track.

What happened?

You would not be the first to ask this question. Mars's retrograde motion was a troubling piece of data—what scientists call an *anomaly*—because it didn't fit within the accepted theory of the universe. If all of the heavenly bodies—the Sun, the Moon, the stars, and the planets—revolve around Earth in the same way, how is it possible for Mars to move backward?

It took more than a thousand years for astronomers to answer this question. An untold number of theories were developed and refined over that time. But the more sophisticated the theories became, the more anomalies they encountered. By the time of the Renaissance, astronomy had become an embarrassing collection of extremely complicated theories that did not fit together very well.

Then came Copernicus. In the introduction to his revolutionary treatise, he complained, "Those who put their faith in [an Earth-centered universe] have in large measure solved the problem of the apparent motions [of the planets]. But meanwhile they introduced a good many ideas which apparently contradict the first principles of uniform motion. [It is] just like someone taking from various places hands, feet, a head, and other pieces, very well depicted, but not for the representation of a single person; a monster rather than a man would be put together from them."

Copernicus had an idea that would make all the anomalies instantly disappear — but it would also change everything about our understanding of the universe. While everyone was busy trying to devise the next clever variation on the Earth-centered theory of the universe, Copernicus simply moved Earth to the side. He put the Sun at the center of the universe and had Earth orbit it, just like the other planets. He solved all of astronomy's problems in one fell swoop.

That was the Copernican revolution. One small idea that moved the world.

It seems baffling that no one saw it before. But scientific progress often hinges not just on the correctness of a new idea but also on whether people accept it. And Copernicus's simple solution met with massive resistance. It wasn't just the Church, which objected to the theological implications of Copernicus's theory. Even other scientists refused to believe Copernicus. It took more than a hundred years for his elegant solution to be widely accepted.

Copernicus's new theory didn't depend on complex mathematics. In fact, it was *less* sophisticated than many of the accepted theories of the time.

But the problem that was holding back astronomy was not mathematical. It was social. If Copernicus was right, all the scientific theories and concepts that had been developed to solve the problem of the wandering planets would suddenly be rendered meaningless. Copernicus didn't just add a new idea to the existing scientific conversation. He changed the conversation. In fact, he changed the language that the conversation was in. He caused an entire system of professional competence to come crashing down.

This is what a paradigm shift looks like. The familiar ways of talking and thinking suddenly become obsolete. Years of work are instantly irrelevant. Serious, sophisticated researchers suddenly feel like schoolchildren, unable to maneuver confidently in their professional corridors. It's unpleasant for a lot of people. And it's the reason why the great physicist Max Planck darkly confessed, "A new scientific truth does not triumph by convincing its opponents and making them see the light, but rather because its opponents eventually die, and a new generation grows up that is familiar with it."

With social change, things are somewhat different. People really can change their minds about social norms in large numbers, and relatively quickly. Think of the remarkable way public opinion has shifted in recent decades on topics such as women in the workplace or same-sex marriage. But the same kind of resistance that blocks scientific change can also provide a challenge for anyone who wants to initiate social change. When social norms are disrupted, people's day-to-day feelings of social competence and expertise are replaced by feelings of anxiety and social bewilderment.

Remember Chris and his seemingly mundane workplace dilemma—to fist bump or not to fist bump?

After years of professional expertise, Chris suddenly did not know how his behavior would be interpreted. Would a fist bump be perceived as au courant or impertinent? Would a handshake be seen as respectful or uptight? Chris had gone from being a native speaker of his professional language to someone who couldn't hold up his end of a professional exchange. He had lost fluency. He could no longer read his clients' minds.

For social change to succeed, a revolutionary movement must ferry people across these uncertain waters to a new set of expectations and a new sense of competence.

The secret to doing this successfully comes from seeing how language works, and what it reveals about how social norms take hold.

Wittgenstein Goes to Kindergarten

In the autumn of his thirty-third year, philosopher Ludwig Wittgenstein became famous. Wittgenstein was a gaunt, severe-tempered Austrian intellectual, virtually unknown until he announced his presence on the world stage with a short, almost impenetrable treatise that altered the course of philosophy. Following in the footsteps of his mentor, British philosopher Bertrand Russell, Wittgenstein had developed a tight analytical theory of how language works. He saw language as a logical system that unraveled the mysteries of the world. For Wittgenstein, language was everything. If you understood language, then you understood the world.

His ideas became the foundation for an entire generation of philosophy, linguistics, mathematics, and even sociology. It only heightened Wittgenstein's renown that he had achieved folk-hero status during World War I. As legend has it, he penned the final version of his treatise as a prisoner of war during the last year of the conflict. Returning home, he published his treatise and became an overnight sensation.

But that's not the best part of the story.

After becoming famous, Wittgenstein mysteriously disappeared. He turned his back on academic philosophy and retired to the country.

A decade later, Wittgenstein returned to the University of Cambridge with a new big idea. His long hiatus was a one-man paradigm shift that again altered the course of philosophy—this time in the opposite direction. Wittgenstein's new work claimed that his first theory of the world, for which he had become well known a decade earlier, was complete nonsense. It was a waste of time. He reportedly said that anyone still working on it should quit their job and do something more useful.

The field of philosophy has yet to recover.

Renowned Princeton University philosopher Saul Kripke said of Wittgenstein's second treatise that it is still "the most radical and original problem that philosophy has seen to date." In 1999, a survey asked thousands of philosophy professors to identify the most important and influential work of the twentieth century. The "runaway winner" was Wittgenstein's second treatise.

Wittgenstein continued to believe that language was the key to understanding the world. But he no longer believed that *logic* was the key to understanding language. Rather, language was *social*. The secret to understanding language was to understand how people play coordination "games" with one another.

How could one man's thinking shift so radically from one intellectual extreme to the other? What happened during those years when Wittgenstein was locked away in the country, in retreat from philosophy?

He became a kindergarten teacher.

As his sister is rumored to have said, "It was like using a precision instrument as a crowbar." But he was not hiding, nor whittling away the time. He was experimenting with a new way of doing philosophy.

It turned out that Wittgenstein had been using the kindergarten as a kind of philosophical laboratory. He was observing the children: the way they played, the way they learned, the way they constructed meaning, and the way they followed social norms. Kindergarten was, for him, a laboratory for studying coordination dilemmas and how people solve them.

Wittgenstein's new philosophy was that social life could be distilled into a series of coordination games. Language was the chief "game" that people played, and it defined every other feature of how we think and how societies work.

Here are just a few examples:

1. You and I meet for the first time.

I extend my hand, expecting to shake hands. You smile at me but do not shake my hand.

The next time I meet a stranger, do I extend my hand to shake?

The next time you meet a stranger, do *you* extend your hand to shake?

How many failed handshakes does it take before I stop extending my hand to each new stranger? What do I do instead?

2. You and I are new colleagues.

We are talking cordially at the water cooler.

You mention that your salary is lower than you think it should be, and wonder if our mutual employer is paying people unfairly.

I fall silent, then awkwardly change the topic of conversation.

The next time you are at the water cooler with a new colleague, will you mention your concerns about the fairness of our salaries?

The next time I am at the water cooler with a new colleague, will I awkwardly change the subject if they ask a question about the fairness of our salaries?

How many of my new colleagues need to ask about the fairness of our salaries before I stop censoring them by changing the topic of conversation?

3. You and I are new colleagues.

As you arrive at work, I tell you how attractive you are and comment on the shirt you're wearing.

You're uncomfortable with my comment. You make a joke, saying that it shouldn't matter what you wear as long as you do your job well.

The next time I see one of my coworkers wearing an outfit that I think is attractive, will I tell them they look attractive and comment on their clothes?

The next time a coworker of yours comments on your attractiveness and compliments you on your clothes, will you still appear to be uncomfortable and joke that your clothes should not matter?

How many new coworkers of mine need to look uncomfortable, and make observations about the fact that their clothes should not matter, before I stop making comments about their appearance?

These are all coordination games.

Wittgenstein's remarkably clear insight into these games of language has become the scientific model for understanding every kind of social norm, from handshakes to witch hunts.

Today, Wittgenstein's idea of social life as a series of coordination games has become a central tenet of research on social norms in psychology, sociology, philosophy, and computer science. And it is what allowed me, many years later, to develop a method for studying how new social norms take hold.

My idea was that every coordination game had within it a *tipping point*—the point at which a novel behavior gained enough traction that everyone's opinion about what was acceptable would suddenly change. I was fascinated by the idea. It meant that an entire population could be efficiently ferried from one social norm to another just by triggering a critical number of early adopters. If that were true, it would be possible to make reliable predictions about social change, and about the social norms people are likely to follow—including the words we use, the greeting gestures we offer, and the ways we behave at work.

CHAPTER 9

Wittgenstein, #MeToo, and the Secret of Cultural Change

Today, Rosabeth Moss Kanter is a star professor at Harvard Business School and a world-renowned expert on workplace productivity. But in 1977 she was a young scholar just starting her career. That year she published a study that catapulted her to academic stardom: a groundbreaking investigation of how gender inequities affect organizational performance. Would firms be more productive if they offered more equitable pay? Would companies be more innovative if women were given greater voice through leadership roles? Kanter set out to answer these questions by conducting a careful ethnographic study of the nuanced dynamics among the men and women working at a powerful industrial company. Along the way, she discovered a key insight for social change.

Kanter noticed that when women were only a small minority of the firm, they were invariably subject to an oppressive culture of discrimination, unequal pay, and sexual harassment. At those companies, it seemed as though very little could be done to increase women's status or improve their working conditions. However, Kanter's ethnography also revealed a way forward: when women occupied a certain percentage of leadership roles in the organization—somewhere between 20 and 35 percent—the culture of the firm could dramatically shift. In other words, that percentage would be a tipping point.

You are probably familiar with the general notion of a tipping point, a term popularized by Malcolm Gladwell in his book of the same name. But I am using it somewhat differently, to refer to the scientific theory that there is a measurable critical mass in organizations and populations that, once reached, can trigger a sweeping change in people's behavior. Kanter, for instance, believed that if women could reach critical mass in the upper echelons of an organization's hierarchy, they could disrupt the gender norms that licensed discrimination, and establish new norms enforcing gender equality.

She identified several telltale signs of organizations in which the number of women was *below* the hypothesized tipping point. Most notably, women in these organizations occupied a "token" role. They were conspicuous at meetings and in conferences, and as such were regarded by their male colleagues as representatives of their gender. As tokens, their behavior was taken to be emblematic of all women generally. They became symbols of what women could do and how they were expected to act.

At the same time, these women were required to conform to a series of highly ritualized social norms. They were obligated to show deference to their male colleagues, to demonstrate exaggerated masculine or feminine behaviors as the situation demanded, and to attend informal social events with greater frequency than would be expected of their male colleagues. By following these social norms, and conforming to their peers' expectations of how they should behave as representatives of their gender, women avoided failures of coordination.

There were several measurable consequences of these social norms on women's careers. Women were informally punished when they didn't show deference to their male colleagues. As a result, there was a higher dropout rate of women than men from their companies. In addition, because of their small numbers, women lacked proper mentorship. They often experienced "role conflict" when trying to figure out how to adopt the strategies for advancement that worked for their male colleagues—and that were advocated by their male mentors—but that conflicted with the social norms for how women were expected to act in the organization. This conflict, and the impossibility of resolving it, resulted in a lower rate of promotion for women. The most egregious signs that a company was below the hypothesized tipping point were the familiar norms of unequal wages, sexual harassment, and sexual assault.

Following Kanter, other scholars extended these findings to the political domain. Detailed studies analyzing changes in the fraction of women in Scandinavian legislatures found that when the number of women in a legislature was below the hypothesized tipping point, their ability to advance new political causes, and to address the specific concerns of women in the polity, was effectively crippled.

The greatest problem for women politicians who were token minorities was that they were not accepted as legitimate actors on the political stage. This lack of legitimacy subjected them to a political culture—and a style of discourse—that aggressively dismissed the value of women's contributions to legislative debates. As token members of the legislature, women who were successfully elected often found themselves ineffective at achieving their policy goals. Disillusioned, these women showed disproportionately higher dropout rates, as they voluntarily decided not to run for reelection as incumbents.

For token minorities both in business and in politics, an essential problem was that they lacked a sufficient critical mass to create legitimacy for the topics they cared about. Women were therefore unable to shift the professional discourse to address the key issues that affected them, such as childcare or sexual harassment. A report from the Danish parliament found that "most politicians did not have a vocabulary to speak about women's position, discrimination, inequality, women's diseases, unpaid labor, division of work between the sexes, sexual harassment, or sexual violence against women." Consequently, male members of parliament felt uncomfortable having these topics discussed in session. When female legislators would explicitly try to raise these issues, they encountered strong opposition. Unable to speak authoritatively on these subjects, their male colleagues deemed the topics inappropriate for parliamentary debate. In essence, the language of politics, and therefore the substance of politics, was governed by the gender of the politicians.

Kanter's big idea was that all of this could change if women could just reach the tipping point. It was—and is—a stunning hypothesis. And it has powerful implications for what #MeToo and other social-change movements can achieve: if the right percentage of people stand up and say that they will not tolerate inappropriate sexual conduct in the workplace, even a small minority may be able to trigger a major cultural shift.

It's an inspiring prospect. But does it work?

When I was first introduced to these ideas, I was transfixed by the possibility they held for explaining how social change happens. The idea of finding a precise tipping point for change is something of a holy grail for social science. The belief that "thresholds" or tipping points exist is nearly a century old. The question has been actively debated among scientists and philosophers at least since the 1950s, long before Kanter's groundbreaking research on gender dynamics gave it new life. On a more practical level, the search to find the size of the critical mass needed for change is something that activists, entrepreneurs, and policymakers have struggled with for generations. Everyone wants to know: Is there really a tipping point for social change? If so, what is it?

For me, the challenge boiled down to two basic questions. First, how can we show that tipping points really exist? There are, after all, many factors that might explain why social change happens—demographic shifts, new legislation, dropping unemployment rates, innovative workplace technologies, fluctuating housing prices—and a variety of other forces that inspire change. How can we know for sure that a critical mass of activists *caused* a social norm to shift by reaching a tipping point?

Second, if we *can* determine that a tipping point exists, is there a way to figure out where it sits, mathematically? How *much* social reinforcement is needed? Can we identify an exact critical point at which social change will happen?

I found the solution to these challenges in the work of Ludwig Wittgenstein. He might seem an unlikely source: what does an austere Austrian philosopher from the first half of the twentieth century have to do with understanding Rosabeth Moss Kanter's study of gender in organizations in the latter part of the century, or the success of the #MeToo movement today?

A lot, as it turns out!

As we saw in chapter 8, Wittgenstein believed that the way people make sense of the world—how we act and what we believe—is at base a coordination game. For me, this meant that the tipping point was really just the point at which people could no longer coordinate with one another without changing their behavior. For instance, the tipping point for the fist bump would be the point at which people could no longer successfully manage their professional encounters without switching from handshakes to fist bumps. Even though the social norm of shaking hands embodies a long and venerated tradition in American business culture, my belief was that when it comes to social norms, our need for *social coordination* is more powerful than our love of tradition—and that that need was the key to social change.

To test this hypothesis, I needed to study how people's behaviors would change in a real-world coordination game. Wittgenstein had found a "philosophical laboratory"—a kindergarten class—for studying social behavior. Could I find— or create—a "sociological laboratory" for testing the theory of tipping points? Not with children learning norms, as Wittgenstein used, but with adults who were *already* using norms, to see whether reaching a critical mass of activists could force people to change the norms they would follow?

My idea was to build a community online where people played the same kind of social-coordination games we regularly play in our daily lives, following norms of language and civility. In the same way that we all figure out how to behave in the various spheres of our social lives—at work, in an intimate relationship, when out with friends, or when meeting strangers— I thought I could create a social community on the internet where I could observe this process of social coordination in action. It would be a social petri dish in which I could observe a "culture" emerge among the people interacting there. Once everyone had established a set of normal behaviors for communicating with one another, I would see if I could successfully disrupt it—to get everyone to adopt a *new* pattern of behavior— by inserting a group of "activists" into the community. Which eventually led me to the essential question: How many change-makers does it take to make change?

The Name Game

When Kanter was studying organizations in the 1970s, she and a growing number of sociologists and economists were beginning to embrace the idea that it was possible for a modest fraction of the population to trigger change, even when a majority was still resisting it. Kanter's ethnographic studies led to the hypothesis that the critical mass needed to "tip" social norms would be around only 20 to 35 percent of the population. Years later, my own research on networks built on these ideas, showing that if enough social reinforcement was concentrated within a social network, it might trigger a broad contagion of social change, eventually spreading to everyone. My colleagues and I believed that we could use the theory of complex contagions to derive an exact mathematical prediction for the tipping point.

Our approach was to think of someone like Chris. How many times would he need to encounter a new behavior like the fist bump before abandoning his trusted handshake? Although Chris had a long history of shaking hands, his recent encounters were likely to be more relevant than older ones when he was deciding how to approach a new situation. We reasoned that if the fist bump became the most frequently encountered behavior in Chris's recent memory, he would change his behavior and use the fist bump in his next meeting.

How many early adopters were needed to trigger a chain reaction that would ultimately "tip" the population? The prediction we derived was right in line with Kanter's original studies: we predicted a tipping point of 25 percent. Once one-fourth of a population adopted a new belief or behavior, we posited, the others would quickly follow.

At the time of our study, this was a controversial prediction. A group of physicists had recently predicted that the tipping point for social change could be as low as 10 percent of the population. At the same time, many social scientists were seriously speculating that tipping points may not exist in society at all. These scholars believed that the process of coordinating on social norms might simply be too complex to measure. Given these varying conjectures, our 25 percent prediction was far from certain. But it seemed a good place to start.

To test the theory of tipping points, we created ten independent online communities. They ranged in size from twenty to thirty people. In each community, we connected the participants together into a social network.

Each community played a "language game" in which they would try to come up with an appropriate name for a random person. We gathered the pictures of ten unknown people and gave one picture to each community. Some communities were given a picture of a male face; others saw a female face. Then we asked: What do you think that person's first name might be?

We began each round with members of each community randomly paired with one of their network neighbors. So in a network of twenty people, we would create ten random pairs each round. The players in each pair had twenty seconds to come up with a name for the pictured face. Everyone played simultaneously.

If you were playing the game, as the round started you would see the pictured face, then a space where you could type any name you wanted. You could not see your partner or what they were typing. You knew only that both of you had twenty seconds to choose a name, and that you were trying to coordinate with each other. At the end of the round, each player would see the name his or her partner suggested. Then you'd be paired with a different member of your community, and you'd play again.

If you and your partner chose the same name, you would both get a cash payment. But if you and your partner chose different names, you would both *lose* money. People hate losing money, so they were highly motivated to coordinate.

Players in the game were just like Chris trying to figure out whether to shake hands or fist bump—or do something else. Chris wanted to coordinate with his new clients. But more than that, he didn't want to *miscoordinate*. In each new encounter with a client, Chris would learn something about the behaviors that people in his professional circle were using; he would then use these experiences to make an informed decision about how to greet the next person he met.

It was the same in our game.

The fun thing about the game was that there was no right answer. People could suggest any name they wanted to (and they did!). But that was the hard thing about it, too: You had no idea what anyone else would do. You could see only the name that your partner in the previous round had entered. You did not know the names other people in the community were using. You did not even know how many people were in your community, nor how many people you were going to meet. Just like Chris, you couldn't use population-level information to infer what the next person you met was going to do.

Our game went on for fifty rounds. Round after round, you had to keep trying names until you were lucky enough to coordinate. But, just like Chris, coordinating with one person did not tell you what to expect from anyone else. Each round, you had to make an informed guess about what the next person would do.

At first there was chaos. In the first few rounds, a community of twenty-four people might produce more than sixty names without finding any common ground.

It was H-Day all over again.

But every once and a while, a pair of players would randomly coordinate—on, say, the name *Mia*. Having suffered so many early failures, both players were thrilled to finally succeed. On the next round, they would both try *Mia* with their new partners. Even if *Mia* didn't work on that round, they would probably both try it for at least one or two more rounds.

Here's where networks come into play. If both of the players using *Mia* were interacting with each other's contacts, those contacts would then encounter the name *Mia* from them. Now, suppose those people were then partnered with each other.

Because *Mia* had recently been reinforced for each of them, they might both try it.

Surprise! They would succeed.

Now, both of *these* players would try to use *Mia* in their next few rounds.

You can see where this is going. The more times *Mia* was reinforced in a community's network, the more likely it was that additional people would start trying it—and the likelier they were to succeed. All of which made it more likely that *Mia* would keep spreading, until ultimately everyone was using *Mia* in every round.

How long do you think it took for a group of twenty-four people to establish their own social norm? Ten minutes? Twenty minutes? It typically took less than *five* minutes. Sometimes it was even faster.

Each community started off in anarchy. But small sparks of coordination quickly led people to coordinate on the same behavior that their peers—and their peers' peers, and their peers' peers' peers—were using. By Round fifteen, every time someone met a stranger, they would immediately know how to coordinate.

Once a norm took hold, everyone knew what to expect from one another. Just like shaking hands.

A few chapters ago, I told you about the spread of birth control in Korea. The most surprising fact in that story was that although each community converged on a contraceptive norm, the particular behavior they agreed upon differed from village to village. Some were "IUD villages"; others were "pill villages"; and still others were "vasectomy villages." The success of contraception in Korea did not depend upon the particular method of contraception, but simply upon social coordination within each community. It was the social norm that mattered, not the specific method.

The same thing happened in our name-game experiment. Each community successfully converged on its own social norm, but the norm was different in each case. Even when we tried giving two different communities the same pictured face, the name that each community coordinated on was different. One community would coordinate on *Elizabeth,* while another converged on *Mia.* In a way, each community established its own culture.

Once everyone was coordinating, they had good reason to stick with the norm they had established. If they tried something new and failed to coordinate, they would lose money. But if they kept using the same name, they would rake in more payments round after round until the game was over.

What would *you* do?

As you can imagine, once a norm took hold, it didn't budge. The players had dozens of rounds still to go, and there was a lot of money to be made by sticking with the norm. And a lot of money to be lost if they started deviating.

Enter the activists.

We then seeded each of the ten communities with a unique

group of "activists." The activists were actually secret members of my research team. They had one job: to overturn the established social norm. They were immune to social influence. Every round, regardless of whom they interacted with, the activists would use only the name that they wanted to become the new norm. For example, if everyone in a community had converged on the name *Mia,* the activists suddenly appeared and started using the name *Ingrid* on every round. They were committed to social change.

Across the communities in our study, we experimented with activist groups of different sizes. The smallest activist group constituted 17 percent of the population (well below our predicted tipping point). The largest activist group was 31 percent (well above it). We called them a *committed minority* because they were determined to stick with *Ingrid* no matter what. These were the ten communities:

Community 1: 17 percent committed minority.
Community 2: 19 percent committed minority.
Community 3: 19 percent committed minority.
Community 4: 20 percent committed minority.
Community 5: 21 percent committed minority.
Community 6: 25 percent committed minority.
Community 7: 27 percent committed minority.
Community 8: 28 percent committed minority.
Community 9: 28 percent committed minority.
Community 10: 31 percent committed minority.

In communities 1 through 5 (17 percent to 21 percent), the committed minority was useless. Although we had predicted this, it was still disappointing to see. Dozens of rounds of continuous activism had no effect on the larger population. Even when the activists composed 21 percent of the group, they barely had any impact on the other players. People were following the established social norm as if the activists weren't there. No matter how loud the activists shouted *Ingrid!*, the *Mia*-loving majority just ignored them.

In Community 6, we increased the fraction of activists ever so slightly to 25 percent...and that did it.

Tipping point. The *Ingrid* minority defeated the *Mia* majority.

And even though we had predicted this too, it was no less stunning to see.

The difference between "failed" Community 5 and "successful" Community 6 was a mere 4 percentage points. Increasing the number of activists from 10 to 14 percent, or from 17 to 21 percent, had no effect on the population. But as soon as the 25 percent tipping point was reached, this small change in the size of the committed group had a disproportionate impact on the rest of the population. In Communities 6 through 10, the committed minority succeeded every time as well.

This is why tipping points are so remarkable. And why social change often appears abrupt. Because *below* the tipping point, even large increases in activism have no effect on the rest of the population. A jump from 10 to 20 percent, for example, has no significant impact. But even a small increase in activism that pushes the fraction above the tipping point? That affects everyone.

Sixteen years before the Arab Spring uprisings surprised the world, the economist Timur Kuran wrote a prescient article entitled "The Inevitability of Future Revolutionary Surprises." He argued that when activist groups are just below the tipping point, society appears to be stable—but in fact it's a mirage. The activists are on the verge of social revolution, even if no one yet knows it. With just a little more effort, social change will erupt, and it will come as a complete surprise.

This is exactly what happened in Egypt in 2011.

Back in 1995, Kuran's article goaded social scientists into making predictions about whether Hosni Mubarak's brutal rule of Egypt would ever be overthrown. If so, when?

Even in 2010, nobody was predicting 2011.

Surprising revolutions happen far more often than unsurprising ones. The fall of the Berlin Wall in 1989. The rise of #MeToo in 2016. The decriminalization of marijuana.

These social changes were surprising because decades of protests and activist efforts seemed to have had very little impact. But once the tipping point was reached, these movements suddenly affected everyone.

After a Tipping Point

As powerful as tipping points are, some norms seem so entrenched that they could never change. For several generations, it looked as though gender bias in politics would be one of them. The challenges confronting women in politics appeared insurmountable.

Earlier, I showed you what life was like for women in the Danish parliament below the tipping point. Women were not seen as legitimate political actors; their concerns were not seen as valid topics of political discussion; they had higher dropout rates, less efficacy in achieving their goals, and little capacity to introduce new language that would address their constituents' concerns, such as women's position, sexual harassment, and domestic violence. Could these norms really change if women reached a tipping point in government?

Yes, they could. And they did.

Studies of women in Scandinavian legislatures found that open opposition against women in politics decreased significantly once women passed the tipping point and were no longer token minorities. One reason for this is that stereotyping becomes harder when there are more women in government. Greater representation among women makes it more difficult to satirize women as a category rather than criticize a particular individual. In Denmark, increasing female representation in the legislature led to a complete disappearance of open opposition to the idea of female politicians. This is not to say that clandestine forms of discrimination were eliminated. However, people no longer felt comfortable *publicly* disparaging candidates on the basis of their sex—a clear sign that the social norms about women in politics had changed.

An essential feature of a successful committed minority is not just their numbers. It is their *commitment*. One of the greatest concerns among scholars studying women's increasing involvement in politics was that as women's role grew, they would simply be assimilated into men's political culture. If women were able to address only the topics that concerned their male counterparts, the impact of women's political participation on women's lives and women's issues would be negligible. In effect, women would be playing the role of men. Thankfully, this is not what the studies of tipping points show.

In Sweden, as women reached a critical mass of 25 to 30 percent of local legislatures, they were able to effectively coordinate with one another to advance novel topics that addressed women's concerns. Not only did this make women more effective as legislators; it also allowed them to better manage their own political careers. Dropout rates among women in politics, previously quite high, fell to the same level as those of men. Men and women of equal seniority were reelected at equivalent rates. Women were able to introduce issues such as childcare, women's reproductive health, and equal pay into the political discussion. These reforms significantly reduced women legislators' own conflicts between their family life and professional life, allowing them to become more productive members of parliament.

Once the tipping point was reached, the norms of political discourse in Scandinavian legislatures changed. In many countries, women's issues became part of the accepted political platform for all professional politicians—regardless of gender. The resulting institutional changes saw the creation of Equal Status Councils within the government, with the mandate to ensure that equality policies were enforced throughout the legislature.

Tipping points offer inspiring potential for social change. But as with all social science, they come with a warning. Tipping points can go the other way, too: rather than liberating a population, tipping points can be used as a tool for social control.

Drowning Out a Tipping Point

In June 2013, violence erupted in China's Xinjiang province. In the remote city of Lukqun, citizens armed only with knives and homemade torches attacked police stations and government offices. The rioters killed seventeen police officers and officials. Government forces retaliated by fatally shooting ten of the rioters.

Xinjiang province is nestled between Mongolia and Kazakhstan in the farthest reaches of China's northwest corner. It is more ethnically diverse than the rest of China. The local Uighur population is more culturally similar to the citizenry in neighboring

Muslim countries than it is to China's dominant Han population. The Uighurs speak Turkic (a central-Asian language more akin to Turkish than Chinese) and observe the religious and cultural practices of Islam. Their perceived threat to Chinese cultural unity is not taken lightly. The local government has instituted uncommonly strict policing policies throughout Xinjiang province. In cities such as Lukqun, harsh economic and social sanctions prevent the sale of Islamic religious garments and provide limited employment opportunities for non-Han residents.

The Chinese government is well aware that the only real threat to its seemingly unstoppable global expansion comes not from foreign competition but from internal dissent. China's international dominance hinges on its national unity. The 2013 Lukqun uprising was the worst outbreak of civil violence that the Xinjiang province had seen for several years, and China's leaders believed it demanded swift action. The government quickly responded both through its official media channel, *The Global Times,* and through social-media sites such as the Chinese version of Facebook, Weibo.

The government's disinformation campaign was clear and compelling. The official party line was that the Lukqun uprising was in fact a random terrorist attack committed by Muslim extremists from Syria. This is the kind of disinformation strategy that we've come to expect from authoritarian regimes. Placing the blame on foreign extremists serves several ends. It fosters national unity. It further alienates and shames the remaining Muslim population in Xinjiang. And it creates the appearance of an external danger.

The truth about the Lukqun uprising is more disquieting. Local reports from citizens of the Xinjiang province indicate that policing in the region had intensified over the months preceding the attacks. A spate of detentions by the local authorities had resulted in the disappearance of many Uighur men from Lukqun. The June outburst was a response to these increasingly oppressive policing tactics.

China's attempt to conceal this internal dissent was nothing new. But in the age of social media, China's social-control strategy was woefully antiquated. The government was using a media playbook that was nearly a century old, and it was not fooling anyone.

But then China did something that no one expected.

As the conversations and reports about Lukqun began to heat up on social media, Chinese government officials, posing as regular citizens, started to flood Chinese social media with fake user posts. These posts were not filled with disinformation about the attacks. Nor with criticisms of independent news reports about Lukqun. Instead, many of the posts offered exuberant praise for a local parade. Other posts started a heated political debate about China's new economic development plans. Still others began teasing their fellow "netizens" to offer their opinions about President Xi Jinping's recent "China Dream" speech.

What did any of this have to do with the Lukqun uprising?

Nothing.

These were strategic non sequiturs. They were part of China's cleverly designed and massively deployed nationwide campaign for social control. Instead of using social media to combat views that disparage the regime, or to debate the nature of the events that took place in Lukqun, Chinese government officers simply created sufficient amounts of random chatter on social media to distract citizens from their legitimate grievances.

It was both ridiculous and brilliant. Imagine what would have happened if, in the midst of the Ferguson protests, people had responded to the #BlackLivesMatter posts with comments about local parades, or enthusiastically shared commentary on recent speeches by the Republican leadership. These people would have been ignored—or, more likely, reviled.

But only if they were a small minority of the conversation.

China's new strategy exploited the theory of tipping points. The country's leaders deployed tens of thousands of coordinated government actors—concealed by fake user accounts—simultaneously posting and forwarding stories and comments that were intended to be distractions from the Lukqun uprising. These government actors are known as the Fifty Cent Party in reference to their payment of fifty cents (in Chinese jiao) for each post they make.

Their efforts were so eerily effective that today the Fifty Cent Party remains one of China's primary social-control strategies. Over the course of a given year, Fifty Cent Party members make an estimated 448 million posts on Chinese social media. Compared with the approximately 80 billion posts made annually on Chinese social media, that boils down to a ratio of one fake Fifty Cent post for every 178 genuine posts. And that ratio turns out to be even higher when the government's tipping-point strategy is taken into account.

Instead of government actors spreading their 448 million posts evenly over the year, they strategically release their messages in coordinated bursts of activity. Immediately after the Lukqun uprisings, Fifty Cent Party members sent thousands of posts and cross-posts aimed at shifting the discourse on social media. Their tactic was exactly the same as Kanter's idea. If you coordinate enough people on a single behavior, others will start to see that behavior as legitimate—and other behaviors as less acceptable.

On social media, the power of tipping points is that people can talk to one another only if they're part of the same conversation. If a committed minority of "activists" (or secret government employees) work together to shift the topic of the conversation, it becomes difficult for others to resist coordinating with them. After all, language is a coordination game.

The Fifty Cent Party is notably different from the censorship strategies used by twentieth-century authoritarian regimes. In fact, it's the opposite of censorship. China is not burning seditious books so much as it is flooding the market with the appeal of pulp fiction.

In April 2014, there was another attack in the Xinjiang province, this one at the Urumqui railway station, killing three people. This time the Chinese government didn't waste time blaming Muslim extremists. Instead, a burst of activity by the Fifty Cent Party generated thousands of posts extolling the virtues of China's new housing policies. Building on that theme, Fifty Cent Party members started several new threads about economic-development opportunities in the Xinjiang province, swamping citizens' posts about the attack.

One of weirdest and most powerful distraction tactics used that day was to initiate a theoretical discussion of Maoist doctrine. Fifty Cent Party members began a rousing debate about how China's leadership should incorporate the opinions of the masses into the government's decision-making architecture. A wide-ranging and thoughtful discussion of Communist principles ensued. The Urumqui railway station, still engulfed in flames, was forgotten.

Unlike the tactics used in Nazi Germany or Stalinist Russia, the strategy of China's Fifty Cent Party is not to stop the flow of information. Rather, it is to control the way that information is received and interpreted. Their strategy is to permit the exchange of ideas while shaping the social norms that govern the value of those ideas.

It would seem that in order for this social-control strategy to be effective, the Fifty Cent Party would need to be a secret.

But the strangest thing by far about the Fifty Cent Party is that it is not a secret. Everyone in China knows about it. In fact, the government tells them about it. When my colleagues in the Government Department at Harvard University published a study exposing China's Fifty Cent Party, the Chinese government posted an official response taking credit for the party's dutiful efforts to "guide public opinion" in ways that benefit China. Instead of denying the party's social manipulations, the government was extolling its virtues!

Why do these tactics work if everyone knows about them?

The bizarre truth is that the Fifty Cent Party is successful only *because* everyone knows about them.

China's strategy is a cunning twist on a witch hunt. In a witch hunt, people are forced to conceal their true beliefs for fear of being called witches. Once people can no longer read one another's minds, everyone believes that their peers support the witch hunt—even when no one does. The looming paranoia of being accused of witchcraft leads even the most skeptical citizens to accuse others of being witches.

On Chinese social media, a citizen's only "proof of sincerity" is to accuse others of being secret government conspirators. The Fifty Cent Party uses this tactic in reverse. Party members essentially accuse regular Chinese citizens of supporting pro-government views. They create multiple identities and post arguments on both sides of a debate, engaging in heated exchanges with themselves and with other Fifty Cent Party members. They even make distracting comments on discussion threads that accuse other participants of making distracting comments. Some of these accusations are true, identifying actual posts made by other Fifty Cent Party members. But, of course, most of them are fake.

The result is the same as a witch hunt. Mind reading becomes impossible if you cannot tell who is false and who is sincere. Everyone winds up coordinating on whatever behavior appears to be accepted among their peers—even if that behavior is a government-created fiction.

The genius of this strategy is that the government's complete *transparency* about the existence of the Fifty Cent Party creates a remarkable *lack* of transparency about citizens' actual beliefs. Conspiratorial accusations become so banal on Chinese social media that they are toothless. The effect is to eliminate any possible proof of sincerity.

Since China first began experimenting with this strategy in 2004, dozens of academic researchers and media outlets have attempted to contact Fifty Cent Party members to have them comment on their tactics of social control. No one had ever been able to secure an interview. But in 2011, the well-known Chinese artist and activist Ai Weiwei finally succeeded. While he was imprisoned in a Chinese detention camp, Ai Weiwei managed to contact and interview a member of the Fifty Cent Party.

In one of the most telling moments, Ai Weiwei asked the party member about the issue of sincerity and social manipulation.

"Do you think the government has the right to guide public opinion?" Ai asked.

Yes, the party member replied. In China, "the government absolutely must interfere and guide public opinion. The majority of Chinese netizens…don't think for themselves and are deceived and incited too easily by false news."

In a revealing moment of self-contradiction, the Fifty Cent Party member then dispassionately confessed that he deliberately spreads false news.

Ai Weiwei continued: "Do you have to believe in the viewpoints you express?"

"I don't have to believe in them," the party member said. "Sometimes you know well that what you say is false or untrue. But you still have to say it, because it's your job."

Activists don't even need to be sincere to trigger a tipping point. They just need to be committed. In China and elsewhere, the dangers of deception on social media allow coordinated actors, with unsettling ease, to tip social norms without anyone ever realizing it.

CHAPTER 10

The Blind Spot in the Mind's "I": Unexpected Triggers for Tipping Points

In the spring of 2006, forty-four Princeton University undergrads were given the opportunity to evaluate a series of new policy proposals for the university. These policies would have an appreciable impact on Princeton, especially in terms of admissions. One proposal, for instance, suggested changing Princeton's "Early Decision" policy from binding to nonbinding. The new policy would offer applicants greater flexibility in their financial-aid process, but it would significantly increase the number of early applications that Princeton received, potentially reducing Princeton's power to secure the best applicants. It was a controversial proposal. Would the students support it or reject it?

This poll wasn't merely a census of the upperclassmen. It was a controlled experiment. It was similar to the conformity studies that you've seen before. As the students evaluated each proposal, they were also shown the opinions of other students. The obvious question was whether students would make a choice that conformed to that of their peers, or whether they would make a different choice. But this study had a couple of twists.

As you would expect, the experimental results showed that students were significantly more likely to support the proposals that their peers had supported. But the researchers weren't interested in merely identifying people's conformity with social norms; they wanted to see whether the participants recognized their own social conformity. The next part of the study therefore asked students *why* they had made their choice to either support or reject each proposal.

Was their choice a result of peer influence? Was it due to a specific feature of the proposal? Was it because of benefits they anticipated for the university (or for themselves as alumni)?

Students replied, almost unanimously, that their choices were based on the quality of the proposals and their potential impact on the school. Rarely did they list peer influence as a major reason for their decisions.

The final twist in the study is the most interesting. Students were then given profiles of students who had voted in the same way that they did. They were then asked to evaluate the reasons why *those students* had made their decisions. Were *their* choices due to peer influence, the quality of the proposals, or anticipated benefits for themselves or the university?

This time, the responses were notably different. Participants were significantly more likely to explain other students' decisions in terms of peer influence. Many other studies have shown the same effect. People often explain other people's choices as a desire to conform to social norms but rarely believe it about themselves. When it comes to their own decisions, most people are certain that their choices are based on intelligent reasoning and personal preferences. This observation has since become known as the *introspection illusion*.

Another example: In a 2004 *New York Times* article about the growing trend of extravagant indulgences among middle-class Americans, a reporter wrote about one New Jersey woman's choice to purchase a $7,000 stove. "It was not keeping up with the Joneses that made her want a Viking range, she said. It was because, as a serious cook who likes to entertain, it had the features she needed."

The vast majority of the time, the social influences altering people's behavior take place beyond their field of vision—in their blind spot. Over the last several decades, social-science experiments have become increasingly good at pinpointing these blind spots and measuring their effects on people's behavior. The introspection illusion offers a clear insight to help us understand this blind spot: people explain their own behavior in terms of what they feel inside, rather than what is happening outside. This simple observation has big implications for the science of social norms. It means that people's beliefs about what will motivate them to change their behavior are often not a reliable guide for helping them to actually change. In fact, people's beliefs about their own motivations may be the *least* reliable explanation for their behavior.

In 2007, an ingenious two-part study showed how the introspection illusion creates a sand trap for public policy, and how to successfully maneuver around it. In the first part of the study, nearly a thousand California residents were asked about their willingness to adopt energy-conservation strategies in their homes. At the time, several programs were being developed to increase energy conservation. These included publicizing financial incentives for homeowners, advertising the dangers of global warming, and trumpeting citizens' moral responsibility for future generations. The California residents were asked what would make them most likely to improve their energy-consumption practices: 1) their environmental values and sense of social responsibility; 2) money-saving opportunities; or 3) the social norms among their peers.

As you might now predict, everyone reported that their motivation to adopt sustainable practices in their homes came from either their desire to save the environment or to save money. No one gave much weight to social norms—though just like the Princeton students, these California residents conceded that *other people* might be influenced by social norms.

Then the researchers launched the second part of their study. Using a second group of California households similar to the first, the experimenters conducted a three-step experiment. First they recorded each household's actual energy usage. Second, over the next few weeks, they gave every household door-hanger pamphlets with information about energy-saving practices (such as turning off unused lights, taking shorter showers, using fans instead of air-conditioning units, and so forth). They divided the households into three groups. One group also received information about the social and environmental benefits of the recommended practices. Another group instead received information about the money they would save by adopting these new practices. And a third group was told how many of their neighbors had used these practices to reduce their energy-consumption levels.

A month later, the researchers followed up. They interviewed each of the residents, and also recorded any changes in residents' household energy usage by inspecting their homes' energy meters. This allowed the researchers to compare people's *beliefs* about the impact of each behavior-change strategy with their actual changes in behavior.

During the follow-up interview, the homeowners were asked which kind of policy nudge they thought would be most effective for them—receiving persuasive messages about the social and environmental impact of energy-conservation practices, receiving information about the money they would save through reduced energy consumption, or receiving information about what their neighbors were doing.

Once again, people responded that the best way to influence their household behavior would be to provide them with information about social and environmental benefits or with facts about how much money they could save each month by, for instance, taking shorter showers or turning off unnecessary lights. Everyone believed that information about their peers' behavior would be the least likely factor to affect their household routines.

What did the researchers find?

In fact, the *only* households to show significant reductions in their energy consumption were the homes that were given information about their peers' behavior. Remarkably, the people in the social-norms group—the ones whose behaviors had been directly influenced by their peers—still believed just like everyone else that the other strategies would be more effective.

If that seems too odd to be true, think about what *you* would say if a researcher asked you what would affect your energy-consumption behavior: Would you rate environmental protection as a primary incentive? What about saving money? Or would you believe that you would just follow the herd without knowing why?

The important finding from this study is not simply that people's opinions about their own motivations are a poor guide for understanding their behavior. I don't think anyone is terribly surprised to hear that (at least about other people). The striking finding is that the strategy that people earnestly believed would be the *least* likely to influence them wound up being the *most* effective way to change their behavior.

For years, these blind spots have undercut a variety of renewable-energy initiatives. Innovators trying to move the US toward more-sustainable policies have been baffled by their ineffectiveness, particularly in light of well-documented accounts of Americans' pro-sustainability preferences. Equally baffling are the outlying success stories from countries that seemed to face identical challenges.

What advice can these countries offer? What strategic lessons can be learned from governments that have successfully tipped social norms toward new sustainable practices?

Watching Your Neighbors

In the early 1990s, Europe was teetering on the cusp of a transformative shift toward solar energy. Switzerland, Germany, France, Italy, and other European nations had pioneered some of the most progressive legislation in the world. But social norms regarding rooftop household solar power still had not changed. People were reluctant to make the shift.

This is the paradox of tipping points: How can you trigger a tipping point if everyone is waiting for everyone else to go first?

The most common strategy in these cases is to use financial incentives. Since 2008, the Swiss government has provided enormous incentives for homeowners to put solar panels on their houses. Done properly, the system is ingenious. Homeowners can install solar panels on their roofs—which, along with a small inverter, deliver power directly into the local energy grid. The Swiss government then pays homeowners above-market prices for their self-generated power, which not only supplies energy to both the house and the community but also turns a handsome profit for the homeowner. It's a win-win!

To launch the initiative, the Swiss government deployed an extensive informational campaign publicizing the environmental importance of solar energy. It also ran nationwide advertisements trumpeting the cost-saving benefits of household solar power. This strategy was effective for generating an initial wave of uptake among a few early-adopting Swiss homeowners. But then the wave petered out. It failed to reach the tipping point.

The problem, as researchers later discovered, was that Swiss citizens' choice to adopt solar panels was ultimately determined not by financial incentives or informational awareness, but by the number of neighbors who had installed panels in their community. The more neighbors who adopted, the more that citizens believed it was *expected* of them. In communities with low levels of uptake, future investments in solar power remained low—or disappeared entirely.

Germany faced the same challenge in the late 1980s. Environmental organizers and industry innovators had spent nearly a decade developing legislative initiatives and financial incentives to stimulate Germany's production of solar cells. Again, the real problem was on the consumer side: how could the government tip social norms among the citizens to trigger widespread acceptance of solar energy?

Germany wanted to spread solar power in the same sweeping way that televisions, VCRs, smartphones, personal computers, email, the internet, and social media had also spread—namely, to everyone. The history of these successful technologies shows a telling pattern. The diffusion of each one was affected by the obvious factors of price, availability, and awareness. But the adoption of each was also clustered socially. People started using these technologies when their friends, neighbors, and colleagues did. The same principle holds true for renewable energy.

Of Shotguns, Silver Bullets, and Snowballs

Do you remember the story of the campaign to spread acceptance of contraception to every community in Korea? Suppose that we went back in time to right before the Korean initiative began.

Imagine that you are a government official responsible for the campaign's success. Your job is to devise a strategy to "tip" the contraceptive norm.

Now further imagine that in each Korean village of 1,000 people, you have a network diagram showing you the exact pattern of social ties among all the village residents. Using this diagram, your task is to target people in the social network who can maximize the impact of your social-change campaign.

You have a limited budget: for each village you have only ten dollars to work with, which you can allocate any way you like. You can concentrate your resources, giving all ten dollars to one person. Or you can distribute your resources across the network, giving one dollar to each of ten people. Once you decide which approach you want to pursue, you have a second question: Which individual (or which ten individuals) do you choose to give the money to?

My colleagues and I have spent the last decade looking for the best answers to those two questions. Dozens of tactics have been proposed, from viral campaigns to influencer marketing. But this wide array of approaches boils down to three core strategies: the shotgun, the silver bullet, and the snowball.

The easiest tipping strategy to implement is the **shotgun strategy.** It is based on the principles of viral marketing. To use this strategy, you distribute your resources broadly, like a shotgun blast. You select ten people in each village to be targets, or "change agents" for spreading contraception. You give each person one dollar to adopt contraception and spread the word about it. The key to this strategy is that your ten change agents are chosen from widely distributed parts of the village's social network—as distant from one another as possible. This should create maximum exposure for your innovation.

The shotgun strategy would work exceptionally well for spreading the measles. Suppose you selected ten people who were widely dispersed throughout the network, and infected each of them with the measles virus. Each person would then spread the disease to their immediate group of contacts, resulting in ten independent outbreaks in the village. Each outbreak would expand rapidly, reaching every corner of the population. The collective effect would be a village-wide pandemic.

This is the idea behind viral marketing. The shotgun strategy gives the contagion maximum exposure, which should enable it to reach the greatest number of people in the shortest possible time.

But the essential problem with the shotgun strategy is that each selected change agent is surrounded by a sea of non-adopters. The initial *reach* of a change effort is increased by maximizing change agents' exposure to the population. But this minimizes *redundancy* in the change agents' networks.

For the spread of the measles, that would be ideal. The shotgun strategy provides each measles carrier with the richest possible environment for spreading the disease.

But if your contagion is not a pathogen but a social norm, the shotgun strategy would be defeated by people's resistance to change.

If you deployed the shotgun strategy in the Korean contraception campaign, you would soon encounter several obstacles. The first is the lack of social reinforcement. Change agents are far away from one another in the social network, making each one the only person in their social circle to adopt the innovation. If the change agents' peers do not see birth control as a socially accepted practice, a lone change agent cannot do much to change that perception. Similarly, a lone change agent cannot offer much evidence about the credibility or safety of contraception, particularly if their peers know the change agent was incentivized to adopt it. Moreover, if everyone in the village already agrees on the status quo regarding family planning, a single person in their social circle adopting contraception does not provide any reason to think there will be social currency in adopting it, since no one else they know is using it.

These were the same obstacles that Germany's solar-power initiative needed to overcome. Solitary change agents had little hope of spreading normative support for solar power in neighborhoods where there was only one adopter. A single homeowner cannot establish the legitimacy, credibility, or social currency of an innovation that no one else in their neighborhood is using.

The second problem with the shotgun strategy is that even well-incentivized change agents are not immune to peer pressure. The issue is not the incentives themselves, but rather how those incentives are strategically deployed. Used properly, incentives can help trigger a change in social norms. But by isolating change agents in different parts of the social network, this strategy pits each change agent's incentives to adopt contraception against the social norms held by their peers. The consequence is that not only will your change agents be unable to spread contraception, they will in all likelihood abandon it themselves.

The third problem is that once this battle has been fought and lost, people do not forget. Do you remember the story of Google+? Google+ achieved massive awareness. At one point, everybody had a person or two in their social network who was using it. But it simply lacked enough social reinforcement to tip the population away from the established norm of using Facebook. So not only was everyone aware of Google+, but they were aware that *almost no one had adopted it.*

The optics of this aren't good. If you succeed in creating massive awareness for your innovation but generate low uptake, there is the danger of a backfire effect. The result for Google+ was that its market share dropped so low it was forced to close its doors.

This can be a serious problem for the shotgun strategy. If word of your social innovation rapidly spreads far and wide but the innovation itself is slow to win adopters, this can leave a vacuum in the minds of the public. People are left with the impression that the innovation failed, and a need to explain why. Once people come to believe there's something wrong with an innovation—that it's too costly, or difficult, or unpopular—it is easy for them to justify not only why they did not adopt it in the past, but also why they would not adopt it in the future. These lingering doubts about the innovation can cripple future campaigns.

Thankfully, there are two other tipping strategies to consider.

The **silver bullet** is a popular alternative to the shotgun strategy because it avoids the problem of spreading your resources too thin. Instead, it concentrates all your resources on a single target.

This is the influencer strategy. For Korea's birth-control campaign, this would be tantamount to finding the most charismatic and highly connected person in the social network and giving them the full ten dollars to promote contraception to everyone they know. This strategy is based on the idea that there is an individual in each village so remarkably well-connected and influential that they can trigger a chain reaction that transforms the entire community's social norms.

At the beginning of this book, I told you about the myth of the influencer. One of the main challenges of using the silver-bullet strategy is that a highly connected person is surrounded by far more countervailing influences than a regular person. Whereas a regular person in the Korean village may have ten contacts, all clustered together in the social network, the influencer might have fifty contacts, widely distributed throughout the population. Because all of the influencer's contacts are following the established social norms of family planning, a highly connected person is unlikely to be incentivized to come out publicly against the status quo.

But for the sake of the thought experiment, let's suppose that the ten-dollar incentive does the trick, and that a highly connected person is persuaded to adopt and promote contraception. The influencer would then convince all fifty of their contacts to adopt and promote birth control. What happens next?

At this point, the silver-bullet strategy becomes quite similar to the shotgun strategy. Except that instead of having ten widely distributed change agents, there would now be fifty. For a simple contagion like the measles, this strategy would be amazingly efficient for creating a "viral" pandemic. This is why influencer marketing has become so popular.

But what if the contagion is a social norm? The influencer's fifty contacts would be in the same position as the ten change agents from the shotgun strategy—surrounded by resistance and without even the one-dollar incentive.

Just like the shotgun strategy, the same factors that make the silver-bullet strategy so effective for spreading the measles are also what cause it to fail for spreading contraception. First, each of the influencer's widely distributed contacts are far apart, and therefore lack social reinforcement from other adopters to help spread the innovation. Second, the influencers' contacts face countervailing influences from all of their peers who still follow traditional norms of family planning.

But let's play devil's advocate.

These problems arise only if the influencer's contacts are widely distributed. What if the influencer's contacts are connected together? Instead of spreading the word far and wide, perhaps the influencer could instead focus their efforts on a few small clusters of reinforcing neighbors?

It's not a bad idea, but it would defeat the entire point of using the silver-bullet strategy. The idea of this strategy is that the high price tag of hiring an influencer is justified by their ability to extend the reach of an innovation across an entire population. It would not make sense to pay so much money for an influencer, then restrict their change efforts to a few small clusters of people. As I will show you in a moment, the notion of targeting small social clusters is indeed the key to success. But there is a much easier, cheaper, and ultimately more effective way to do to this than hiring influencers.

Before abandoning the silver-bullet strategy entirely, let's imagine one more way that it might succeed. Consider what would happen if an influencer's reach across the population was far greater than we thought: What if the influencer was personally connected to so many people that they could trigger the tipping point all by themselves? In a village of 1,000 citizens, for example, perhaps the influencer might have 250 personal contacts whom they could directly influence. Or in a country with sixty million voters, suppose the influencer had fifteen million personal contacts, each of whom would be directly influenced by this single person. (That would indeed be amazing.) It's easy to see how this might work for a simple contagion. But in the Korean birth-control initiative, each of the influencer's contacts is surrounded by people who follow traditional norms of family planning. A lone influencer is unlikely to have much success convincing their contacts that contraception is credible and legitimate, or has social currency, when no one else in their social networks is using it. The only way for the influencer to succeed would be to persuade every one of their contacts to disregard the social norms held by their friends and neighbors. It's an unlikely prospect.

The final observation about the silver-bullet strategy is not about its success, but about backfire effects. If the silver-bullet strategy succeeds in spreading the word to everyone but doesn't gain much traction for adoption, it risks the same backfire effect that haunted the shotgun strategy. But it would be even worse this time. A failed influencer campaign may not only numb people to the advantages of an innovation. It may actively turn people against it.

Remember Google Glass?

The Glass campaign used the silver-bullet strategy. A small group of high-status influencers was incentivized to adopt Google's futuristic eyewear. But Glass had a blind spot: the social norms among non-adopters.

Google's high-status influencers violated non-adopters' social norms so egregiously that people's *implicit* social expectations about face-to-face interaction and social surveillance boiled over into an *explicit* culture war. Glass became a stigmatized technology that nobody wanted to be associated with. The campaign backfired not only in terms of Glass sales, but also in terms of people's negative impression of Google.

While no one wants to design a change campaign that fails,

you really don't want to design one that hurts the reputation of your organization. Here is the take-home lesson for the silver-bullet strategy: if your social innovation challenges established social norms—for instance, regarding birth control or alternative energy—tipping strategies can invite backfire if they prioritize the spread of awareness over the goal of establishing local support.

Fortunately, the third and final tipping strategy offers a solution. This is the **snowball strategy.**

Compared with the reach and scale of the shotgun and silver-bullet strategies, the snowball strategy seems relatively pedestrian. But although it's not glamorous, this strategy has legs.

Instead of targeting *special people* who can spread an innovation far and wide, the snowball strategy is based on targeting *special places* in the social network where an innovation can take hold. The goal of the snowball strategy is not to convince everyone to adopt at once. Rather, it is to incubate support for your innovation. It is to grow a critical mass.

To use the snowball strategy for the Korean contraception initiative, you would select ten change agents and give each of them one dollar to adopt and promote birth control, just as in the shotgun strategy. However, unlike the shotgun strategy, instead of picking ten people who are dispersed far and wide in the network, you would choose ten change agents who are all part of the same social cluster. The key to the snowball strategy is that all of your change agents know one another.

This would be a terrible strategy for spreading the measles. For any simple contagion, the snowball strategy would be a waste of resources. Your change agents would simply wind up telling *each other* about the innovation. What's the point of that?

But for spreading a social norm, this redundancy is remarkably efficient.

With the snowball strategy, each of your change agents no longer faces a sea of countervailing influences. Instead, they are able to talk to one another about their decisions to adopt contraception. They are able to share their experiences and reaffirm their mutual commitment to using birth control. This makes it less likely that they will abandon the innovation.

The snowball strategy doesn't just help the change agents stick with the innovation. It also helps them to spread it. Because your change agents are all part of the same social cluster, they have social connections with the same non-adopters. This enables change agents to coordinate their efforts to increase the legitimacy and credibility of contraception among their mutual friends and shared neighbors. Moreover, the social currency of contraception is strengthened within the change agents' peer group by the fact that their contacts can observe them coordinating with one another on their use of birth control. The snowball strategy establishes contraception's foothold in the social network.

Once a new social norm takes hold within the change agents' social cluster, it does not stay there for long. Contagion infrastructure is the key to what happens next: social reinforcement across wide bridges enables a new norm to propagate by spilling over from one social cluster to another. This is how the snowball strategy succeeds: A small cluster of early adopters snowballs into a social movement that can tip the social norms for an entire community.

This is in fact how the Korean birth-control initiative succeeded. Tightly knit clusters of women's groups within each village coordinated with one another to explore the opportunities for contraception. Once an initial cluster of women adopted, contagion infrastructure took over. The new behavior then spread—snowballed—from the early adopters to other groups of women, and from them to other groups, until contraception became accepted throughout each village.

Danish physicist Sune Lehmann and his team used this same strategy to deploy their thirty-nine bots on Twitter. They connected their bots together to form a reinforcing cluster of support for their new hashtags, which successfully spread their social innovations, such as #Getyourflushot and #highfivea-stranger, among thousands of people. This is also how the Pals Battalions were mobilized in World War I. Recruitment grew through clusters of mutual friends, whose reinforcing ties triggered cascades of enlistment through their neighborhoods and towns.

It is how the Arab Spring uprisings took hold of Egypt, how Facebook's popularity spread across college campuses, and how Twitter membership expanded throughout the United States. From innovative technologies to revolutionary movements, new social norms spread by gaining traction within social clusters and expanding until the tipping point is reached.

What does this mean for sustainability? Could the snowball strategy really change a country's social norms about sustainable technology?

In 2010, the government of Malawi, along with a group of US economists, decided to find out.

The Malawi Experiment

The small African nation of Malawi is nestled between the stunning grassland plateaus of Tanzania to the east and Zambia to the west, with the tropical inland forests of Mozambique to the south. From north to south, the countryside gradually softens from rugged, mountainous terrain to gentle, rolling hills, down to the southern low country. The serpentine Lake

Malawi provides a fertile inland coast along nearly two-thirds of the country's border, creating an abundance of arable land and healthy crops.

But, as elsewhere on the African continent, food is still a problem. Since the 1990s the government has struggled to spread conservationist farming practices throughout Malawi. Traditional farming techniques, such as ridge planting, have been used for generations. Ridge planting involves dividing your land into even strips of hills and troughs. The crops are planted in a row upon the hills, while water collects in the troughs. This technique can work well in the short term, but it does not efficiently hold water in low-rainfall years, and it leads to soil erosion and decreasing annual yield. With increasing urgency, the Malawi government has worked to persuade farmers to adopt a new farming practice. But it has not been easy. Tipping farmers' social norms to a more sustainable technology has become one of Malawi's important economic and social challenges.

Nor is it just Malawi. Across several African nations, food production is far below the capacity of the existing farmland. In 2008, Malawi's productivity gap was the greatest, with their traditional-farming techniques producing an estimated one-fifth of what their farmland was capable of yielding. Part of the solution to this problem is called *pit planting*, which forgoes the ridges and simply requires digging a larger hole for each plant. The holes are filled not only with the plant but with manure and fertilizer, which make efficient use of rainwater and add nutrients to the soil. It's a remarkably simple solution to help address Malawi's food problem.

But as with any social innovation, the real challenge is not developing the solution but convincing people to use it. In Malawi villages, the new method of pit planting was not well received.

The government's campaign to spread the more sustainable and higher-yield pit planting technique cut against the practices that farmers had learned from their parents, and their parents' parents. Despite years of government and NGO-sponsored information campaigns and village-outreach efforts, in 2009 less than 1 percent of Malawi farmers had adopted pit planting.

Just like homeowners in Germany considering solar panels and California residents evaluating their household energy practices, information campaigns and government outreach efforts were not enough. These strategies couldn't convince people to adopt a behavior that no one else around them was using.

In 2010, an ambitious group of scientists led by Northwestern economist Lori Beaman decided to test a *social tipping point* approach to the problem. Their idea was to run a real-life version of the same thought experiment that you just did a few pages ago—but with 200 villages throughout Malawi. Partnering with the Malawi Ministry of Agriculture and Food Safety, they conducted a four-year, nationwide experiment on social tipping strategies.

In year one, Beaman and her team went household to household conducting surveys and interviews. They asked people to list others in the village whom they knew, whom they trusted, and whom they talked to about farming. They gathered all of the peer-relationship data they would need to analyze the social networks in each of the 200 villages (approximately 200 people per village). It was a massive undertaking. But the resulting network diagrams would allow them to identify the right network locations to target when selecting their change agents.

In year two, they coordinated with the Malawi government

to train a small group of farmers who became their "change agents" in each village. Each change agent was given the resources and training they would need to adopt the new pit-planting technique, and was encouraged to advocate for it in their community.

Beaman and her team randomly divided the 200 villages into four groups. Each group of fifty villages used one of the four tipping strategies: shotgun; snowball; an alternative version of the snowball strategy, which I'll call the *snowball-neighborhood* strategy; and the Malawi government's existing silver-bullet strategy.

In group one, all fifty villages used the shotgun strategy. Change agents were selected at random and thus were widely dispersed across each village.

In group two, all fifty villages used the snowball strategy. Beaman and her team selected change agents in the same social cluster, who were connected to one another and had shared friends in common.

In the third group of fifty villages, the scientists used the snowball-neighborhood strategy. Instead of using the social network to identify their targets, the scientists selected change agents who all lived within a single residential neighborhood. The neighborhoods in each village were large enough that it was unlikely that arbitrarily targeted individuals would be socially connected. But compared with the shotgun strategy, the snowball-neighborhood strategy offered better odds of fortuitously creating a social cluster of change agents. Moreover, if the snowball-neighborhood strategy worked, implementing the snowball strategy would be much easier in the future. Rather than spending valuable time collecting social-network data, policymakers could simply target change agents who lived in the same residential neighborhood.

In the last group of fifty villages, the scientists used a version of the silver-bullet strategy. It was based on the outreach campaigns that the Malawi government was already using. The government would identify well-known "influencers" in each village and encourage them to become change agents for pit planting. Because this strategy was already used elsewhere by the Malawi government, this final group of villages became the benchmark, or control group, against which the other three groups of villages were evaluated.

For three years, from 2011 to 2013, the scientists visited each of the 200 villages to evaluate the uptake of pit planting. They were trying to answer two questions. First, did any of these tipping strategies affect whether farmers learned about pit planting? And second, did they actually trigger people to adopt it?

The first thing to figure out was whether pit planting was a simple or complex contagion. Would hearing about it from one change agent be enough, or would farmers need to come into contact with multiple change agents?

By the end of the first year, it was clear that the new farming practice was a complex contagion. Farmers' willingness to even learn about the new technique depended on social reinforcement. Farmers who were connected to *more than one* change agent were over 200 percent more likely to know what pit planting was and how to implement it than farmers who were connected to only one change agent.

By the end of the second year, this knowledge had translated into behavior. Farmers who were connected to *more than one* change agent were over 200 percent more likely to have *adopted* the pit-planting technique than farmers who were connected to only one change agent.

What did this mean for each of the tipping strategies?

By the end of the study, there was a clear ranking of outcomes across the each of four groups of villages, particularly among the villages that had never before been exposed to pit planting.

At the bottom of the ranking, the government's default "influencer" strategy finished in *last place*. Both in terms of the spread of knowledge about pit planting and in terms of actual uptake, this strategy had almost no impact on farmers' acceptance of the innovation.

In *third place* was the shotgun strategy. These villages fared only slightly better than the control group of villages using the government's silver bullet strategy.

In *second place*, the snowball-neighborhood strategy produced a 50 percent increase in adoption compared with villages using the shotgun strategy. It was an improvement, but the ultimate impact on social norms was negligible.

In *first place* by a wide margin was the snowball strategy—the one that relied not on physical proximity but on network architecture. It produced a nearly 300 percent increase in adoption levels compared with the shotgun strategy. It also spread knowledge about pit planting much more effectively. Even beyond the villagers who adopted the new technique, more farmers knew about pit planting and how to implement it in the villages using the snowball strategy than in any other group of villages.

Perhaps the most remarkable thing about the Malawi experiment is the number of change agents they used. How many change agents do you think they had in each village? In our thought experiment in Korea, we imagined there were ten change agents in each village.

In Malawi, there were only two!

How could such a small number of change agents have such strikingly different effects in each group of villages?

The answer is social redundancy.

You saw the same thing happen with the spread of *Mia* in the name-game experiment. In the Malawi experiment, the snowball strategy targeted change agents with shared contacts in common. Each of these contacts would observe two of their peers adopting pit planting. This made them more willing to learn about the new technique. Once they visited their peers' farms and saw the pit-planting method in action, they became more likely to adopt it. What happened next was just like what happened with *Mia:* together with the change agents, the farmers who adopted pit planting increased the credibility and legitimacy of the new technique among the other farmers in their social cluster. These other farmers then became more interested in visiting their colleagues' pit-planting farms and learning about the innovation. Which in turn increased their likelihood of adopting it as well.

That's the power of a snowball. Just a little social reinforcement can grow into something much larger. And more reinforcement can make it go even faster.

For the snowball strategy, two change agents are the absolute minimum requirement to create social redundancy. In this respect, the four-year experiment in Malawi was the most stringent possible test of whether the snowball strategy could have a direct impact on the spread of a sustainable technology. And it did. But with more change agents, this strategy could have been even more effective for triggering a cascade of social reinforcement.

That's not the case for the shotgun or silver-bullet strategies.

For both, the principle is the same—*reach over redundancy*. This means that the change agents are chosen to be as widely distributed as possible. For complex contagions, the resulting lack of social reinforcement, and constant pressure from countervailing influences, causes these tipping strategies to fail, regardless of whether there are two change agents or ten.

By contrast, the *snowball-neighborhood* strategy is the most sensitive to the number of change agents. Choosing more change agents in the same geographic area would significantly increase the odds of randomly selecting people who were part of the same social cluster. This would allow social reinforcement to take hold within a targeted neighborhood, then spread to others.

For both the snowball and snowball-neighborhood strategies, greater numbers means greater social reinforcement. Imagine if there had been four change agents in each village instead of only two. The critical mass would have been twice as large, exponentially increasing the overall impact of the change agents in their village networks. Or what if there had been six, or ten? This would have enabled the creation not only of larger clusters of change agents, but also multiple clusters in each village. It's exciting to think about how effective a small group of change agents might be with the right tipping strategy.

The implications extend far beyond Malawi. We can imagine lots of ways in which these ideas could be applied, for instance, to spread sustainable technologies in Europe or the US.

But do the findings from Malawi villages really apply in modern industrialized settings? Communities in the US enjoy sophisticated mass-media communications and well-organized, well-funded government and corporate outreach programs. Don't these differences suggest that there are better strategies for spreading sustainable technologies?

Surprisingly, they don't. In fact, the historical spread of sustainable farming practices in the US has uncanny parallels with the findings from Malawi. The story of one of the greatest transformations of sustainable farming technology in American history shows how effective a social tipping strategy can be, even in a modern industrialized setting.

It is the story of hybrid corn.

The Corn Revolution

Millions of dollars were spent in the United States in the 1920s developing and marketing hybrid corn. Yet despite all of the scientific ingenuity and marketing efforts that stood behind it—and despite farmers' desperate need for it—hybrid corn was, at first, a complete flop.

Eventually, this near-fiasco was transformed into one of the most successful change campaigns of the twentieth century. As so often happens, the ultimate success of hybrid corn was an accident. It was a fluke of social networks, a fluke that shines a rare light on why even the best-marketed social innovations can fail, and what can help them succeed.

It began during the Great Depression. For two long years after the market crash of 1929, the country had been sinking into economic chaos. By 1931, entire industries had collapsed. In urban settings such as New York and Chicago, the grinding halt of the market was evident all around. And in rural Midwestern towns, farmers and their children were suffering in an additional way: an endless, seemingly biblical drought had crippled farms throughout the region.

In John Steinbeck's famous novel, *The Grapes of Wrath*, the opening lines tell of environmental disaster descending upon an unsuspecting American farm community. "The sun flared down on the growing corn day after day until a line of brown spread along the edge of each green bayonet....The surface of the earth crusted, a thin hard crust, and as the sky became pale, so the earth became pale, pink in the red country and white in gray country."

And then came the winds — relentless winds, sweeping away farms and families and the great American dream of prosperity.

Within a few years, millions of people were homeless and starving. The expanding Dust Bowl — massive soil erosion caused by drought, wind, and poorly managed crop rotation — spread north from Texas and Oklahoma into Kansas and Nebraska. Farmland was literally carried away on the wind, as lethal microparticles of dust infected the lungs of everything that breathed — livestock, farmers, and infants.

The devastation would eventually spread east from Nebraska. By the mid-1930s, airborne blight would loom on Iowa's horizon. But in the early 1930s, before the dust arrived, Iowa's corn farmers had another problem: the corn itself.

The corn plants they had used for decades had become inbred. Pollination patterns had given rise to generations of corn seed that were spawned from sibling plants. By the mid-1920s, the problem had become painfully obvious. The soft stalks hunched over as they grew, making the corn difficult to harvest. The plants were susceptible to disease and unsuited for changes in climate or the hardships of drought. For many farmers, over half of their annual crop went to waste each year. Now, with the Depression sinking in around them, and the expanding drought and soil erosion in their neighboring states, farmers' corn yields were becoming catastrophically low.

A decade earlier, scientists had anticipated these problems with the corn. Years of research and development using cross-pollination and fertilization techniques had yielded a new kind of corn seed: hybrid corn. Based on classic principles of artificial selection through crossing family lines, this new generation of corn seed was highly resistant to drought. It produced high yields and grew in tall, firm stalks that could be easily harvested. In 1927, after years of testing, hybrid corn was ready for market. Farmers in Iowa were desperate for a solution. Hybrid corn was the answer.

Starting in 1929, the campaign to market hybrid corn in Iowa followed all the principles of both traditional media advertising and viral marketing. Frequent radio commercials were supplemented with door-to-door sales reps who visited farmers' homes to explain the value of the new corn seed and give farmers an opportunity to try it. Widespread market penetration was the goal. The thinking at the time, just as it is today, was that greater exposure would yield greater adoption. The wider the marketers cast their net, the more likely it was that the innovation would catch on.

By 1931, over 60 percent of Iowa farmers had received information about hybrid corn from both media advertisements and local sales reps. By 1933, nearly 70 percent of farmers had heard about hybrid corn. The awareness campaign was remarkably successful.

The problem was that nobody was buying it. In 1933, less than 1 percent of farmers had adopted hybrid corn.

Something had gone horribly wrong. Hybrid corn had seemed as though it would be a huge hit. It was obvious to the producers that the innovation solved an urgent problem for the farmers. They needed hybrid corn. Marketing departments had gone all-in on promoting their innovation. With resource-intensive and time-consuming investments in home visits, paper-pamphlet distribution, and media advertising, it was an all-out assault on the market.

But their efforts were in vain. Why weren't farmers adopting?

First, hybrid corn was expensive. Replanting standard corn cost farmers nothing because they could simply gather seeds from their current crop. But new seed for hybrid corn had to be purchased, and it wasn't cheap. Budgets were already tight.

Each year, farmers were struggling just to break even. Going into debt to buy hybrid corn was a big risk.

Second, of course, was the fear of the unknown. The only way farmers could justify the cost of purchasing hybrid corn would be if it significantly outperformed anything that they or their neighbors had ever seen before. It seemed an unlikely prospect.

And then there was the looming Dust Bowl. The possibility of harder times ahead only increased farmers' wariness about switching to an unknown kind of corn seed. Ironically, hybrid corn was actually less vulnerable to Dust Bowl conditions than standard corn. The expanding drought should have weakened farmers' resistance to hybrid corn rather than strengthened it. But as so often happens with social norms, the straightforward scientific reasons for adopting a valuable innovation were eclipsed by the complex social reasons for rejecting it.

Such is the nature of uncertainty. When people are scared, they hold on to what they know. For farmers on the brink of bankruptcy, the worsening drought was a reason to stick with the established way of doing things rather than take a risk on an unknown product.

In addition to the economic reasons for resisting hybrid corn, farmers' unfamiliarity with the innovation gave rise to other kinds of resistance.

The third reason why farmers rejected hybrid corn was that it looked odd. The ears weren't the same color as normal corn. Nor did they have the perfectly symmetrical rows of kernels that were the hallmark of a good corn crop. Sociologists studying the spread of hybrid corn at the time summed it up succinctly: "It was not, in physical appearance, the type of ear which would lead farmers to exclaim, 'This is *real* corn!'"

As part of their study, the sociologists interviewed farmers about their reasons for resisting the innovative corn seed.

One farmer reported, "I had good seed, so why change?"

Another said, "A man doesn't just try anything new right away."

Resistance to adopting hybrid corn came in all the standard forms: suspicions about marketers' claims; reluctance to try something new. And, of course, waiting for social confirmation. One of the most common responses was, "I just figured I'd let the neighbors try it first."

But the problem was that the neighbors were not trying it. And that was the final obstacle. You've seen it many times already—the problem of countervailing influences. The more successful an awareness campaign is, the more conspicuous it becomes if no one adopts the innovation.

Farmers would have been worried about how their peers would see them—in particular, how their peers would judge the quality of their decisions and the soundness of their investments. Particularly in tough times, farmers relied upon banks, stores, and their fellow farmers to maintain their credit while they struggled alongside everyone else. If they took a bad risk on an innovation that everyone else had rejected, that wouldn't just make them look unlucky; it would make them look foolish, gullible, and incompetent. And gaining a reputation for incompetence is not only personally embarrassing but can be economically fatal, particularly in a challenged industry. It can affect future loans, lines of credit, and ultimately sales. Corn yields may vary season to season, but reputations are enduring.

These influences fell in farmers' blind spot. But the farmers still needed to justify their decisions. Just like California homeowners rationalizing their household energy consumption, or Swiss and German citizens legitimizing their failure to install solar panels, farmers in Iowa cultivated a list of appealing reasons for not adopting hybrid corn. Speculation circulated in the farming community that something must be wrong with the new seed. Rumors spread that hybrid corn was not the size or shape required for consumption, and that it had the wrong consistency to be used for livestock. Farmers agreed that it was likely to be harsh on the soil, or "too flinty" for normal use. These rumors spread quickly throughout the same word-of-mouth networks that had been targeted by the advertising campaigns.

Ultimately, the marketing strategies that lived by simple contagions also died by them. Marketers' efforts to spread new scientific evidence to counter the farmers' rumors served only to strengthen farmers' suspicions that something was amiss. Word of hybrid corn had achieved fantastic reach, but so had the rumors undermining it.

By 1934, the companies promoting hybrid corn had all but given up. They had depleted their marketing budgets and achieved nearly zero acceptance for the innovation. They were ready to leave Iowa and its farms behind.

Then something unexpected happened.

A small group of daring early adopters in Iowa created a social cluster of innovation. Sociologists observing it at the time described it as a "community laboratory," in which farmers could experiment with the new corn while being supported by one another and somewhat protected from the countervailing influences of non-adopters. These early-adopting farmers became the change agents in their social network. They were, in effect, "seeds" for the spread of the innovation.

Once hybrid corn took hold among this cluster of Iowa farmers, the same considerations that had originally led farmers to *resist* the innovation became the most powerful reasons for them to *adopt* it. Farmers could see the success of their neighbors who had adopted hybrid corn, making the innovation more credible. This social confirmation made the cost of the new corn seed seem like less of a risk. The more neighbors who adopted, the more legitimate the new corn became. The odd-looking corn and the farmers who adopted it were less subject to rumor and speculation. The social norm began to tip. Hybrid corn became an increasingly accepted innovation for farmers struggling to weather the drought.

It was a social transformation. The secret ingredient that turned the tide for hybrid corn was not its price, nor its marketing campaign. Rather, it was the networks of early adopters who triggered a tipping point in the social norm. Within a decade, hybrid corn was transformed from an abject failure—used by only 1 percent of Iowa farmers in 1933—to an unrivaled success, used by 98 percent of farmers in the state.

Nor did it stop there. Once hybrid corn took hold in Iowa, it spread across the country, reaching 100 percent market saturation nationwide.

Hybrid corn became the new norm.

The 1,000-Roof Strategy

Let's get back to Germany and its solar-energy campaign. Remember, it was 1990, and Germany was far behind on its renewable-energy goals. The country's leaders needed a way to maneuver around people's blind spots and jump-start a nationwide solar-power initiative.

But they were trapped by the classic problem of tipping points. Germany was waiting for a change that everyone wanted, but that seemed destined never to reach a critical mass.

Then the German government devised a clever solution to this paradox. It was called the "1,000 roofs" initiative. In just a few years, the government oversaw the installation of roof-mounted solar panels in more than 2,000 grid-connected homes across the country. For a country with nearly forty million households, that is a small drop in a very large bucket. But you can guess by now that the crucial factor for Germany's renewable-energy future was not the total number of homes that were targeted, but rather how those homes were clustered together within the social network.

Studies of solar-panel adoption in Texas, Connecticut, and California have all found the impact of peer influence to be remarkably localized. The more social reinforcement people receive in their immediate neighborhood, the more likely it is that solar technology will catch on and spread from street to street. The German government didn't have the snowball strategy in mind when they devised their plan, but that was the spirit of their initiative. If they installed solar panels in enough neighborhoods, perhaps they could trigger a massive shift in people's acceptance of solar power.

A 2016 study of the spread of solar power in Germany reported the results of their initiative. In neighborhoods where a critical mass of early adopters was formed, the entire region grew into a dense concentration of solar installations. Reinforcing social expectations within neighborhoods spurred the adopters' neighbors, and their neighbors' neighbors, to install solar power. Crucially, these social-reinforcement effects were not limited to the targeted communities. This process of social coordination spilled over from one community to the next—through what were essentially wide bridges between communities, which extended across state lines and even national borders. The key to the growth of solar power was not the particular provinces or states in which citizens lived, but the social reinforcement among communities that enabled acceptance of solar power to spread from each neighborhood to the neighborhoods around them.

From 1992 through 2009, solar installations in German households grew from 2,000 homes to more than 576,000 homes. By 2016, Germany led the world in solar-energy production per capita. The German government worked hard to advertise the advantages of solar power. They designed incentive systems that would motivate industry producers to develop novel solar technologies—while also incentivizing household consumers to purchase installations.

But Germany's success was not caused by these incentive programs and informational campaigns alone. The 2016 analysis of Germany's successful initiative found that neighborhood-level social influences were essential for the speed and scale of the country's transformation. The regional spread of social reinforcement—all the way down to the particular blocks and streets that people lived on—played a crucial role in tipping Germany's social norms toward a nationwide transition to solar power.

In the last few years, investigations of successful alternative energy–adoption campaigns in other countries have found these same snowball dynamics at work. In the UK, neighborhood effects account for a significant part of the growth of solar power. Social spillover between neighborhoods increased not only the number of installations but the rate of installation. Similarly, following in Germany's footsteps, the Japanese government invested in a "70,000 roofs" program. A 2014 analysis of solar adoption in Japan found the same neighborhood effects at work: the strongest predictor of whether Japanese residents would adopt solar power was not their access to information nor the incentives they received, but rather the number of people in their neighborhood who had already installed solar panels.

The promise of these successful initiatives extends far beyond sustainability. They inform social policies for promoting vaccination, voter turnout, and economic development, all of which are influenced on a national scale by the norms established within people's neighborhoods.

Germany's story shows that the snowball-neighborhood strategy can be effective for creating transformative change. But the success of this strategy depends upon two crucial elements.

First, there need to be enough adopters in a small segment of a neighborhood—on a specific street or a block—to make adopters' neighbors feel pressure to coordinate on a new behavior. And second, the behavior needs to be visible, just as rooftop television antennas were two generations ago, and blue recycling bins were in the most recent generation. For the strategy to work, when people adopt a new norm, their neighbors need to be able to *see* it.

The snowball-neighborhood strategy is ideal for spreading household solar power. The more people in a community who have installed solar panels atop their homes, the more conspicuous their neighbors are who have not. As the number of installations on each block multiplies, residents without solar panels become increasingly aware of the changing social expectations in their community.

This is how solar power succeeded in spreading not just in Germany but across Europe. (The map below shows the growth

Spread of Solar Panel Adoption

of solar power from 1992 to 2014 for countries producing at least 0.1 watts of solar energy per capita.)

If you glance back at the map on page 39, you will be surprised to see that the spread of solar-panel installations in Europe bears an uncanny resemblance to the spread of the Black Plague six centuries earlier. It might seem unlikely that anything would still spread this way. The Black Plague had spread geographically because at that time there weren't any long-distance weak ties for it to exploit. COVID-19 didn't have this limitation, so it could jump across the world at an alarming rate.

But those are simple contagions.

For the spread of complex contagions, even at the turn of the twenty-first century, innovations still gain legitimacy, credibility, and social currency by being reinforced within people's close social networks. European nations worked hard to develop policies that would promote solar energy. But those policies alone could not trigger change. Particularly for a technology such as household solar power, the most efficient way to trigger widespread acceptance was to spread social norms within residential communities.

PART IV

DISCORD, DISRUPTION, AND DISCOVERY

CHAPTER 11

Optimizing Innovation: Social Networks for Discovery

What does the science of complex contagions tell us about how to design better and more creative work teams? How should you structure your own organization to accelerate discovery of the next great innovation?

As this new science has grown and spread in recent years, practitioners and leaders in a wide variety of fields have sought to harness the network dynamics of social learning to promote new forms of innovation. Engineers searching for technical solutions, medical researchers and practitioners seeking groundbreaking treatments, musicians striving to invent the next great sound, and businesses developing new products— all of them rely on networks of colleagues and collaborators to discover innovative approaches and opportunities. This chapter explains how the concepts I've described in earlier chapters—including bridge width, relevance, reinforcement, and social clustering—can be used to boost creativity and innovation in any kind of organization.

The Magic of Hamilton

When *Hamilton* arrived on Broadway in 2015, it was an immediate game changer. Within weeks, the new musical was credited with redefining the art form for an entire generation. President Obama, foreign heads of state, industry leaders, and the royalty of Europe traveled to the small Richard Rodgers Theater to watch history unfold before their eyes. No one was disappointed.

The big idea behind *Hamilton* seems impossible to pull off. It was a rap-based, historical account of the US Founding Fathers, focusing on the often-overlooked character of Alexander Hamilton. It recounted everything from his love life to his conceptual model for the US Treasury. All of the main characters were played by persons of color, including famous slave owners such as George Washington and Thomas Jefferson. The story needled historians and scholars by turning revered American hero Thomas Jefferson into a wandering playboy foil for the earnest, heroic Hamilton. In a word, it was irreverent.

That was especially true in the way *Hamilton* portrayed famous historical debates. You probably remember these debates from your high school and college history classes—the endless points of contention among Jefferson, Washington, Hamilton, Madison, and all the others about federalism and taxation and banking regulations.

What could possibly make any of this new or interesting?

Well, in *Hamilton* the Founders hold forth on the fate of American democracy by engaging in rap battles. Picture Kanye West versus Eminem, battling over how to respond to new taxation regulations from England. Hard to imagine? Then also consider that each political figure's unique cunning and intelligence—Jefferson, Washington, Hamilton, Madison—is represented by his own distinctive lyrical style and rhythmic deftness.

As Jefferson and Hamilton lock horns, the tempo quickens. A circle of peers surround them, cheering and mocking the great historical figures, amplifying the sting of each parry and riposte. Jefferson attacks first in simple rhyming verse, delivered in standard 4/4 time (think of Run DMC). Hamilton responds, escalating the duel with crowd-pleasing alliterations and double entendres, delivered in masterly, almost savage 3/16 time. The circle of taunting peers falls into awestruck silence.

New York Times theater critic Ben Brantley reported, "At this point, it would be almost a relief to report that *Hamilton* has shrunk beneath the bloat of its hype."

He then conceded without hesitation, "Yes, it really is that good."

Hamilton sold out its entire Broadway run and was nominated for a record-breaking sixteen Tony awards. It also won a Pulitzer Prize.

The questions that everyone wants to answer are, *Where does this kind of innovation come from? And how can we reproduce it?*

How Broadway Harmonizes

The story of Broadway's rise to international prominence, which is also the story of how the science of innovation works, begins with *Oklahoma!*

In 1943, Richard Rodgers and Oscar Hammerstein II's smash hit ushered in the modern era of musical theater. *Oklahoma!* was the biggest success the industry had ever seen. And Rodgers and Hammerstein were just getting started.

Their next effort, *Carousel,* further reinvented the genre, reimagining the way plot devices, songs, and narratives were woven together. It was an even bigger hit than *Oklahoma!*, receiving *Time* magazine's recognition for "best musical of the century."

The musical duo kept going. *The Sound of Music* came next, followed by *South Pacific,* whose influence extended far beyond Broadway, winning the 1950 Pulitzer Prize for Drama and making three million dollars in its debut year (which was a lot of money in 1950).

There are two ways of measuring success on Broadway. The first is whether the show is a critical success: Are the songs innovative? Is the story compelling? Does the work push the genre, or develop new insight into important social or existential themes? Critical success comes in the form of Tony Awards and, on rare occasions, a Pulitzer Prize.

The second measure is commercial success. Put simply, did the show make a lot of money?

It's clear that these two measures of success are not always compatible. But in order for a Broadway show to be truly considered a hit, both are required. The real power of innovation — on Broadway or in the boardroom — is making something profoundly new that is also commercially successful.

In the world of Broadway musicals, there are a few well-known hits and hundreds more unknown flops. Many of us know the hits: *Hamilton, The Lion King, Chicago, A Chorus Line,* and so on. Most of us have never heard of the flops, but they far outnumber the hits. Despite their failure, the flops had top talent, big backers, and enough interesting songs and plot devices to merit a run on Broadway.

In order for a show to make it to Broadway at all, a lot of people need to believe it's going to succeed. In fact, at the start of a Broadway run, the hits and the flops cannot be distinguished from each other. They both have all the key ingredients for success.

Given that, it's shocking how wide the gaps are between failure and success. One of Broadway's biggest hits, *The Lion King*, has been running continuously for over twenty years and has grossed more than $1.5 billion. By contrast, the legendary musical team of Rodgers and Hammerstein, who essentially invented the genre of the modern musical, followed *South Pacific* with *Pipe Dream*, which lasted fewer than 250 performances and lost money, grossing less than it cost to produce.

Marketers and scholars have worked for decades to figure out what the key ingredients are that set the hits apart from the long list of flops. For a long time, this question seemed unanswerable.

But times have changed.

In the early 2000s, sociologists Brian Uzzi and Jaret Spiro spent several years adapting the analytic strategies of network science to identify the key features that underwrite creative success on Broadway. Their breakthrough produced some remarkable new insights into the science of creativity.

Their major finding was that individual artists were not the factor that determined a creative success on Broadway. Nor was it the particular songs, nor the palette of colors, nor the costumes, nor even the themes that were developed. Rather, hits came from the particular dynamics among the collaborative teams behind a show. Successful productions grew out of collaborations in which talented people managed to balance the common lessons they had learned from their previous collaborations with the new ideas they were inventing together on their current one. Successful innovation comes from social networks that balance coordination with creativity.

The strange history of Broadway musicals provides a rare glimpse into exactly what these successful networks look like.

Just like the prices of commodities sold on the New York

Stock Exchange, the track record of successful innovation on Broadway has been meticulously chronicled.

Before Rodgers and Hammerstein's breakthrough in 1943, Broadway musicals were frequent, but not terribly inventive. The genre did not command much critical or commercial attention. *Oklahoma!* changed all that. It not only ushered in a new wave of artistic and financial success but also birthed a new era of collaboration. Broadway musicals enjoyed high times through the 1940s, 1950s, and into the 1960s. Show after show was a hit.

This rising wave ultimately crashed at the end of the 1960s, followed by an era when hit musicals were rare indeed. It appeared that the heyday of the Broadway musical was over, and that the industry might die entirely. But then an unexpected revival brought new life to the industry. In the late 1970s and 1980s, massive hits like *A Chorus Line, Annie, Cats, Les Misérables,* and *Phantom of the Opera* reinvented the genre of musical theater, with *Phantom of the Opera* setting the record for the most popular Broadway musical of all time (more than 13,000 performances and counting).

But why? What's the story behind these historical peaks and lulls in innovation on Broadway? Insight into this question comes from an unlikely place: a close look at the changing pattern of social networks within the industry.

Just like innovative efforts in science or in engineering, innovation in the arts frequently comes from teams of people with complementary skills. The basic formula for creating a musical is well known. You need a composer to write the music, a lyricist to write the lyrics, a librettist to write the plot of the story, a choreographer to plan the dancing, a director to communicate the team's vision to the actors, and, finally, a producer to pay the bills. Most teams have one person per role, but team size can vary. A typical team for developing a Broadway musical ranges from five to nine people. In the parlance of social networks, a single team is what I refer to as a "social cluster."

The most obvious question is, what features make a successful team? Does team size predict success? It does not. Nor does the particular composition of the team; each individual composer and director and choreographer has plenty of hits and flops. The feature that *does* predict success is how a team is connected to the larger network of Broadway's creative professionals.

During Broadway's periods of peak innovation, the network of industry collaborations has been composed of tightly clustered teams with wide bridges between them. It resembles the network pattern among international research centers working on the Human Genome Project and Silicon Valley corporations during the best years of open innovation. In all these settings, creativity has been sustained by a contagion infrastructure that enables the transfer of knowledge across teams, leading to an explosion of innovation.

But Broadway wasn't always like that. Before the heyday of the 1940s, the network pattern on Broadway was a dense web of fireworks displays. Everyone worked with everyone. The social clusters were not very distinct. There was not a great deal of diversity in the industry. A few strong personalities and dominant themes pervaded every team. Musicals largely followed a standard formula, with a familiar boy-meets-girl plot and a big, love-focused musical number toward the middle of the show. Despite Broadway being flush with talent at the time — Rodgers, Hammerstein, Gershwin, Porter, and others were all hard at work — hits such as *Show Boat* were surprisingly rare. Ninety percent of shows were flops.

It was difficult to innovate in 1930s Broadway for the same reason that it was hard to spread hybrid corn in 1930s Iowa.

The standard formula had an established track record of decent success. Everyone was surrounded by countervailing influences that favored the status quo. People with new ideas were often pushed aside or forced to conform.

All that changed in the 1940s. Rapid economic growth and increased social mobility expanded the audience for Broadway shows. At the same time, the loss of many of Broadway's talented artists during the Second World War created a vacuum, bringing an influx of new blood into the New York City creative scene. Social networks within the Broadway community began to diversify. Distinct clusters began to take form, from which new artistic styles emerged. Broadway had developed a contagion infrastructure. Social clusters preserved creative diversity, while connections across teams enabled experienced artists and newcomers to coordinate their efforts to innovate. Newly emerging wide bridges combined ideas from people who had never worked together before. Novel approaches and traditional techniques were mixed together in the creative cauldron of Broadway's new social networks. Broadway had achieved that magical balance between coordination and creativity—the recipe for successful innovation.

After Rodgers and Hammerstein's run of successes, Broadway's musical hits just kept on coming. The 1957 hit *West Side Story* featured a first-time collaboration between the award-winning composer and lyricist Stephen Sondheim and the librettist Arthur Laurents. *Time* magazine called the show "a milestone in musical-drama history." It was the first musical to use choreography as a central narrative element, and it changed the way Broadway shows were produced. Sondheim and Laurents worked together again in 1959 on the hit musical *Gypsy*. *Gypsy*'s creative success combined the lyrical and narrative elements that Sondheim and Laurents had developed on *West Side*

Story with new styles of choreography and direction. Renowned theater critic Clive Barnes called *Gypsy* "one of the best musicals of all time." *Gypsy*'s success led its director, Jerome Robbins, to collaborate again with Laurents on the 1967 hit *Fiddler on the Roof*. This production combined the directorial style and narrative elements that Robbins and Laurents had developed in *Gypsy* with the new lyrical and musical approaches of Sheldon Harnick and Jerry Bock. *Fiddler on the Roof* became the most successful Broadway musical of its time, with more than 3,000 performances.

Broadway's new dynamic network of collaborations led to the exploration of radical new terrain, allowing artists to tackle cutting-edge issues of racism, political oppression, gender relations, and homosexuality. Teams reimagined industry conventions in ways that were at once recognizable and novel. Choreographic ideas that originated in *West Side Story* evolved into novel techniques that were expanded in *Gypsy*, and later evolved into other hit shows.

Broadway in those postwar years seemed to have an inexhaustible capacity for creativity and success. How could it ever collapse?

The answer: television and Hollywood.

In the late 1960s, the growing popularity of television and increasing economic opportunity in Hollywood were attractive draws for Broadway's talent. Within a few years, the industry's social networks were decimated. Writers and directors and producers left New York City altogether in search of other commercial markets. Teams became balkanized, and knowledge transfer across productions broke down. Coordination stalled out and innovation became much less common. Occasionally there were individual hits, but the industry as a whole hit a slump that grew deeper by the year.

You could see the decline reflected on the streets. Along Broadway's once-sparkling "Great White Way," petty crime became a cliché, deterring tourists and talent alike. Each new problem fueled others. Fewer hits led to lower audience turn-out, which led to fewer investments by wealthy producers, which led to a less appealing work environment, which led to even greater difficulty attracting new talent.

Broadway's boom appeared to be over. Indeed, Broadway might never have recovered but for a strategic series of efforts to rejuvenate New York City in general, and Broadway in particular.

In the early 1980s, an aggressive initiative to clean up Broadway coincided with an enormous public-advertising campaign to bring droves of international tourists to New York City. (Remember the I ♥ NY marketing campaign?) The city's push for international tourism attracted new investors for Broadway shows, and with them new resources to lure talented writers, composers, actors, and directors back to Broadway. Within a few years, industry-wide collaboration networks began to re-form into the familiar network pattern that had supported innovation so effectively in the 1940s and 1950s.

Newly constructed wide bridges in the creative industry enabled coordination among diverse teams and supported the recombination of talent into novel collaborations. Knowledge transfer across these teams gave rise to cooperative ventures among new and experienced artists, ushering in another explosion of innovation. Hits such as *A Chorus Line, Cats, Les Misérables,* and *Phantom of the Opera* were produced, followed a few years later by the breakout success *The Lion King,* which featured entirely new elements in a Broadway musical and became the highest-grossing musical of all time.

The New Science of How Teams Work

The concept of contagion infrastructure gives us a way to think about how an entire industry or firm might be organized to promote creativity and innovation. But what about small-scale teams? Individual managers rarely have control over the network structure of an industry, or even of their organization. But they do have control over their teams.

What can network science tell us about how team members — scientists working on prototypes for the Mars lander, artists working on new Broadway productions, or engineers developing new kinds of personal computers — should be connected to one another in order to maximize their capacity for innovation?

The conventional wisdom says that the more efficient a team's communication networks are for information spreading — meaning the more weak ties there are in the social network — the more effective they will be at collaborating. In fact, this wisdom says that the harder the problem is that a team is trying to solve, the more important weak ties are for innovation. A team that is connected in a network pattern resembling a fireworks display should be most effective for sharing information, keeping everyone up to speed, and accelerating the team's discovery process.

It is clear why the conventional wisdom recommends a network structure that optimizes information sharing. Any good idea discovered by one member of a team can rapidly spread to the rest of the group, accelerating the entire team's ability to converge on the new idea and innovate further.

It seems obvious. So obvious, in fact, that decades of management practice have dutifully followed this idea. Management routines that ensure rapid information exchange — weekly meetings, regular check-ins, and high-contact office spaces — are designed to keep everyone up to speed on the latest and greatest breakthroughs among their team members.

But do the strategies learned from solving simple problems really generalize to teams solving complex ones?

What if you're managing a team of biochemists working on a new cancer medication? Or you're running a team of data scientists at Amazon or Target trying to develop a better algorithm to predict customers' product interests? What if you're managing a team of physicians striving to develop the best protocols for a new opioid substitute? These are complex problems. How should you structure your team to maximize its capacity to discover innovative solutions?

These were the questions I wanted to answer.

To do so, I would need a way to study how the structure of research teams influences their creativity and productivity. Was there a way to replicate the process of innovation so that I could study it scientifically?

Around 2014, I was lucky enough to start working with a talented graduate student named Devon Brackbill, who was also interested in this idea. We started dreaming up ways to construct the same kind of "sociological laboratory" I had used to study tipping points. Could we create a laboratory for studying the process of innovation and scientific discovery?

Remarkably, Devon found a way to do this. He borrowed an approach that was popularized in the early 2000s by Netflix — a strategy that not only helped to solve Netflix's core business problem at the time but inadvertently helped to establish the modern field of data science.

The Power of Fishing-Net Teams

In 2005, Netflix was regularly providing its customers with recommendations for new movies to watch, based on their previous rentals. The problem was that Netflix wasn't doing a very good job of recommending movies. It was an important goal: suggest the right titles and customers will keep using Netflix; suggest the wrong ones and customers will get bored and drift away. The company's data analysts had used tens of millions of company records—years of customer viewing and rating data— to develop their own internal recommendation system, called Cinematch. But Netflix had outgrown Cinematch. It couldn't keep up with the changing universe of new content and evolving consumer tastes. As a result, Netflix was seeing an alarming drop-off in customer engagement. The writing was on the wall: *do something drastic or subscription revenues will plummet.*

Netflix decided to turn its internal corporate problem into a public scientific problem. They would crowdsource an answer. The idea of holding public competitions to find solutions to challenging engineering problems had been pioneered decades earlier by engineering firms such as Boeing and GE. But Netflix did something different. They did not simply announce their problem and see who came to them with the best solution. They made their precious data on customers' movie-watching behavior and rating histories public, inviting teams of data scientists to hack through it and come up with an effective algorithm for generating movie recommendations.

On October 2, 2006, the Netflix Prize was launched, promising a one-million-dollar purse to the team that could deliver the best movie-prediction algorithm. The competition ran for three years. Tens of thousands of professional programmers from around the world joined in. University students spent their summers working on it, professors built classes around it, and entrepreneurs launched companies dedicated to solving it. It became the most talked-about problem in computer science since the search-engine problem of the mid-1990s. (As we all know, Google solved that problem and took over the search-engine market.)

In 2015, Devon and I were hunting for the secret recipe for managing innovation when Devon suggested the Netflix competition as a potential source for insight. We were less intrigued by Netflix's specific movie-recommendation problem than by their solution-seeking strategy. In the years since 2009, when the Netflix Prize was finally won, the field of data science had become inundated with Web-based competitions emulating the idea of the Netflix Prize. Websites such as Kaggle, Crowd-ANALYTIX, Innocentive, TunedIT, and many others were providing a kind of digital posting-board for companies, governments, and private individuals to advertise public competitions for data-analytical problems, with prizes typically ranging from $50,000 to $500,000.

This new social space—public competitions for solution discovery—offered Devon and me a remarkable opportunity to look behind the curtain and see how high-stakes creative collaborations work and how the connectedness of teams affects their capacity for innovation. Would it be possible to "manage innovation" by designing the right kind of social networks among teams of data scientists? Would building a contagion infrastructure within collaborative teams offer a useful way to accelerate the discovery of better solutions?

With generous funding from the National Science Foundation, Devon and I constructed our own version of the Netflix Prize, called the Annenberg Data Science Competition. Similar to the Netflix challenge, we constructed problem-solving teams composed of globally distributed researchers, and tasked them with accelerating breakthroughs in machine learning, artificial intelligence, and statistical and computational analysis. Unlike the Netflix challenge, our goal was not to figure out how to generate better movie recommendations. Instead, our competition gave us a way to see whether arranging the network connections among our teams of researchers into different patterns would alter the researchers' capacity for innovation. Would using the principles of complex contagion—connecting the researchers in a fishing-net pattern—yield greater innovation? Or would teams perform better if we instead designed researchers' networks for rapid information-sharing using a fireworks pattern?

We recruited 180 data scientists from university campuses and job boards, and randomly divided them into sixteen teams— eight organized into fireworks patterns and eight into fishing-net patterns. On the eight fireworks teams, the researchers (or "contestants") were completely connected with their teammates. Information flow was maximized. The team network was a dense pattern of fireworks explosions. Everyone on a team could see all of their teammates' best solutions as they discovered them.

On the eight fishing-net teams, by contrast, each contestant was connected to only a few members of their team. They could see only the solutions of teammates to whom they were directly connected. So to learn about a discovery by a remote team member (several steps away in the network), they would have to wait for the idea to travel across a few wide bridges before it finally reached them.

Like the Netflix Prize, the contestants in our competition were playing for prize money. Researchers' rewards were allocated based on the quality of their final solutions. The best solution won the most money.

But we added a twist. Teams had only fifteen minutes to solve the problem.

The competition started when we provided each of the teams with highly detailed sales and product data drawn from publicly available performance records of Fortune 500 companies. Contestants were asked to discover the best predictive model for explaining the success of the companies' products.

What predicted shoe sales? Was it price, style, celebrity endorsements, or some unknown combination of factors? What determined beer sales? Was it advertising, flavor, alcohol content, regional targeting, carbonation levels, or a combination of other factors? Every factor interacted with the others; lower prices seemed to drive shoe sales, until you took celebrity endorsements into account, at which point *higher* prices increased sales. The data sets had more than fifteen thousand possible solutions.

The competition was a good approximation of what life is like for any research team working in a fast-paced industry. The contestants were all smart, well-trained, highly motivated data scientists. And they were all under severe time pressure to solve a challenging technical problem.

So how did they fare?

At first the eight fireworks teams quickly jumped ahead. Good solutions reached everyone within only a few minutes, and team members quickly coalesced around a shared strategy. The problem was that whereas each team's early discoveries were invariably *good* solutions, they were far from *the best solution possible.* And once everyone on a team had adopted a good solution strategy, their future explorations were all fairly similar to one another. Everyone started looking at the problem the same way. Innovation stopped.

Devon and I discovered that the problem with the fireworks network was that good solutions were spreading *too quickly.* People stopped exploring radically different and potentially innovative approaches to the problem.

What we learned was that discovery, like diffusion, requires *social clustering.*

The reason is that clustering preserves diversity. Not demographic diversity. But informational diversity.

Because fishing nets were *less efficient* for spreading information, they prevented news of an early, pretty good discovery from reaching everyone on the team too quickly. By slowing down information, the fishing net "protected" researchers from exposure to solutions that might take them off the track of discovering something truly innovative that no one else was anticipating.

The networks that were less efficient for *information* were more efficient for *exploration*.

At first this result puzzled us, but then it started to make sense. We realized that one of the greatest obstacles to innovation is that familiar solutions are *simple contagions*. They are easy to understand and easy to spread. They fit into our preexisting picture of how the world works. These predictable solutions sprint across teams that are connected in a fireworks pattern.

We organized the competition so that each team was equal, composed of data scientists with the same technical-skill levels, professional experience, and financial motivation. The teams were all given identical problems to solve. But by the end of the competition, all eight fishing-net teams had found better solutions than all eight fireworks teams. In fact, each fishing-net team found a solution that was better than the *best* solutions found on any of the fireworks teams.

On every team, researchers furiously explored large combinations of variables, trying to find the best predictive model, right up until the last seconds of the competition. But on the fireworks teams, people converged so quickly on the same approach that all of their explorations rarely improved upon the early, pretty good discovery.

The fishing-net teams started out the same way. Early discoveries would begin to propagate around each team's network.

But as these solutions were spreading, other team members who were off exploring alternative approaches would find *better* solutions. As those new discoveries started to spread slowly, researchers in another part of the network would find even better solutions. By slowing down the spread of information, the fishing-net pattern increased the efficiency with which teams could explore new ideas.

The fishing-net teams did so well, in fact, that Devon and I started to wonder how their solutions would compare with computer-based approaches to solving these complex problems. In fields such as engineering and medicine, the promise of artificial intelligence (AI) has been a welcome relief for managers trying to solve complex, time-critical problems. Would that also be true for the problems in our competition?

To find out, we recruited a new contestant: the supercomputer cluster at the University of Pennsylvania, which we used to run comprehensive AI algorithms to solve the same data questions the human teams had taken on.

We were not surprised to find that the AI algorithms often outperformed the human teams. But we *were* surprised that that was true only for teams with *fireworks* networks. Teams with a fishing-net pattern typically outperformed the computers!

It turned out that the algorithms suffered from the same problem we'd found in the fireworks networks: they knew too much.

The AI algorithms we used were unrelentingly systematic. A typical algorithm would evaluate every predictive model for one variable at a time. It would select the best variable, then move forward looking for the next variable to add. It would methodically add or exclude each variable until it arrived at the best solution.

But this approach can fall into the same trap that tripped

up the humans in the fireworks-network teams. If a highly predictive variable is discovered early on, all future solutions will include that variable. And that's not always the right approach. There may exist a bizarre combination of variables, each of them individually unpromising but collectively providing a superior solution. A researcher could discover this unlikely solution only if she was protected early on from being exposed to other, more conventional, promising ideas. Only people who were able to explore variables that seemed unlikely to succeed would eventually figure out the optimal solution. That's an approach that neither our AI algorithms nor the fireworks networks would be likely to follow.

The hallmark of a well-designed team is that it preserves intellectual diversity while enabling coordination. Much like Broadway in the late 1940s and 1950s, the perfect balance between coordination and creativity is a network of wide bridges among clusters of independent innovation. In well-designed teams, team members are *protected* enough to preserve informational diversity. This enables them to explore unlikely terrain in sufficient depth to discover something unexpected. But it leaves them *connected* enough that innovative ideas can be reinforced once they are discovered.

For managers, this means that when problems are complex, teams with smaller, less frequent meetings may outperform teams that maintain constant information flow through larger, more frequent meetings. Amazon's CEO, Jeff Bezos, has made clever use of this idea with his impromptu "two-pizza rule." He reasoned that meetings should be small enough to feed everyone with two pizzas. If meetings required more pizzas, they were probably too big; the networks were probably too connected; and the potential for informational diversity, exploration, and innovation was probably being lost.

China's Fireworks Problem

In his 1999 Pulitzer Prize–winning study of the history of civilizations, *Guns, Germs, and Steel,* Jared Diamond poses the question of why over the last several centuries European civilizations have triumphed over civilizations from other continents. A key factor in the explanation is the capacity of societies to effectively develop and spread innovations. A particularly sharp paradox arises from the case of China.

In the first millennium AD (from 0 to 1000), China developed, and productively used, gunpowder for firearms, compasses for navigation, the printing press, and paper. By AD 1300, Chinese scholars had developed detailed treatises on the proper military uses of fire arrows, rockets, firearms, land mines, naval mines, cannon, and two-stage rockets. Europeans were still fighting each other with broadswords.

The Chinese advantage wasn't just in warfare. All the way back in 8500 BC, China had already routinized food production on a massive scale. In the centuries that followed, China led the world in the unprecedented consolidation of political power across a vast geography, enjoyed unrivaled success in global navigation, and achieved dominance over the seas.

Covering as much territory as it did, China had all the geographic ingredients for a successful civilization. It had a stable, fertile, and diverse ecology, which enabled the development of diverse crops and livestock. China's massive system of food production has been remarkably stable for the last 10,000 years.

As Diamond writes, "A historian who had lived at any time between 8500 BC and AD 1450, and who had tried to predict future historical trajectories, would surely have labeled Europe's eventual dominance as the least likely outcome." Throughout the long history of the development and spread of innovations,

China dominated Europe. How, then, did the backward states of Europe come to dominate the world only a few centuries later?

The answer involves a surprising feature of social networks. The pattern of the informational networks in China was a lot like that of the *fireworks* teams that we studied in the Data Science Competition. Any good idea that was discovered in China was immediately connected to the capital, then spread around the nation. This centralized system of information flow accelerated the spread of technologies around the country with blazing speed. This gave China a big head start, enabling the rapid development of arms, agriculture, and government. The capacity for rapid diffusion can give a highly connected population an early lead. But connectedness also comes with long-term downsides, which can be observed in the history of China.

Centralized control in China led to rapid convergence on good ideas. But these efficient networks for informational access and political control in China also meant that independent innovation could be controlled, and stopped, by the central government. Any leader who wanted to slow the process of discovery, or preserve a particular technology or cultural practice, could unilaterally prevent all progress throughout the country. And this is precisely what happened. As Diamond puts it, "China's connectedness eventually became a disadvantage, because a decision by one despot could and *repeatedly did* halt innovation."

Europe, however, was a different story. It was composed of many different states, each with its own capacity for invention and exploration. The European states more closely resembled fishing-net networks. National borders slowed down the spread of innovation, preventing a popular innovation that happened to take hold in one European state from commanding authority over all the others. Innovations eventually spread across

Europe, but far more slowly than in China. Meanwhile, every state was free to keep exploring its own ideas. This informational and cultural diversity enabled vastly more exploration. Even though China had a head start of hundreds of years (and in some cases thousands of years), once Chinese innovations reached Europe, European states could adopt them but also keep innovating. They could continue to experiment and explore in ways that their fellow European states could not imagine, and that the Chinese government did not permit for its own citizens.

Only a few hundred years after Chinese innovations reached Europe, rapid European exploration and innovation led to historic new developments—and an expansive new Western frontier. Europeans soon invaded the Americas, then prepared to move east as well.

It could just as well have been China exploring these frontiers. In the early 1400s, decades before Christopher Columbus's famous triad of ships sailed for the New World, Chinese fleets composed of hundreds of ships sailed across the Indian Ocean as far as Africa. The Chinese had such an enormous head start, why wouldn't they be the ones to reach the Americas first?

At the time, between AD 1405 and AD 1433, there was a power struggle in China. The factions that controlled the training of crew and captains were not the factions that controlled the harbors. To wrest control from the captain-training factions, the harbormaster factions closed all harbors in the nation and forbade shipping entirely. In Europe, such a dispute would have closed ports only within the disputed region—southern Italy, say, or western Scandinavia—without disrupting shipping or marine exploration in any other nation; in China, the massive connectedness of the nation meant that the power struggle for dominance affected the entire country, resulting in a complete shutdown of all shipyards nationwide. All Chinese harbors closed, and remained closed for decades. Within the last few years of that century, the crucial window for China's world dominance was lost. By the time China began to rebuild its shipping industry a few generations later, Europeans had already settled in the New World and were expanding their exploration of China.

Networks that facilitate the spread of ideas are necessary for innovation. The networks that brought Chinese innovations to Europe were essential for the European Renaissance, and Europe's eventual emergence from the Middle Ages. But if innovations spread too rapidly, or if connectedness is too great or too centralized, societies lose the capacity for independent exploration—a vital requirement for any successful enterprise trying to solve complex problems under competitive time pressures. Just as we saw in the history of hybrid corn, an essential strategy for successful social change—both for the discovery of innovations and for their spread—is to protect the places in the social network that incubate innovation. A contagion infrastructure composed of cohesive social clusters with wide bridges between them accelerates innovation by enabling new ideas to take hold—and then to take off.

CHAPTER 12

Bias, Belief, and the Willingness to Change

In a now-famous scene from the classic Woody Allen film *Annie Hall,* Alvy Singer, played by Allen, is asked by his psychotherapist how frequently he has sex with his girlfriend, Annie. Frustrated, he replies: "Hardly ever, maybe three times a week." When Annie, played by Diane Keaton, is asked the same question by her own therapist, she says (in a split screen), "Constantly, I'd say three times a week."

Funny, yes. But also telling. Two people can interpret the exact same event or information in starkly different ways. So can two groups of people, such as C-suite executives and salaried workers, or opposing political parties. People's social networks often reinforce their belief systems, which can make it difficult for people who see the world differently to come to a shared agreement on contentious issues.

The previous chapter showed how contagion infrastructure was essential for the discovery of new ideas. This chapter will show how it can also be essential for the *acceptance* of new ideas—particularly ideas that certain groups are far more predisposed to accept than others.

NASA's Climate Roadblock

NASA's recent findings on global trends in Arctic sea ice are a case in point. Arctic sea ice is perhaps the best indicator we have to evaluate global climate change. The more rapidly sea-ice levels decline, the more immediate the danger from rising sea levels, warming atmospheric temperatures, and reduced ocean salinity. Each of these indicators threatens the survival of coastal and deep-sea marine ecologies around the world. If these ecologies fail, so does the rest of the planet.

Over the last thirty years, NASA has used orbital satellites to document these Arctic trends. In 2013, the results were released to the public. To NASA's scientists, they presented a definitive scientific demonstration of the rapid decline in Arctic sea ice and the need for swift, decisive action. Remarkably, although NASA's graph showed a clear downward trend in Arctic sea-ice levels, plummeting much faster in the last fifteen years, public interpretations of the graph were alarmingly contradictory: some groups took the graph as evidence that the threat of climate change had been overhyped.

To examine this phenomenon more closely, two of my graduate students (Douglas Guilbeault and Joshua Becker) and I conducted a study in 2017 in which liberals and conservatives were asked to use NASA's data to forecast Arctic sea-ice levels in 2025. Most liberals understood the graph to mean that Arctic sea ice was decreasing. But nearly half of conservatives concluded that Arctic sea-ice levels were *increasing*. They predicted that Arctic sea-ice levels in 2025 would be far above our present-day values. If they were right, it meant that all of the concerns the data had raised about the need to develop aggressive technological and public-policy strategies for handling (and hopefully slowing) an impending climate crisis could be safely dismissed.

NASA officials had thought their findings would demonstrate the looming perils of climate change. So how did their decades-long study communicate just the opposite to a significant percentage of the population?

How Networks Affect Bias

The answer can be found in the work of a world-renowned psychologist, Leon Festinger. Festinger used the term *motivated reasoning* to describe the way an individual's psychological and political biases can significantly skew their interpretation of otherwise neutral information. As he put it: "A man with a conviction is a hard man to change. Tell him you disagree and he turns away. Show him facts or figures and he questions your sources. Appeal to logic and he fails to see your point."

This specific form of cognitive bias leads some people to be significantly less likely to rationally process new scientific data about climate change. What's worse, the bias is exacerbated by social networks. Because social networks are the channels through which so much information is communicated, they act as filters on how we *interpret* new information, both in face-to-face interactions and on social media. The fate of many hot-button topics is now governed, to an unnerving degree, by the social networks through which information travels—even if that information contradicts the most impeccable scientific research. Because we live in a time of politically homogeneous and polarized "echo chambers," partisan bias is often reinforced through repeated interactions among like-minded peers.

As I studied the reaction to the NASA findings, I began to realize that echo chambers are exactly what organizational scholars refer to as *silos*. Silos emerge when there are no bridges between groups, preventing valuable information from traveling between them. As you saw in chapter 6, a narrow bridge can spread information, but it is often not enough to transfer knowledge between groups. That requires wide bridges.

A potential solution to the problem of echo chambers (and the misguided beliefs they can foster) is to increase the bridge width across the polarized communities. Perhaps a little social reinforcement across the aisle can help to mitigate the alarming rise of cultural and political divides. This is precisely what our 2017 study on climate change set out to do.

Once we had discovered how dramatically conservative and liberal interpretations of NASA's climate-change graph differed, we brought people from both groups together in social networks where they could interact directly and discuss their very different opinions about climate trends. Each social network had forty people (twenty Republicans and twenty Democrats) connected in a fishing-net pattern. We replicated our study twelve times (using twelve independent networks, for a total of 480 people). We decided at the outset that only if there was bias reduction in all twelve networks would we be able to conclude that wide bridges had worked to reduce political polarization.

So, did these interactions solve the problem? Did people learn from one another and coordinate on a new understanding of climate trends?

No, they did not.

In all twelve replications of our study, both Democrats and Republicans failed to learn anything new or change their ideas at all. Polarization was steadfast, and there were no significant improvements by either group in their capacity to understand or interpret the climate-change data from NASA. Wide bridges across party lines had failed to solve the problem.

But then we noticed something.

We had designed our experimental interface to resemble a social media site, such as Twitter. In the lower left corner of the screen, we included an image of the Republican Party logo (a red-white-and-blue elephant) and the Democratic Party logo (a red-white-and-blue donkey). These images did not serve any purpose. They did not indicate whom people were interacting with, or provide party-affiliation information for anyone in the study. They were just fun, eye-catching graphics.

That shouldn't have made a difference, right?

But then we looked at a different group of Democrats and Republicans.

They were just as polarized on the topic of climate change as the first group. We connected them in social networks just like before: 480 people divided into twelve networks, each network half-Republican and half-Democrat, each one connected in a fishing-net pattern with wide bridges across the political communities.

This time, however, we removed the political imagery from the screen.

And this time everything was different.

Cross-party interactions in these networks not only improved the "intelligence" of the group—everyone's ability to read the graph properly—but also completely eliminated belief polarization. By the end of the study, the forecasts of *both* liberals and conservatives had become far more accurate than we had thought possible. Astonishingly, both groups reached nearly 90 percent accuracy in their interpretation of NASA's data!

All twelve replications showed the same thing. Political polarization disappeared. In every group where we connected Democrats and Republicans together into a network of wide bridges across the aisle, we saw dramatic improvements in their ability to interpret climate trends—on both sides.

But if wide bridges are so effective, why did this strategy fail so utterly the first time, when the party logos were included?

Anyone who has ever tried to resolve disputes between warring companies, or address tensions between longtime rivals, knows that simply connecting conflicting groups together will not solve their problems. Done incorrectly, these social interventions can backfire—making the conflict far worse.

When *bias* is at work, wide bridges are only the first part of the solution. There are two other factors that matter. The second is *framing* and how it determines relevance.

In chapter 7, you saw that feelings of group solidarity and belonging could be remarkably contagious when they were socially reinforced. You saw how they were used to create fictional group boundaries between American preteens at an Oklahoma summer camp. Even superficial lines of similarity (such as dividing the boys into Rattlers and Eagles) could be used to spread emotional contagions that triggered intergroup violence. Similarly, the study done among Christian and Muslim teenagers in Beirut showed that creating fictional group boundaries between a Blue Ghosts team and a Red Genies team led Muslim and Christian teenagers to bond together on the Red team in violent confrontations with Muslims and Christians on the Blue team.

We see the same effects in the "real world" of social media. Democrats and Republicans interact all the time on social media, frequently with terrible results. Incivility and growing hostility exacerbate group polarization, deepening the enmity across party lines.

Our findings showed that the cause of this intergroup

enmity is not the interactions themselves, but how those inter-actions are framed. On social media, people interact within a sea of videos and images that remind them that the world is polarized. Party logos, political icons, and viral memes fill the Twittersphere with images that frame people's thinking in terms of their party identity. These images shape people's sense of who is relevant and who is not. They determine who is seen as the in-group and the out-group and implicitly define the boundaries of social influence.

We discovered that these seemingly irrelevant features of social media—specifically, graphics that remind people about their party loyalties—have a powerful influence on how social networks operate. Wide bridges across groups can facilitate learning and mutual understanding, but only when these inter-actions are framed in a way that makes diverse participants rel-evant to each other. If interactions are framed in a way that stirs feelings of political loyalty, even by introducing something as trivial as a graphic of a donkey and an elephant, it reduces people's ability to listen to diverse opinions, and even to see the facts clearly.

For any social-change campaign, designing a compelling message is important. But framing effects can determine what people actually hear. As NASA found out, framing effects can have a bigger impact than the message itself on what people ultimately believe.

Wide bridges and framing effects are two essential pieces of the puzzle for understanding how bias operates in social net-works. The third and final piece of the puzzle is *network central-ization*. At the beginning of this book, I introduced you to the idea of highly connected influencers at the "center" of a social network. The more connected these people are relative to everyone else, the more *centralized* a network is. A centralized social network resembles a single firework explosion. One highly connected person—a social star—is at the center of the conversation. This individual wields disproportionate influence over the flow of information among everyone else. Voices from the periphery are easily silenced.

The polar opposite is a fishing net. Instead of being centralized, this network is *egalitarian*.

In an egalitarian network, everyone has an equal voice in the conversation. In essence, everyone is part of a large, interconnected periphery. People typically interact in small clusters, and ideas flow across wide bridges between them. The key feature of an egalitarian network is that new ideas and opinions can emerge from anywhere in the community and spread to everyone without being blocked by a powerful social star at the center of the network.

In earlier chapters, you saw why centralized networks are excellent for spreading simple contagions but not very effective for spreading complex ones. Now I want to show you why this feature of centralized networks makes them prone to increase bias in people's opinions—and what you can do about it.

In our experiments on how people interpret NASA's climate-change data, we had placed Democrats and Republicans into fishing-net patterns. To see how network centralization would affect our findings, we conducted a new series of studies. We tested what would happen if we ran our second experiment again—the one *without* political imagery. But this time the Democrats and Republicans would be placed into a centralized network—a single firework explosion—rather than a fishing net. We experimented with randomly choosing different people to be in the center of the network—sometimes a Democrat, other times a Republican.

This time, polarization wasn't a problem. But bias was. If

the central person had any bias, it was amplified throughout the rest of the network. Network centralization made the entire population—both Democrats and Republicans—biased toward the central person's viewpoint.

There is a silver lining to centralization. If the person in the center of the network has a perfectly unbiased opinion, their influence can reduce the bias of the entire group.

But it's a very thin silver lining. Even small biases or errors by the central person can increase the entire population's tendency toward a biased opinion.

We found this problem to be less severe in more diverse groups, such as networks composed of both Democrats and Republicans with a wide range of views. Their diverse viewpoints can help mitigate the bias of a central individual.

Centralization is a far greater problem in groups of similarly minded people. When communities are organized along lines of shared political, social, or cultural beliefs, ideas that reinforce a community's existing beliefs are simple contagions: they are easy to understand, and easy to spread. Within political echo chambers, highly connected influencers at the center of the conversation can easily spread misinformation that plays to a group's biases.

By contrast, contentious ideas that *challenge* a group's biases are complex contagions: these ideas face strong opposition and are therefore unlikely to emerge from highly connected individuals facing a sea of countervailing influences. New ideas that challenge the status quo emerge more commonly from the moderately connected network periphery—where everyone's voice is equally heard, and where new ideas can be reinforced among peers and protected from too many countervailing influences.

The problem of bias affects everyone, from powerful CEOs to

the country's most vulnerable citizens. The natural asymmetry in the influence of influencers—they're good at spreading simple contagions but poor at spreading complex ones—can be particularly consequential for the spread of misinformation that exploits a community's biases. For instance, research on underserved communities, in particular African American and Latina women, has found that the members of these communities report disproportionate levels of distrust toward mainstream medical care— often because of years of poor and discriminatory treatment. As a result, highly connected influencers in these communities can be effective for spreading misinformation that amplifies people's distrust of current preventive health measures, such as birth control, vaccination, and COVID-19 prevention measures. The easy spread of that misinformation can, in turn, further exacerbate health inequities, making communities that are already distrustful of mainstream health care increasingly vulnerable to suffering negative but preventable health outcomes.

It's not just in public health.

As you'll see in the pages ahead, centralized networks can increase bias—and egalitarian networks can reduce it—among corporate managers, political leaders, and professional sports coaches. Even among physicians making life-and-death decisions.

Most of us have been taught to think of bias as a feature of individual people's beliefs—some people are biased and others are not. But the most consequential forms of bias are not in people's heads, but rather in their social networks.

A (Very Slow) Medical Breakthrough

In 1929, Werner Forssman was an ambitious twenty-five-year-old cardiologist working at a small hospital in the remote German town of Eberswalde. He had a big idea that would change the field of cardiology. His idea was about the little plastic tubes that physicians call *catheters*.

Since the late 1800s, catheters had been used intravenously in urology and related fields to help fluids such as blood and urine flow out of the body.

Forssman's strange new idea was that this technique might also be used *inside* the heart. What if you could push these catheters from a patient's arm all the way up into their chest cavity? That would allow physicians to examine the quality of a patient's cardiac muscle, identify diseased tissue, and even deliver life-saving medications directly to the pericardium.

There was one good reason *not* to do this—namely, that the entire medical community agreed that pushing a plastic tube into a person's heart would immediately kill them.

Everyone but Forssman.

He had read about the procedure being performed on animals and saw no reason why it should not work just as well on people. At the time, there were no operating rooms or laboratories set up to handle such a procedure. Was it really possible to insert a five-foot-long plastic tube into the arm or leg of a patient and guide it all the way into their heart—without killing them? How could you even see when the tube had reached the vena cava, or the right atrium? And even if you managed to navigate it up there, how would you use it for diagnosis or treatment?

Forssman had a few ideas.

He persuaded a nurse, Gerda Ditzen, to help him. Forssman told her he planned to perform the procedure on himself. That seemed liked suicide to Ditzen, so she insisted that he perform the procedure on her. That way, if anything started to go wrong, he could abort the procedure before it became life-threatening.

He agreed. Once she provided him with access to the surgical room and all of the sterile materials he needed for anesthesia, incision, catheterization, and extraction, he used the surgical restraints to secure her to the operating table. She was ready to begin.

But she didn't feel anything.

She waited for the incision, anticipating the dull feeling of the plastic tube sliding into her arm. Forssman leaned over and appeared to begin the procedure. It looked like he was making his cut and inserting the tube. But she still couldn't feel anything. It did not take her long to realize that he had cunningly placed his arm next to hers. Instead of cutting her, he had made the incision in himself!

She was helplessly tied to the table as the young cardiologist fed the plastic tube into his own forearm. She watched in horror as he pushed the catheter farther and farther into his body, searching for his own chest cavity.

She was terrified. It looked like he would kill himself.

But the young doctor had a plan.

He asked Ditzen to come with him downstairs to the X-ray room. She agreed. He released her from her restraints. The two of them hurried from the surgery office down the long hallway to the X-ray department, several feet of coiled plastic tube still protruding from Forssman's left arm. Forssman positioned himself in front of the X-ray imaging machine and observed his own chest cavity on the monitor as he guided the catheter up into his torso, around his pericardial sac, and into his right ventricle. He had Ditzen snap an X-ray photo of his work. It showed the plastic tube running into Forssman's left forearm, extending up into his shoulder socket, through his chest cavity, and comfortably resting inside his heart. Forssman's daring experiment had worked.

Weeks earlier, Forssman's boss, the hospital's chief surgeon, had forbidden Forssman from attempting this procedure. What did the chief think of it now?

He was both furious and delighted. Furious that Forssman had been so reckless with his own well-being (and had disregarded the chief's directive so flagrantly). But the chief couldn't help being delighted by the fact that it had worked. He knew that the small hospital in Eberswalde was on the verge of making medical history.

Anticipating outraged reactions from their peers, Forssman and his chief decided to demonstrate the therapeutic value of the procedure. They used Forssman's catheter method to deliver cardiac medication directly into the right ventricle of a terminally ill cardiac patient. The method proved to be far more therapeutically effective than the standard approach of intravenous injection. With this demonstration successfully completed, Forssman felt ready to announce his game-changing idea to the world.

He submitted his report on the procedure to a well-known German medical journal. Within only a few weeks, it was accepted for publication.

It appeared that Werner Forssman was on his way to fame and fortune. That year, he had moved from the small hospital in Eberswalde to the prestigious Charité Hospital in Berlin, where he planned to continue his pioneering work on cardiac catheters.

And then the article came out.

As soon as his groundbreaking findings were published, his career began to crumble. The medical establishment did not take kindly to this upstart surgeon recklessly using a self-administered procedure to challenge the received wisdom in cardiology.

In 1929, the social norms in medicine were already well

established. Forssman had clearly violated them. The more attention Forssman's groundbreaking paper garnered from the international press, the more resentment he received from his peers in the medical community. His new boss, the Charité Hospital's chief surgeon, ordered Forssman's immediate dismissal. The young surgeon was fired.

Over the next thirty years, Forssman bounced around, working in cardiology, urology, and other departments, never quite settling into a proper career in medicine.

Maybe you remember the twist in this story from the beginning of this book. A few decades later, Forsmann, now in his fifties, had secured a post as a urologist at a local hospital in the small German town of Bad Kreuznach. On a chilly autumn evening in 1956, nearly thirty years after his only major publication, Forssman was enjoying a drink at the local pub. His wife phoned the pub to tell him to come home because a reporter was trying to reach him. But Forssman was not interested in talking to reporters, so he rejoined his friends for another round of drinks. Around 10 p.m., when Forssman finally arrived back at his modest country home, he received the call informing him he'd won the 1957 Nobel Prize in Medicine and Physiology.

Today, cardiac catheterization is one of the most routine procedures in medicine. It is used for diagnosis and treatment in every major cardiology department in the world.

But it took a long time to get there.

A few chapters ago, I showed you how social norms operate, and why they can be so hard to change. You might imagine that social norms would not play any role in how doctors make decisions. After all, medical science is supposed to be objective and empirical.

Unfortunately, doctors are just as susceptible to the influences of social norms as everybody else. Perhaps even more so.

In chapter 10, you saw how farmers were reluctant to adopt hybrid corn partially because there were reputational consequences that might haunt a farmer who made an unwise decision. As the stakes become higher, the social risks of making an unpopular decision are greater. In professions that involve both tremendous uncertainty and high stakes—such as finance and medicine—successful people are acutely aware of the social norms in their professional community. The higher the stakes and the greater the uncertainty, the greater people's conformity to social norms.

In 2020, a groundbreaking study of this phenomenon, led by Nancy Keating of Harvard Medical School, showed that physicians' willingness to use new biologic therapies to treat cancer patients depends crucially on the social networks within their medical community.

Keating and her team examined the treatment decisions of more than 800 physicians, across 432 practices, located in more than 400 different medical communities. Over the course of their four-year study, starting in 2005, Keating's team examined the reasons why physicians switched their cancer patients from traditional chemotherapy treatments to the new biologic therapy, bevacizumab. Keating found that neither the nature of a patient's illness nor the characteristics of a physician's background and experience could explain why some patients received the new treatment while others did not. Even the size of a physician's practice did not seem to matter. Clinically identical breast-cancer patients—treated by similarly trained physicians with similar pedigrees and in similar kinds of practices—were receiving starkly different treatments. The obvious explanation was money. But, strikingly, Keating's analysis found that no standard economic theory or medical guideline could explain why some medical communities adopted the treatment but others didn't.

They finally figured it out.

The explanation was neither medical nor economic.

It was social.

Physicians' use of bevacizumab was determined by reinforcement in their social networks. Once a treatment reached a critical mass in a clinician's community, it was socially acceptable to use. If the treatment had not taken hold within a physician's social network, they typically would not use it.

Keating and her team found that it wasn't informational awareness that determined whether oncologists used the new treatment. They needed to see that the treatment was considered legitimate within their social network before they would prescribe it. The more reinforcement they received, the more likely they were to prescribe the treatment.

This is not necessarily a bad thing. As you saw in our study of Democrats' and Republicans' evaluations of NASA climate data, social influence from peer networks can significantly improve people's judgments. With the right social network, it's not a bad idea for physicians to rely on the wisdom of their peers when there is uncertainty about a new treatment.

But with the wrong network, it can also go horribly wrong.

A Color Line in Catheters?

By the 1990s, Forssman's Nobel Prize in Medicine and Physiology had become the stuff of legend. His story had been repeated for decades as an inspiring tale for young, maverick physicians. The procedure of cardiac catheterization had become well established. US medical guidelines stipulated when it was required, and every major hospital in the US had surgery rooms designed for it.

In 1997, though, a group of social scientists and physicians at the University of Pennsylvania, Georgetown University, and the RAND Corporation began to investigate a suspicion they had developed. They believed that this life-saving procedure was not being used fairly. They suspected there was systematic discrimination, according to race and gender, in how doctors recommended who received cardiac catheterization and who did not.

Earlier research had established the destructive power of unequal medical care in the United States. Bias in medical care is often rooted in genuine disparities in medical statistics, which show that health outcomes vary widely based on wealth, diet, environmental factors, and race. These factors are often correlated. Once these correlations become well known within the medical community, doctors frequently accept them as inevitable. Then social norms take over: physicians begin to develop expectations about their patients based on their patients' race, which their peers often unconsciously reinforce. The result is that poor health outcomes for Black patients are more likely to be attributed to their lifestyle or background than they are to clinicians' inadequate treatment. Doctors sometimes make similar lifestyle-based assumptions for white patients as well, but not nearly as often. White men, in particular, are the least likely group to suffer the effects of these kinds of biases.

The reason it is hard to correct these biases is that they are often unconscious, or *implicit*. The problem with implicit bias is that it does not live within the hearts and minds of bigoted doctors and nurses; it lives within professional social norms and the networks that reinforce them. Dozens of studies over the last several decades have found that implicit bias pervades medical decision-making throughout the US. Studies routinely find that women of color get the worst of it. Even affluent, educated, and respected women of color are not treated with the same standard of care as white men.

The cardiac-catheterization researchers therefore had good reason to suspect that doctors were making decisions about patient treatment unequally. But how could they show it? No cardiologist in the US would believe that they had made a racist or sexist clinical recommendation, let alone admit to it on a survey.

The scholars came up with an ingenious plan to see if cardiac catheters were indeed being prescribed equitably. They set up private computer booths at the 1997 annual meetings of the American College of Physicians and the American Academy of Family Practice. Booths like this are a common sight at physicians' annual meetings. Attendees are typically given small monetary incentives to participate in ongoing surveys and research studies. The researchers cleverly designed their booth to resemble a voting booth, surrounded by thick curtains, so that physicians could participate anonymously.

Each participant in their study was shown a video screen in which a patient described their symptoms. It was like a virtual doctor's-office visit. The clinicians were then asked to respond to a series of questions about the patient's condition, and finally asked to determine whether the patient should receive a cardiac catheter.

This kind of "virtual patient" scenario is the bread and butter of medical training. Throughout medical school, residency, and fellowship, physicians are regularly exposed to standardized-patient experiences like this one. Either in person or by video, physicians are asked to diagnose the actors who are pretending to be patients. The actors portray the symptoms, body language, and even slurred speech (for instance, for a brain-injury case) that would be typical of a real patient with that condition. The doctor's job is to figure out the problem, make the correct diagnosis, and prescribe the correct test or treatment. It's such a common practice that some actors make a good living as full-time standardized patients for well-known hospitals. There's no deception involved: the doctors know the actors are actors. But they also know they're being evaluated based on their performance, so they take the test seriously.

What the clinicians who were participating in this study didn't know was that there were dozens of different variations of the patient video. In each variant, patients presented with slightly different symptoms, histories, and medical records. This enormous number of variations made it unlikely that any two clinicians who bumped into each other at one of the annual meetings could compare notes on their experiences, since the cases they saw were likely to be different.

Also unknown to the physicians, most of these variations were not the true purpose of the study. The real experimental design systematically varied the race and gender of the patients in the videos to see whether those features of the patient affected the clinicians' recommendations.

The article hit the *New England Journal of Medicine* like an atomic bomb. The findings showed that Black women were significantly less likely to receive cardiac catheterization than white men. It was the first controlled experiment to demonstrate a direct effect of racial and gender bias in clinicians' treatment recommendations. Dozens of news stories and commentaries were written about it, and hundreds of subsequent articles cited it. The results sharpened everyone's thinking about inequity in health care. Implicit bias was now at the center of the conversation.

The question ever since has been what to do about it.

De-Biasing Networks

You've already seen how egalitarian social networks were able to eliminate bias among Democrats and Republicans evaluating NASA's climate data. I believed that this would also work for clinicians evaluating patients.

The question was how to show it.

An unexpected answer came from the *New England Journal of Medicine (NEJM)*.

It turns out that practicing clinicians spend an awful lot of time taking professional quizzes. Sometimes these quizzes are done for money, similar to the ones offered at the annual meeting of the American College of Physicians. In other cases, clinicians receive professional credit for taking quizzes that demonstrate they are up-to-date on new medical advances. Each issue of *NEJM* includes these quizzes in the back pages of the journal. Physicians write in with their answers, then eagerly check the following week's issue to see if their responses were correct.

In 2016, I had the idea of designing a similar kind of quiz game to evaluate bias in clinicians' medical reasoning. I would run the study nationally, across hundreds of practices. It would be just like the cardiac-catheterization study conducted two decades earlier, but instead of clinicians watching videos of make-believe heart patients in a voting booth at an annual convention, they would watch them and make their diagnosis-and-treatment decisions on the internet. I gathered a team of colleagues from the University of Pennsylvania and the University of California, San Francisco, and together we worked to design such an experiment.

The first thing we realized was that to recruit practicing clinicians, we would need to make the incentives worth their while. We decided to pay them hundreds of dollars if they got the answers right but give them no payment at all for getting them wrong. It worked: our recruitment was remarkably effective. Thousands of clinicians from across the country eagerly registered with our study and downloaded our app.

Over the course of two months, we conducted seven replications of the experiment. Each one began by sending notifications to every clinician who had registered. They could ignore the notification if they were busy, or click the link if they wanted to join a quiz. Hundreds of clinicians typically responded each time.

When each study started, the clinicians would see a patient video, just like the ones used in the cardiac-catheterization study. There were two versions of the video, and the actors in each followed the same script. They complained about having tightness in their chest, and a family history of heart problems. But in one video the patient was a Black female, in the other a white male. The clinicians were then asked to select the best treatment option. Options ranged from sending the patient home, to referring the patient to the emergency department for immediate evaluation, to recommending immediate cardiac surgery.

There were four conditions in each trial. The doctors in the first two conditions worked alone, just like the doctors in the original 1997 study had. The first group was composed of forty independent clinicians who watched the video of the Black female patient and indicated their recommended treatment. A second group of forty independent clinicians watched the white-male video and did the same. After being given time to reflect on their decision, the clinicians in both groups were allowed to revise their answers if they wanted, then provide their final response.

We expected that those two groups alone would produce some useful data on implicit bias in medicine. But my real interest was in how network dynamics might affect those biases. Our hope was that the two remaining groups might provide some answers. One group was shown the Black-female video, the other the white-male video. Again, each group of forty clinicians independently provided their initial recommendation. Then we connected each group into its own egalitarian network. In each network, clinicians could anonymously share their initial treatment decisions with their contacts, see their contacts' decisions, then revise their answers if they wanted. Last, the clinicians were asked to provide their final recommendations.

The initial responses in every group revealed a distressing degree of bias. The correct recommendation was to refer the patient to the emergency department for immediate evaluation. However, we found that white men were nearly twice as likely to be referred for immediate evaluation as Black women. That's a staggering amount of inequity. It meant that Black women who needed immediate cardiac monitoring were regularly being sent home instead.

In the control groups, when clinicians were given a chance to reflect on their responses before providing their final recommendations, nothing changed. Their final responses were just as biased as their initial ones. It was disheartening.

But the experimental groups showed something remarkable.

After clinicians exchanged their opinions in egalitarian networks, the rate at which Black women were referred for immediate evaluation nearly doubled. By the end of the study, there was no significant difference in the rate of referral for white men and Black women. In fact, we found that for *both* patients, clinicians in the egalitarian networks were a staggering eleven times more likely than clinicians in the non-networked groups to switch from initially undertreating the patient to ultimately providing the correct care. In practical terms, this means that a clinician who would have *incorrectly* discharged a patient with a dangerous heart condition was now 1,000 percent more likely to make the *correct* decision, referring the patient to the emergency department. Simply as a result of their social network.

In addition to the cardiac study, we conducted more than half a dozen versions of this experiment using different clinical cases—ranging from opioid prescription to diabetes treatment. All told, we ran more than 100 replications. The results were consistent: doctors who compared notes in an egalitarian network were not only less biased in their treatment recommendations; they were also more likely to provide better treatment to their patients of all races and backgrounds.

Experts on the Outer Rim

One of the most unexpected findings from these experiments was that clinicians who scored high on some quizzes scored low on others. The best individual clinician varied from quiz to quiz. In the fishing net, these changes in individual performance from quiz to quiz did not affect the network-wide improvements in everyone's performance on each quiz. But this variation highlights one of the key (and unavoidable) problems with centralized networks: the same person is always at the center. A highly authoritative surgeon is likely to be disproportionately influential even on clinical topics that fall well outside their expertise. When they're wrong about something—as they sometimes will be—their wrong ideas will quickly spread.

How can this problem be solved in real life? How can we increase the influence of people in the network periphery? Can a centralized network really be made more egalitarian?

In 2018, former US president Barack Obama addressed this very question in a lecture to the Sloan School of Management at MIT. He was speaking about how leaders make good decisions in situations of uncertainty.

He described being seated around a table with his Cabinet members, facing a difficult policy decision. He noted how the deep, polished oak of the table and the tall leather chairs where he and his Cabinet members were seated commanded authority. Jokingly, he noted, "It all felt very presidential."

He remembered how an army of staffers lined the dimly lit periphery of the room. These were the low-level grunts—the data analysts, policy wonks, and writers, with "binders and notes," whose job it was to prepare the materials that the Cabinet members would use to make their recommendations. Mr. Obama remarked pointedly that the "important" people sitting around the table did not have time to look at the data. Rather, they would skim the high-level policy information prepared by their senior staff members, and then, Mr. Obama noted only partially in jest, "explain it, probably inaccurately."

He conceded that the enormous complexity of the modern world necessitated this kind of distillation in order to condense hundreds of pages of research into useful information for the president.

But then he drew our attention to his core insight into how decision-making succeeds or fails. It's all about the network periphery.

"One trick I had was that I would make a habit of calling on these people in the outer rim"—namely the staffers hidden around the room's edges—"because I knew that they were doing all of the work." The staffers were terrified, and had been told by their bosses not to speak. But when the president explicitly called on them, they were forced to comply, bringing their useful bits of wisdom from the periphery of the network into the center of the conversation.

Mr. Obama added, "If you want a broad set of voices, you will get them." They are there in the periphery—in the "outer rim." But he emphasized that leaders have to be intentional about bringing those voices into the conversation. Mr. Obama concluded, "In today's culture, if you are not deliberately doing that, then you are going to fall behind. That is true in politics and it is true in business."

How to Change a Coach's Mind

A few years ago, I received a phone call from the Philadelphia 76ers' Director of Performance Research and Development. He had seen some of my research on social networks and wondered if my work might be helpful for the NBA.

The problem, he explained, was scouting.

If you've read *Moneyball* by Michael Lewis (or seen the film starring Brad Pitt and Jonah Hill), you'll immediately understand the problem: professional sports scouting, not unlike medicine, has long been an old boys' club. Most professional scouts are former players or managers. They have well-established biases regarding how to evaluate players. Long-standing norms in scouting can privilege certain kinds of players (who tend to fail) and ignore other kinds of players (who may succeed).

Moneyball describes the way the Oakland A's threw out the venerated norms of scouting and devised an entirely new way of building their team roster. The new scouting strategy led the A's to break the record for the longest winning streak in American League history.

The question the Philadelphia 76ers had for me was, "Can we do that too?"

In the NBA, there are some fairly famous stories of professional scouting gone horribly awry. In 2011, the very last pick in the NBA draft—literally, the last person to make it onto a team—was Isaiah Thomas. That name sounds familiar to many because he was named after the 1980s-era Detroit Pistons Hall of Famer, Isiah Thomas. This Isaiah Thomas—the five-foot-nine, 2011 late-stage draft pick—was not a major college star like his eponym. In fact, he had been lucky to get a spot on the Sacramento Kings' roster. Many thought he would disappear soon after. But he rose through the ranks of the NBA, ultimately becoming an NBA All-Star in both the 2016 and 2017 seasons and winning the prestigious All-NBA Team honor in the 2016/17 season.

By contrast, in 2013 the very first pick in the NBA draft—the highly coveted "number one overall" pick—was Anthony Bennett. At six foot eight, the UNLV power forward invited comparisons with basketball great Larry Bird. Bennett was poised to be an All-Star. Four years later, in 2017, just as Isaiah Thomas was making his second appearance on the NBA All-Star team, a series of disappointing seasons for Bennett saw him drop down to the minor leagues.

In 2017 Bennett played for the Maine Red Claws, and in 2018 he was traded to the Agua Caliente Clippers of Ontario—teams most of us have never heard of.

When the Philadelphia 76ers called me, they had an NBA championship on their mind. They wanted to know how they could improve their scouting procedures to help them identify the unlikely Isaiah Thomases of the world, while avoiding the unfortunate Anthony Bennetts.

Even before the phone call was finished, I knew what they had to do. I just didn't know if they would be willing to do it.

At the time, the Sixers already had a large staff of data scientists analyzing everything about their players, from the total number of seconds played by each player in each game, to the total distance traveled by each player, to data showing players' postures and body language during the games. With all of those data points at their disposal, it seemed there must be a way to find the secret algorithm that would bring them success—the needle in the haystack that would lead them to victory.

My approach was different.

It was based on the idea that although data science is an essential part of the puzzle, there is also a lot of tacit human knowledge that is never included in the data analysis—mostly because it's hard to know which bits of knowledge matter and which don't. If the right bits are never recorded, they can never make it into the algorithms.

I was interested in the hidden insights that might lie within the human social networks among the Sixers' staff. Was there untapped knowledge in the "outer rim" of Sixers' coaches that could be used to improve their scouting?

The main challenge was that organizational networks in professional sports are highly centralized. Just like successful managers, politicians, and physicians, coaches work in a hierarchical world. Some members of the coaching staff are more powerful than others. Influence flows from the people at the center of the network (like the head coach or general manager) to everyone else. My goal was to see whether changing the pattern of these networks might lead to better predictions about player performance.

You may be wondering if this is really possible. On a professional sports team, there are hundreds of millions of dollars at stake each year. The chain of command is difficult to disrupt. While the president of the United States can be intentional about bringing in diverse voices from the network periphery, what could a sociologist possibly do to make the Sixers' networks more egalitarian?

My idea was to take the same approach that had worked for the medical study: we would turn the coaches' scouting problem into a quiz game.

My research team and I developed a simple application so that when the coaches logged in, using either their phones or laptops, they would be connected together in a fishing-net pattern. They would then be asked questions about the performance of the draft prospects the Sixers were actively considering.

Scouting season was already underway, and the Sixers had started to look over their top prospects for the upcoming draft. For the duration of this study, I was sworn to secrecy. Any leaks by me or my research team could result in the Sixers' draft prospects receiving additional media attention that might draw another team's interest during the draft.

Over a period of several weeks, the Sixers were flying in their top prospects to visit their training center. They would run the players through a series of drills, including brief two-on-two and three-on-three games, free-throw shooting, sprints, three-point shooting, and so forth. The Sixers were bringing in new NBA prospects several times a week, and there was intense interest in identifying the best "shooters."

Each day, either I or one of my graduate students would arrive at the Sixers' training facility in Camden, New Jersey, typically in late morning. The training sessions and drills would already be underway. Once we had set up our materials, our team contact would ping all of the coaches to let them know that it was time to join the study. At that point, there would be one more drill left to do in the day. It was the three-point shooting drill.

We ran a total of five of these studies on five different days. Each one worked the same way. Once the coaches were alerted that the study was going to start, each would log on to the site and see the profiles of that day's prospective recruits. The quiz asked them enter their predictions—based on everything they had seen so far that day—for each player's three-point shooting percentage in the upcoming drill.

Just as in the medical study, after the coaches made their initial predictions, they could see the anonymous predictions made by the other coaches to whom they were connected in the network. They could either ignore that information and stick with their first instinct, or use their colleagues' opinions to revise their guess. They would then submit their final response.

That was it.

Each quiz took about ten minutes. Then the coaches would get back to work. A few hours later, the players would complete the three-point shooting drill and we could test the coaches' predictions. During the drills, coaches were watching several players at a time. They could readily evaluate shooting form, but they were unaware of accuracy. The coaches had to wait for the results of the study just like everyone else.

The first week's study didn't go over well.

Most of the coaches were indifferent. But some were genuinely annoyed. Their comments were pretty much exactly what you would expect. Lots of jokes.

But after the first week, everyone's attitude improved dramatically. In fact, the coaches *wanted* to participate. A few things had happened after the first week's session that prompted this change of heart.

First, the coaches realized that the quiz was kind of fun. Second, coaches are naturally competitive people, like clinicians. Once they understood the idea of the quiz, and that they could do better or worse than their peers, they were more motivated.

But the main reason that the coaches were more engaged was an unexpected by-product of the fishing-net pattern: the coaches realized their voices were being heard.

The coaches had initially assumed that the higher-ranked people on the coaching staff would dominate the interactions in the quiz game. They didn't know about the egalitarian networks I was using to connect them. After the first session, some of the lower-ranked coaches (from the "outer rim") saw they could exert genuine influence over the group. They felt a sense of empowerment.

I hadn't noticed this idea of empowerment in my previous studies, probably because I had never been able to talk face-to-face with the participants before. I also did not expect it because empowerment seems like an odd concern for a group of six-foot-five ex-athletes. But evidently some of the coaches had been feeling that their voices were not always heard. Talking with them afterward, a few mentioned to me that the quiz was satisfying because they could see their own influence affecting the group's decision, and moving them toward a better answer. But most notable of all, everyone I talked to was glad to see that the group's opinion was not being dominated by the same senior individuals who typically influenced their meetings. This fact, more than anything, helped to create buy-in among the coaches during the remaining weeks of the study.

Once we tallied up the data from all five sessions, the results were striking. In only ten minutes, the coaches' ability to accurately predict a player's three-point shooting significantly improved, going from 57 to 66 percent accuracy. The coaches thought the findings were interesting, but it was the Sixers' management who really sat up and paid attention. The experiment gave them new insights into how the network periphery among coaches and support staff might be used to improve not just scouting decisions but judgments about how much playing time athletes should get, as well as decisions about how long practices should last, and how much recovery time athletes should have between workouts. There's a lot of tacit knowledge hidden in the network periphery, and an egalitarian network offered a new way to collect and use it.

Biases are strange things. They make us more likely to choose answers that are familiar rather than correct, even when those mistakes are costly. Centralized networks tend to reinforce these bad habits of thought. Once biases are established, ideas that resonate with them become simple contagions. They are easy to understand and easy to spread. The real problem is that our biases, and the networks that reinforce them, can prevent us from finding new ways of solving hard problems. They can even keep us from seeing clearly the information that is right in front of us.

Thankfully, the network periphery can, and does, support real social change. In 2001, the Oakland A's were the second poorest team in Major League Baseball, using an oddball strategy to try to gain an edge. Nobody thought it would work.

Today, this oddball idea has been adopted by every Major League franchise. There has been a sea change in the social norms of Major League scouting. And it spread from the periphery.

CHAPTER 13

The Seven Fundamental Strategies for Change

At the start of this book, we talked about the frustrating failures that result from popular myths concerning how change happens. For lack of a better explanation, these failures are often chalked up to bad luck. But by now, you know that luck matters less than many people think for whether a behavior or innovation will be adopted.

Brand-marketing gurus, political strategists, consulting firms, and a whole host of experts claim to know the secret sauce to "going viral." And to some extent, they do: they may know what types of information and products have proven contagion-worthy in the past; they may understand how to select and measure successful media messages. There is a lot of impressive knowledge about spreading simple contagions.

But these strategies fail us when it comes to spreading complex contagions.

So, what if you want to spread a change of your own? Maybe you're a CEO managing a network of teams. Or maybe you just want to spread a new idea in your community or your church group or your state legislature or your pickup basketball team.

What can you take from these breakthroughs in network science to change the behaviors of the people you're connected to? Here are seven useful strategies for how to apply the lessons in this book to your own change initiative:

Strategy 1: Don't rely on contagiousness.

Social change does not spread like a virus. A viral advertising campaign doesn't enable new ideas to take hold. Simply attracting eyeballs will not suffice. Not only that, it can backfire. If word of an innovation reaches everyone but nobody adopts, the unintended effect is to make the innovation look undesirable. Think of Google+. A negative stigma arising from a widely publicized failure can undercut future efforts.

To make your change initiative successful, do not rely on the contagious spread of information to solve the problem. Use strategies that are designed to grow support for complex contagions, which will allow behavior change to take hold and take off.

Strategy 2: Protect the innovators.

Non-adopters are often *countervailing influences.* Any social-change effort that requires legitimacy or social coordination depends as much on limiting skeptical signals from non-adopters as it does on creating reinforcing signals from adopters. Think about hybrid corn.

Innovations that face entrenched opposition from established norms can spread more effectively when early adopters have *less* exposure to the entire network. This is a matter of balance between being *protected* and being *connected.* You need to create enough wide bridges to allow the innovators to work together to spread the new idea, while giving them ample reinforcement from one another so that they do not get overwhelmed by countervailing influences. A good way to do this is to target social clusters in the network periphery.

Strategy 3: Use the network periphery.

Highly connected influencers can be a roadblock for social change. This is because they are connected to a vast number of countervailing influences — that is, people conforming to the status quo. The key to initiating social change is to target the periphery. Think of the Arab Spring. The network periphery was associated both with greater propagation of activist messages and with greater turnout at protest events.

Stop looking for special people, and focus instead on special places. Think of the spread of contraception in Korea. Your resources are precious. Use them in the places where they will have the most impact. People in the periphery are less connected, and therefore more protected. The network periphery is the place where unfamiliar innovations take hold and spread.

Strategy 4: Establish wide bridges.

A narrow bridge typically consists of a single weak tie between groups. Narrow bridges have reach but lack redundancy, which is necessary to spread complex contagions. To spread a new behavior from one group to another, wide bridges are essential for establishing the necessary trust, credibility, and legitimacy. Think of the growth of Black Lives Matter.

Any attempt to coordinate a large and diverse population

should be based on establishing wide bridges between different subgroups—among different divisions within an organization, across different communities and regions, and between different political constituencies.

Strategy 5: Create relevance.

There is no magic bullet for creating relevance, no single defining trait that is *always* influential. However, a few general principles are helpful for understanding how relevance gets established from one context to another:

PRINCIPLE 1: When behavior change requires that people be given social proof that a particular innovation will be useful for them, *similarity with the adopters* is a key factor for creating relevance.

PRINCIPLE 2: When behavior change requires a degree of emotional excitement or feelings of loyalty and solidarity, then, once again, *similarity* among the *sources of reinforcement* will help to inspire behavior change.

PRINCIPLE 3: When behavior change is based on legitimacy—that is, believing that the behavior is widely accepted—then the *opposite* is true: *diversity* among reinforcing sources of adoption is key for spreading the innovation. Think of the equal-sign campaign on Facebook.

When it comes to creating relevance, context is king. Deciding whether the key factor is diversity or similarity (and what kind of similarity) depends upon the barriers to adoption—the kind of resistance that your desired behavior change will be most likely to encounter. Is it an issue of credibility, legitimacy, or excitement? Once you identify the kind of resistance, you will also know how to create relevance.

Strategy 6: Use the snowball strategy.

Clustering is key to triggering tipping points. Strategically target locations in the social network where early adopters can reinforce one another's commitment to your initiative. Remember Malawi. The snowball strategy creates stable pockets of legitimacy for an innovation.

The emphasis here, again, is on *special places,* not *special people.* Incubator neighborhoods allow a new behavior to compete against an established norm. Contrary to the lessons learned from decades of research on simple contagions, too much exposure to non-adopters early on is counterproductive. Clustering change agents together can lower the size of the critical mass needed to trigger social change.

Two principles can help you apply the snowball strategy:

Principle 1: Know the community and its boundaries.

Is your target community composed of farmers in Iowa, homeowners in Germany, or villagers in Zimbabwe? Who are the people you want to reach, what do they believe, and what are the social norms you want to change?

To tip a social norm, you must first determine the boundary of the community that you want to change. Is it a neighborhood, a state, or a nation? Is it an online chat group or a political party? Is it an organizational division or an entire firm?

Once you know the boundaries of your community, the next step is to find the special locations within the network.

Principle 2: Target bridging groups.

Bridging groups are social clusters that establish wide bridges between divisions. Think of a group working between the engineering team, the design team, and the sales team. Bridging groups are special because they are the most *centrally located* groups in a social network.

Individually, the members of a bridging group are indistinguishable from anyone else. They are not highly connected "influencers" or brokers, nor are they even likely to know they occupy a special location. Their influence comes from the fact that collectively they sit amid *more wide bridges* than any other social cluster in the population. This makes these network locations efficient for initiating snowball campaigns.

Strategy 7: Design team networks to improve discovery and reduce bias.

Networks are not neutral. They either foster innovation or they hamper it. They either promote knowledge transfer across groups or they reduce it. The right contagion infrastructure spurs teams to be more creative, and groups to be more cooperative; the wrong one can thwart creativity and cooperation.

Familiar ideas and biased opinions are simple contagions. They are easy to understand and easy to follow. They will spread if you let them. In centralized networks, social stars are effective for spreading these simple contagions.

True innovation requires protecting people from influences that reinforce the status quo. Breaking free of old ideas and discovering new common ground requires a contagion infrastructure that preserves diversity and stimulates the discovery of new knowledge.

Information-based change campaigns often fail because of social networks. Remember NASA's climate data. Networks are prisms that color and shape what people see and what they believe. Networks can either reinforce bias, stabilizing the status quo, or champion new ideas that overturn the status quo.

Untapped knowledge lives in the network periphery. The right contagion infrastructure can bring that knowledge to everyone—and reduce a group's unconscious bias in the process.

How Should You Use These Strategies?

The seven strategies of change require a change in thinking. They require shifting your attention from the goal of spreading information to the goal of propagating norms. The essential importance of this distinction was overlooked in the past because of the centuries-old assumption that if people are given the right information, the rest will take care of itself. But that view of social change does not take social networks into account.

Ideas and beliefs that reinforce existing biases spread easily in centralized networks. Innovative ideas that challenge our biases and improve our thinking benefit from a contagion infrastructure that protects innovators from too many countervailing influences and offers wide bridges to convey innovative ideas.

Egalitarian networks spread social change. But, more important, they allow new ideas and opinions to emerge from anywhere in the community and spread to everyone without being blocked by a powerful social star at the center of the network.

Network strategies for change should be focused on incorporating voices from the periphery. This approach to social change improves equity in health and fairness in political discussions; it creates opportunities for lifesaving innovations to spread where they once failed, making it less likely that inferior innovations will take hold.

The seven strategies of change can draw out tacit knowledge hidden in the "outer rim" of a community, which leads everyone to a clearer, more informed understanding of the problems they face, and the solutions that will work.

As President Obama said, "In today's culture, if you are not deliberately doing that, then you are going to fall behind. That is true in politics and it is true in business."

Acknowledgments

It takes a village to write a book. It is a great pleasure to acknowledge the many villagers who made this project possible. I am grateful to all of my colleagues and readers who provided important comments on these chapters, including Lori Beaman, Cristina Bicchieri, Paul DiMaggio, Deen Freelon, Mark Granovetter, Douglas Heckathorn, Thomas House, Rosabeth Moss Kanter, Elihu Katz, Elaine Khoong, Jon Kleinberg, Hans-Peter Kohler, Sune Lehmann, Aharon Levy, David Martin, Karl-Dieter Opp, Jennifer Pan, Johannes Rode, Urmimala Sarkar, Oliver Sheldon, Peter Simkins, Brian Skyrms, Zachary Steinert-Threlkeld, Johannes Stroebel, Paul Tough, Brian Uzzi, Arnout van de Rijt, Brooke Foucault Welles, Peyton Young, and Jingwen Zhang. Much of the work reported in this book was supported by research grants from the National Science Foundation, the National Institutes of Health, the Robert Wood Johnson Foundation, and the James S. McDonnell Foundation. I would also like to thank my terrific team, including my editor, Tracy Behar, my agents, Alison MacKeen and Celeste Fine, and the wonderful folks at Hachette Book Group and Park & Fine Literary and Media, for helping me bring the idea of this book into concrete form. I also owe a debt of gratitude to the excellent graduate students with whom I have had the privilege of working on several of the projects discussed in these pages, including Devon Brackbill, Joshua Becker, and Douglas Guilbeault, as well as all the members of the Network Dynamics Group, whose enthusiasm for network science and the possibilities it holds for social change keep me enthralled in new and fascinating explorations. Finally, my greatest debt is to my wife, Susana, who inspired this book.

Notes and Further Reading

Chapter 1

Research on opinion leaders began with several landmark studies, including Paul Lazarsfeld et al., *The People's Choice* (New York: Duell, Sloan and Pearce, 1944); Elihu Katz and Paul Lazarsfeld, *Personal Influence* (New York: Free Press, 1955); and Elihu Katz, "The Two-Step Flow of Communication: An Up-to-Date Report on an Hypothesis," *Public Opinion Quarterly* 21 (1957): 61–78. Research related to these ideas was nicely popularized in Malcolm Gladwell, *The Tipping Point: How Little Things Can Make a Big Difference* (Boston: Little, Brown, 2000).

Katz and Lazarsfeld's original notion of an "opinion leader" was not a celebrity like Oprah Winfrey (whom they would consider part of the media) but a personal contact—a sister-in-law or a friendly colleague—who was highly informed about new-media content, and who in turn helped to inform everyone else. The modern notion of the "influencer" extends the idea of opinion leaders to include people who are highly connected (for instance on social media), but not necessarily personally acquainted with their contacts. The history of these ideas is detailed in Damon Centola, "Influencers, Backfire Effects and the Power of the Periphery," in *Personal Networks: Classic Readings and New Directions in Ego-Centric Analysis,* edited by Mario L. Small, Brea L. Perry, Bernice Pescosolido, and Edward Smith (Cambridge: Cambridge University Press, 2021).

Contemporary measures of social influence focus on the concept of network "centrality," as defined in Mark Newman, *Networks: An Introduction* (London: Oxford University Press, 2010). The most popular methods for identifying influential individuals in a social network are: "degree centrality" (individuals with the most connections), "betweenness centrality" (individuals through which most paths must travel, going from one part of a network to another), and "eigenvector centrality" (individuals whose neighbors are highly connected). Recent studies showing the limitations of these measures for identifying influential network positions for spreading social contagions include Eytan Bakshy et al., "Social Influence and the Diffusion of User-Created Content," in *Proceedings of the 10th ACM Conference on Electronic Commerce* (New York: Association of Computing Machinery, 2009), 325–334; Glenn Lawyer, "Understanding the Influence of All Nodes in a Network," *Scientific Reports* 5 (2015): 1–9; Xioachen Wang et al., "Anomalous Structure and Dynamics in News Diffusion among Heterogeneous Individuals," *Nature Human Behaviour* 3 (2019): 709–718; and my commentary on Wang et al., Damon Centola, "Influential Networks," *Nature Human Behaviour* 3 (2019): 664–665.

In Douglas Guilbeault and Damon Centola, "Topological Measures for Maximizing the Spread of Complex Contagions" (working paper; Annenberg School for Communication, University of Pennsylvania, Philadelphia, 2020), we develop the measure of "complex centrality," which provides a formal method for identifying and targeting specific network locations, found in the network periphery, that are most efficient for spreading social contagions. Early empirical work showing the importance of peripheral network locations for the spread of social movements include Karl-Dieter Opp's key studies of the 1989 Berlin Wall protests—including Steven Finkel et al., "Personal Influence, Collective Rationality, and Mass Political Action," *American Political Science Review* 83, no. 3 (1989): 885–903; and Karl-Dieter Opp and Christiane Gern, "Dissident Groups, Personal Networks, and Spontaneous Cooperation: The East German Revolution of 1989," *American Sociological Review* 58, no. 5 (1993): 659–680—and Douglas McAdam's groundbreaking work on the 1964 Freedom Summer—*Freedom Summer* (Oxford: Oxford University Press, 1988); and Douglas McAdam, "Recruitment to High-Risk Activism: The Case of Freedom Summer," *American Journal of Sociology* 92, no. 1 (1986): 64–90.

Recent work showing the power of peripheral network locations for the growth of online social movements include Zachary Steinert-Threlkeld, "Spontaneous Collective Action: Peripheral Mobilization during the Arab Spring," *American Political Science Review* 111 (2017): 379–403; Killian Cark, "Unexpected Brokers of Mobilization," *Comparative Politics* 46, no. 4 (July 2014): 379–397; Sandra González-Bailón et al., "Broadcasters and Hidden Influentials in Online Protest Diffusion," *American Behavioral Scientist* 57, no. 7 (2013): 943–965; and Pablo Barberá et al., "The Critical Periphery in the Growth of Social Protests," *PLoS ONE* 10 (2015): e0143611. More recent work showing the importance of peripheral network locations for initiating organizational change is in Rosabeth Moss Kanter, *Think Outside the Building: How Advanced Leaders Can Change the World One Smart Innovation at a Time* (New York: Public Affairs, 2020).

Chapter 2

The network dynamics of the Black Plague epidemic is presented in Seth Marvel et al., "The Small-World Effect Is a Modern

Phenomenon," *CoRR abs/1310.2636* (2013), which is the data-source for the Black Plague illustration used in this chapter. The general dynamics of modern disease spreading is clearly described in N. T. J. Bailey, *The Mathematical Theory of Infectious Diseases and Its Applications*, 2nd ed. (London: Griffin, 1975). The vast literature on social networks and viral epidemics is nicely condensed in a network anthology, Mark Newman et al., *The Structure and Dynamics of Networks* (Princeton, NJ: Princeton University Press, 2006). Three particularly useful articles on infectious-disease spreading in social networks are: Ray Solomonoff and Anatol Rapoport, "Connectivity of Random Nets," *Bulletin of Mathematical Biophysics* 13 (1951): 107–117; Fredrik Liljeros et al., "The Web of Human Sexual Contacts," *Nature* 411, no. 6840 (2001): 907–908; and J. H. Jones and M. S. Handcock, "Social Networks (Communication Arising): Sexual Contacts and Epidemic Thresholds," *Nature* 423, no. 6940 (2003): 605–606. Excellent studies of the effects of transportation networks on infectious disease dynamics are in Vittoria Colizza et al., "The Role of the Airline Transportation Network in the Prediction and Predictability of Global Epidemics," *Proceedings of the National Academy of Sciences* 103, 7 (2006): 2015–2020; and P. Bajardi et al., "Human Mobility Networks, Travel Restrictions, and the Global Spread of 2009 H1N1 Pandemic," *PLoS ONE* 6, 1 (2011): e16591, which is the data-source for the H1N1 illustration used in this chapter. The spreading dynamics of H1N1 are clearly described in Kamran Khan et al., "Spread of a Novel Influenza A (H1N1) Virus via Global Airline Transportation," *New England Journal of Medicine* 361 (2009): 212–214. The most up-to-date data on the spread of COVID-19 can be found at https://coronavirus.jhu.edu.

Mark Granovetter's classic (and still superb) study of social networks is "The Strength of Weak Ties," *American Journal of Sociology* 78, no. 6 (1973): 1360–1380. The original "six degrees of separation" study is in Stanley Milgram, "The Small World Problem," *Psy-*

chology Today 1 (1967): 61–67. Notably, the term "six degrees of separation" does not come from Milgram but from John Guare's award-winning play, *Six Degrees of Separation* (New York: Random House, 1990). Milgram's original study received excellent theoretical and empirical elaboration in Jeffrey Travers and Stanley Milgram, "An Experimental Study of the Small World Problem," *Sociometry* 32, no. 4 (1969): 425–443; Harrison White, "Search Parameters for the Small World Problem," *Social Forces* 49 (1970): 259–264; Judith Kleinfeld, "Could It Be a Big World after All? The 'Six Degrees of Separation' Myth," *Society,* 2002; Peter Dodds et al., "An Experimental Study of Search in Global Social Networks," *Science* 301, no. 5634 (2003): 827–829; Duncan Watts and Steven H. Strogatz, "Collective Dynamics of 'Small-World' Networks," *Nature* 393, no. 6684 (1998): 440–442; and Jon Kleinberg, "Navigation in a Small World," *Nature* 406, no. 6798 (2000): 845. A general introduction to this literature can found in Chapter 2, "Understanding Diffusion," in Damon Centola, *How Behavior Spreads* (Princeton, NJ: Princeton University Press, 2018).

An excellent analysis of the spread of Twitter is provided in Jameson L. Toole et al., "Modeling the Adoption of Innovations in the Presence of Geographic and Media Influences," *PLoS ONE* 7, no. 1 (2012): e29528. The "Blue Circles" map from Facebook is presented in Michael Bailey et al., "Social Connectedness: Measurement, Determinants, and Effects," *Journal of Economic Perspectives* 32, no. 3 (2018): 259–280, and can be accessed at https://www.nytimes.com/interactive/2018/09/19/upshot/facebook-county-friendships.html.

Chapter 3

The unexpected dominance of inferior products has been nicely analyzed in Brian Arthur, "Competing Technologies,

Increasing Returns, and Lock-In by Historical Events," *Economic Journal* 99, no. 394 (1989): 116–131; Brian Arthur, "Positive Feedbacks in the Economy," *Scientific American* 262, no. 2 (1990): 92–99; Robin Cowan, "Nuclear Power Reactors: A Study in Technological Lock-In," *The Journal of Economic History* 50, no. 3 (1990): 541–567; and David Evans and Richard Schmalensee, "Failure to Launch: Critical Mass in Platform Businesses," *Review of Network Economics* 9, no. 4 (2010). This work was recently elaborated and refined in Arnout van de Rijt, "Self-Correcting Dynamics in Social Influence Processes," *American Journal of Sociology* 124, no. 5 (2019): 1468–1495, which shows that even in the absence of institutional constraints preventing free choice, these market inefficiencies can arise due to the reinforcing effects of social networks.

The term *stickiness* in this chapter refers to the features of innovations that make them more likely to be adopted. A highly engaging discussion of these topics is in Jonah Berger, *Contagious: Why Things Catch On* (New York: Simon & Schuster, 2013), which elaborates on Chip Heath and Dan Heath's excellent book *Made to Stick: Why Some Ideas Survive and Others Die* (New York: Random House, 2007). Reports on the failure of Google Glass and Google+ include Thomas Eisenmann, "Google Glass," *Harvard Business School Teaching Case 814-116,* June 2014; Thompson Teo et al., "Google Glass: Development, Marketing, and User Acceptance," *National University of Singapore and Richard Ivey School of Business Foundation Teaching Case W15592,* December 21, 2015; Nick Bilton, "Why Glass Broke," *New York Times,* February 4, 2015; Sarah Perez, "Looking Back at Google+," *Techcrunch,* October 8, 2015; Seth Fiegerman, "Inside the Failure of Google+, a Very Expensive Attempt to Unseat Facebook," *Mashable,* August 2, 2015; Chris Welch, "Google Begins Shutting Down Its Failed Google+ Social Network," *The*

Verge, April 2, 2019; and the quoted article, Mat Honan, "I, Glasshole: My Year With Google Glass," *Wired,* December 30, 2013. The grapefruit effect was first reported in David Bailey et al., "Interaction of Citrus Juices with Felodipine and Nifedipine," *The Lancet* 337, no. 8736 (1991): 268–269, and was broadly publicized in Nicholas Bakalar, "Experts Reveal the Secret Powers of Grapefruit Juice," *New York Times,* March 21, 2006.

The demographic transitions of the 1960s and the challenges of spreading contraception in developing nations are documented in helpful government and NGO reports, including Warren C. Robinson and John A. Ross, eds., *The Global Family Planning Revolution* (Washington, DC: The International Bank for Reconstruction and Development/The World Bank, 2007); *Trends in Contraceptive Use Worldwide 2015* (New York: United Nations Department of Economic and Social Affairs); and National Research Council, *Diffusion Processes and Fertility Transition: Selected Perspectives,* Committee on Population, John B. Casterline, ed. Division of Behavioral and Social Sciences and Education (Washington, DC: National Academy Press, 2001). Useful studies of how social networks influence the spread of contraception are in Everett M. Rogers and D. Lawrence Kincaid, *Communication Networks: Toward a New Paradigm for Research* (New York: Free Press, 1981); Hans-Peter Kohler et al., "The Density of Social Networks and Family Planning Decisions: Evidence from South Nyanza District, Kenya," *Demography* 38 (2001): 43–58 (which highlights the differential effects of network structure on contraception decisions in rural versus urban communities); D. Lawrence Kincaid, "From Innovation to Social Norm: Bounded Normative Influence," *Journal of Health Communication,* 2004: 37–57; Barbara Entwisle et al., "Community and Contraceptive Choice in Rural Thailand: A Case Study of Nang Rong," *Demography* 33 (1996): 1–11; and

Rhoune Ochako et al., "Barriers to Modern Contraceptive Methods Uptake among Young Women in Kenya: a Qualitative Study," *BMC Public Health* 15, 118 (2015).

The NIAID-supported VOICE study was a series of elegantly designed randomized controlled pre-exposure prophylaxis (PrEP) trials in sub-Saharan Africa that targeted not only Zimbabwe but also South Africa and Uganda, as detailed in Marrazzo et al., "Tenofovir-Based Pre-Exposure Prophylaxis for HIV Infection among African Women," *New England Journal of Medicine* 372, no. 6 (February 5, 2015): 509–518. A helpful video summary of the study is provided at https://www.nejm.org/do/10.1056/NEJMdo005014/full/

Chapter 4

My early research on complex contagions was spurred on by several classic studies of networks and social movements, including Peter Hedström, "Contagious Collectivities: On the Spatial Diffusion of Swedish Trade Unions, 1890–1940," *American Journal of Sociology* 99, no. 5 (1994): 1157–1179; Dennis Chong, *Collective Action and the Civil Rights Movement* (Chicago: University of Chicago Press, 1987); Douglas McAdam and Ronnelle Paulsen, "Specifying the Relationship between Social Ties and Activism," *American Journal of Sociology* 99, no. 3 (1993): 640–667; Michael Chwe, *Rational Ritual: Culture, Coordination, and Common Knowledge* (Princeton, NJ: Princeton University Press, 2001); Roger V. Gould, "Multiple Networks and Mobilization in the Paris Commune, 1871," *American Sociological Review* 56, no. 6 (1991): 716–729; Dingxin Zhao, "Ecologies of Social Movements: Student Mobilization during the 1989 Prodemocracy Movement in Beijing," *American Journal of Sociology* 103, no. 6 (1998): 1493–1529; and Robert Axelrod, *The Evolution of Cooper-*

ation, rev. ed. (New York: Basic Books, 1984). My complex-contagion research was further spurred by the early work on social networks and health collected in Lisa Berkman and Ichiro Kawachi, *Social Epidemiology* (Oxford: Oxford University Press, 2000), as well as by early research on the spatial dynamics of technology diffusion—including Torsten Hagerstrand, *Innovation Diffusion as a Spatial Process* (Chicago: University of Chicago Press, 1968); and William H. Whyte, "The Web of Word of Mouth," *Fortune* 50, no. 5 (1954): 140–143—and by early work studying online behavior, in Lars Backstrom et al., "Group Formation in Large Social Networks: Membership, Growth, and Evolution," *Proceedings of the 12th ACM SIGKDD International Conference on Knowledge Discovery and Data Mining* (New York: Association of Computing Machinery, 2006): 44–54.

My initial theoretical studies of complex contagion include Damon Centola et al., "Cascade Dynamics of Multiplex Propagation," *Physica A* 374 (2007): 449–456; Damon Centola and Michael Macy, "Complex Contagions and the Weakness of Long Ties," *American Journal of Sociology* 113, no. 3 (2007): 702–734; and Damon Centola, "Failure in Complex Social Networks," *Journal of Mathematical Sociology* 33, no. 1 (2008): 64–68. All of these were further elaborated in Damon Centola, "The Social Origins of Networks and Diffusion," *American Journal of Sociology* 120, no. 5 (2015): 1295–1338; Damon Centola, *How Behavior Spreads*; and Douglas Guilbeault et al., "Complex Contagions: A Decade in Review," in *Complex Spreading Phenomena in Social Systems,* Yong Yeol Ahn and Sune Lehmann, eds. (New York: Springer Nature, 2018). The *Complex Spreading Phenomena* volume includes several interesting studies of complex contagions.

The network images used in this chapter are adapted from Paul Baran's classic study of distributed computing, first published in Paul Baran, "On Distributed Communications Networks,"

RAND Corporation papers, document P-2626 (1962). Useful accounts of the Pals Battalions in World War I are provided in Peter Simkins, *Kitchener's Army: The Raising of the New Armies, 1914–1916* (New York: Manchester University Press, distributed by St. Martin's Press, 1988); and Peter Simkins, "The Four Armies, 1914–1918," in *The Oxford Illustrated History of the British Army,* David Chandler and Ian Beckett, eds. (Oxford: Oxford University Press, 1994): 241–262. A helpful description of peer influence in Patients Like Me can be found in Jeana Frost and Michael Massagli, "Social Uses of Personal Health Information within PatientsLikeMe, an Online Patient Community: What Can Happen When Patients Have Access to One Another's Data," *Journal of Medical Internet Research* 10, no. 3 (2008): e15.

My experimental study of the spread of innovation was originally published in Damon Centola, "The Spread of Behavior in an Online Social Network Experiment," *Science* 329, no. 5996 (2010): 1194–1197. An explanation of how I constructed this experiment—and how I have used the method of "sociological laboratories" as a general scientific research tool—can be found in Damon Centola, *How Behavior Spreads,* Chapter 4 ("A Social Experiment on the Internet") and in the epilogue ("Experimental Sociology"). When I was developing this method, it was important to me that my social experiment meet high ethical standards. I wanted every participant to know that they were entering into a university-sponsored study, and that I was collecting data on their behavior. At the same time, I wanted them to have a "natural" social experience so that I could observe how their peers would influence the choices they made. At the time, it seemed like these two objectives—creating a natural social experience and giving people full disclosure about the scientific study—might be in tension with each other. But, in the end, they weren't. Rather than hindering people's interest in my study of innovation spreading, all of my disclosures helped create enthusiasm for it. People reasoned that if a well-known university was sponsoring a study about health and social networks, it would probably offer something useful. And they were right. After the study was over, I was surprised by the number of emails I received from participants thanking me for offering the health-networking site to the public, and remarking on how helpful it was. It was an important step forward for my research to realize that a scientific study may not only provide new knowledge but also offer a useful public good.

For readers interested in applications of this experimental method to public-health research and policy, details can be found in Damon Centola, "Social Media and the Science of Health Behavior," *Circulation* 127, no. 21 (2013): 2135–2144; Jingwen Zhang et al., "Support or Competition? How Online Social Networks Increase Physical Activity: A Randomized Controlled Trial," *Preventive Medicine Reports* 4 (2016): 453–458; Jingwen Zhang and Damon Centola, "Social Networks and Health: New Developments in Diffusion, Online and Offline," *Annual Review of Sociology* 45 (1): 91–109; and in Damon Centola, *How Behavior Spreads*, Chapter 9 ("Creating Social Contexts for Behavior Change"). A useful methodological reference for researchers who want to understand the wide array of new empirical methods for network science is Matthew Salganik, *Bit by Bit: Social Research in the Digital Age* (Princeton, NJ: Princeton University Press, 2017).

Chapter 5

A nice study of the #SupportBigBird event is found in Yu-Ru Lin et al., "#Bigbirds Never Die: Understanding Social Dynamics of

Emergent Hashtags," *Seventh International Conference on Weblogs and Social Media* (2013). The spread of political hashtags was studied in Daniel Romero et al., "Differences in the Mechanics of Information Diffusion across Topics: Idioms, Political Hashtags, and Complex Contagion on Twitter," *Proceedings of the 20th International Conference on World Wide Web* (New York: Association of Computing Machinery, 2011): 695–704. The equal-sign movement on Facebook was studied in Bogdan State and Lada Adamic, "The Diffusion of Support in an Online Social Movement: Evidence from the Adoption of Equal-Sign Profile Pictures," *Proceedings of the 18th ACM Conference on Computer Supported Cooperative Work & Social Computing* (New York: Association of Computing Machinery, 2015): 1741–1750. A related analysis of the spread of voting behavior through online strong ties is in Robert Bond et al., "A 61-Million-Person Experiment in Social Influence and Political Mobilization," *Nature* 489, no. 7415 (2012): 295–298. The Ice Bucket Challenge and related memes were studied in Daniel Sprague and Thomas House, "Evidence for Complex Contagion Models of Social Contagion from Observational Data," *PLoS ONE* 12, no. 7 (2017): e0180802; and the study of bots for social good is detailed in Bjarke Mønsted et al., "Evidence of Complex Contagion of Information in Social Media: An Experiment Using Twitter Bots," *PLoS ONE* 12, no. 9 (2017): e0184148. A comprehensive collection of empirical studies on complex contagion can be found in Douglas Guilbeault et al., *Complex Contagions: A Decade in Review.*

There are several excellent articles addressing the topic of how social reinforcement among social-media bots and "trolls" influences the spread of misinformation and "fake news." Important new studies in the political domain include Kathleen Hall Jamieson, *Cyberwar: How Russian Hackers and Trolls Helped Elect a*

President: What We Don't, Can't, and Do Know (New York: Oxford University Press, 2018); Alessandro Bessi and Emilio Ferrara, "Social Bots Distort the 2016 US Presidential Election Online Discussion," *First Monday* 21, no. 11 (2016): 7; and Norah Abokhodair et al., "Dissecting a Social Botnet: Growth, Content and Influence in Twitter," *CSCW* (2015): 839–851. In the health domain, useful work on this topic includes Ellsworth Campbell and Marcel Salathé, "Complex Social Contagion Makes Networks More Vulnerable to Disease Outbreaks," *Scientific Reports* 3 (2013): 1–6; David Broniatowski et al., "Weaponized Health Communication: Twitter Bots and Russian Trolls Amplify the Vaccine Debate," *American Journal of Public Health* 108, no. 10 (2018): 1378–1384; and my recent policy report on this topic, Damon Centola, "The Complex Contagion of Doubt in the Anti-Vaccine Movement," *2019 Annual Report of the Sabin-Aspen Vaccine Science & Policy Group* (2020).

Chapter 6

Excellent studies of knowledge transfer across organizational boundaries include Deborah Ancona and David Caldwell, "Bridging the Boundary: External Activity and Performance in Organizational Teams," *Administrative Science Quarterly* 37 (1992): 634–665; Morten T. Hansen, "The Search-Transfer Problem: The Role of Weak Ties in Sharing Knowledge across Organization Subunits," *Administrative Science Quarterly* 44, no. 1 (1999): 82–111; and Gautam Ahuja, "Collaboration Networks, Structural Holes, and Innovation: A Longitudinal Study," *Administrative Science Quarterly* 45 (2000): 425–55. Analyses of the role of brokers in organizational networks can be found in Ronald Burt, *Structural Holes: The Social Structure of Competition* (Cambridge, MA: Harvard University

Press, 1992), and in Chapter 7, "Diffusing Change in Organizations," in Damon Centola, *How Behavior Spreads.*

Brief but useful histories of the Human Genome Project are provided in Henry Lambright, "Managing 'Big Science': A Case Study of the Human Genome Project" (Washington, DC: PricewaterhouseCoopers Endowment for the Business of Government, 2002) and in Charles R. Cantor, "Orchestrating the Human Genome Project," *Science* New Series 248, no. 4951 (April 6, 1990): 49–51. The Human Genome Project's connection to open innovation is nicely elaborated in Walter Powell and Stine Grodal, "Networks of Innovators," *The Oxford Handbook of Innovation* (2005), 56–85. A treasure trove of data on the day-to-day logistics of collaboration between centers working on the Human Genome Project can be found in the publicly available government archive: https://web.ornl.gov/sci/techresources /Human_Genome/index.shtml.

Helpful studies of the history of open innovation include AnnaLee Saxenian, *Regional Advantage: Culture and Competition in Silicon Valley and Route 128* (Cambridge, MA: Harvard University Press, 1994); Eric Von Hippel, "Cooperation between Rivals: Informal Know-How Trading," *Research Policy* 16 (1987): 291–302; and John Hagedoorn, "Inter-Firm R&D Partnerships: An Overview of Major Trends and Patterns since 1960," *Research Policy* 31 (2002): 477–492. Excellent studies of social networks and open innovation include: Christopher Freeman, "Networks of Innovators: A Synthesis of Research Issues," *Research Policy* 20 (1991): 499–514; and Walter Powell et al., "Interorganizational Collaboration and the Locus of Innovation: Networks of Learning in Biotechnology," *Administrative Science Quarterly* 41, no. 1 (1996): 116–145. The process of coordination across organizational boundaries is not without complication; see, for instance,

Paul DiMaggio and Walter W. Powell, "The Iron Cage Revisited: Institutional Isomorphism and Collective Rationality in Organizational Fields," *American Sociological Review* 48 (1983): 147–160; and Mark Granovetter, "Economic Action and Social Structure: The Problem of Embeddedness," *American Journal of Sociology* 91 (1985): 481–510.

A nice analysis of the spontaneous #myNYPD movement can be found in Sarah Jackson and Brooke Foucault Welles, "Hijacking #myNYPD: Social Media Dissent and Networked Counterpublics," *Journal of Communication* 65 (2015): 932–952; quoted tweets are from this study. A comprehensive report on the evolution of Twitter networks during the Ferguson protests can be found in Deen Freelon et al., *Beyond the Hashtags: #Ferguson, #Blacklivesmatter, and the Online Struggle for Offline Justice* (Washington, DC: Center for Media & Social Impact, American University), 2016. Twitter quotations from the Ferguson protests are from Sarah Jackson and Brooke Foucault Welles, "#Ferguson Is Everywhere: Initiators in Emerging Counterpublic Networks," *Information, Communication, and Society* 19, no. 3 (2015): 397–418, which provides an insightful analysis of citizens' experiences during the protests and their evolving engagement with the media. Useful elaborations of this work include Munmun De Choudhury et al., "Social Media Participation in an Activist Movement for Racial Equality," *Proceedings of the Tenth International AAAI Conference on Web and Social Media (ICWSM 2016)*, and Sarah Jackson et al., *#HashtagActivism: Race and Gender in America's Network Counterpublics* (Cambridge, MA: MIT Press, 2019). Public opinion polls detailing rapidly growing support for the Black Lives Matter movement are found in Nate Cohn and Kevin Quealy, "How Public Opinion Has Moved on Black Lives Matter," *New York Times,* June 10, 2020.

Chapter 7

My experimental study of similarity and social influence at MIT was published in Damon Centola, "An Experimental Study of Homophily in the Adoption of Health Behavior," *Science* 334, no. 6060 (2011): 1269–1272. The sociologist's term *homophily* has often generated confusion due to its multiple meanings. It refers both to people's preference for making social connections to similar others, and to the observation that people are disproportionately connected to similar others (which may come about through means other than preferential selection, such as organizational sorting); further confusion is created by the term's subdivision into *status homophily* (social connection based on similar circumstances and characteristics) and *value homophily* (social connection based on similar beliefs and attitudes). These multiple senses of homophily have led to overlapping uses and conceptual ambiguity; for details, see Miller McPherson et al., "Birds of a Feather: Homophily in Social Networks," *Annual Review of Sociology* 27 (2001): 415–444; Paul Lazarsfeld and Robert K. Merton, "Friendship as a Social Process: A Substantive and Methodological Analysis," in *Freedom and Control in Modern Society* 18, no. 1 (1954): 18–66; and Damon Centola and Arnout van de Rijt, "Choosing Your Network: Social Preferences in an Online Health Community," *Social Science & Medicine* 125 (January 2015): 19–31. For clarity in this chapter, I use the term *similarity* rather than *homophily*, and discuss settings in which people's similarity on either status or belief can affect the flow of social influence between them. The role of similarity in social influence is circumscribed by the 3 Principles of Relevance.

Relating to Principle 1, an insightful account of how patients' responses to physicians' health advice vary with the characteristics of the physicians is in Lauren Howe and Benoît Monin, "Healthier than Thou? 'Practicing What You Preach' Backfires by Increasing Anticipated Devaluation," *Journal of Personality and Social Psychology* 112, no. 5 (May 2017): 735. An excellent study of the spread of organizational innovations including the poison pill and the golden parachute is in Gerald F. Davis and Henrich R. Greve, "Corporate Elite Networks and Governance Changes in the 1980s," *American Journal of Sociology* 103, no. 1 (July 1997): 1–37. Davis and Greve use the term *cognitive legitimacy,* whereas I use the term *credibility,* to refer to board members' need to believe in the safety and effectiveness of the innovation. Also related to Principle 1, see Lazarsfeld and Merton, *Friendship as a Social Process.*

Related to Principle 2, Heckathorn and Broadhead's network approach to recruiting injection drug users to join an HIV-prevention program is described in Douglas Heckathorn, "Development of a Theory of Collective Action: From the Emergence of Norms to AIDS Prevention and the Analysis of Social Structure," *New Directions in Contemporary Sociological Theory,* Joseph Berger and Morris Zelditch Jr., eds. (New York: Rowman and Littlefield, 2002); and Douglas Heckathorn and Judith Rosenstein, "Group Solidarity as the Product of Collective Action: Creation of Solidarity in a Population of Injection Drug Users," *Advances in Group Processes,* vol. 19 (Emerald Group Publishing Limited, 2002), 37–66. The classic study showing the effects of similarity on the spread of solidarity is Muzar Sherif et al., *Intergroup Conflict and Cooperation: The Robbers Cave Experiment* (Norman, OK: The University Book Exchange, 1961). The follow-up study conducted in Beirut is in Lutfy Diab, "A Study of Intragroup and Intergroup Relations among Experimentally Produced Small Groups," *Genetic Psychology Monographs* 82, no. 1 (1970): 49–82, which is further detailed in David Berreby, *Us and Them: The Science of Identity* (Chicago: University of Chicago Press, 2008). A series of novel studies on bridging groups (also referred to as *gateway groups*) is in Aharon Levy et al., "Ingroups, Outgroups, and the Gateway Groups Between: The Potential of Dual Identities to Improve Intergroup Relations," *Journal of Experimental Social Psychology* 70 (2017): 260–271; and Aharon Levy et al., "Intergroup Emotions and Gateway Groups: Introducing Multiple Social Identities into the Study of Emotions in Conflict," *Social and Personality Psychology Compass* 11, no. 6 (2017): 1–15.

Related to Principle 3, studies of diffusion showing the importance of diverse sources of social reinforcement for establishing legitimacy include Bogdan State and Lada Adamic, *The Diffusion of Support in an Online Social Movement*; Vincent Traag, "Complex Contagion of Campaign Donations," *PLoS One* 11, no. 4 (2016): e0153539; and Johan Ugander et al., "Structural Diversity in Social Contagion," *Proceedings of the National Academy of Sciences* 109, no. 16 (2012): 5962–5966.

Chapter 8

Early explorations of how social norms work, and what happens when they are violated, can be found in compelling descriptions of "breaching experiments" in Harold Garfinkel, *Studies in Ethnomethodology* (Polity Press, 1991); Stanley Milgram et al., "Response to Intrusion in Waiting Lines," *Journal of Personality and Social Psychology* 51, no. 4 (1986): 683–689; and related work in Erving Goffman, *Relations in Public: Microstudies of the Public Order* (New York: Basic Books, 1971). Evocative images of H-Day can be found at https://rarehistoricalphotos.com/dagen-h-sweden-1967/.

Popular accounts of shifting expectations regarding handshakes and fist bumps can be found in Amber Mac, "Meeting Etiquette 101: Fist Bumps, Going Topless, and Picking Up

Tabs," *Fast Company*, March, 14, 2014; Pagan Kennedy, "Who Made the Fist Bump?," *New York Times*, October 26, 2012; and Simon Usborne, "Will the Fistbump Replace the Handshake?," *Independent,* July 29, 2014. The interview with Chris Padgett can be found in Eric Markowitz, "The Fist Bump Is Invading Fortune 500 Boardrooms," *Business Insider,* July 31, 2014. The first contemporary work of philosophy to place the problem of social norms into the language of coordination games was David Lewis, *Convention: A Philosophical Study* (Oxford, UK: Wiley-Blackwell, 1969).

The sociological distinctions among *injunctive norms, descriptive norms,* and *conventions* are elided in this chapter in favor of the generic term *norm.* Some important theoretical work reserves the term *norm* for cooperation equilibria, in which enforcement is required to sustain prosocial behaviors (see, for example, Cristina Bicchieri, *The Grammar of Society: The Nature and Dynamics of Social Norms* [Cambridge: Cambridge University Press, 2006]). However, the empirical cases I consider are coordination games, in which coordination failures are highly consequential. These are situations in which people expect others to do a certain behavior, and believe that others likewise expect they should do that behavior too (for instance, greeting an executive client appropriately). Coordination games that encode standards of etiquette or status involve normative expectations even absent concerns about violating prosocial behavior. This point is pursued in greater detail in chapter 9, which discusses norms for "token" minorities in organizational settings. Excellent resources for further reading about coordination games include Thomas Schelling, *The Strategy of Conflict* (Cambridge, MA: Harvard University Press, 1960) and Martin J. Osborne and Ariel Rubinstein, *A Course in Game Theory* (Cambridge, MA: MIT Press, 1994). The famous rowboat analogy comes from

David Hume, *A Treatise of Human Nature* (London, 1739–40), ed. L. A. Selby-Brigge, revised 3rd edn., ed. P. H. Nidditch (Oxford: Clarendon Press, 1976): 490. Arthur Miller's account of *The Crucible* comes from Arthur Miller, "Why I Wrote '*The Crucible*,'" *The New Yorker*, October, 13, 1996; these observations are explored in depth in my computational study of witch hunts, Damon Centola et al., "The Emperor's Dilemma: A Computational Model of Self-Enforcing Norms," *American Journal of Sociology* 110, no. 4 (2005): 1009–1040.

Important work on scientific "revolutions" is presented in Thomas S. Kuhn, *The Structure of Scientific Revolutions* (Chicago: University of Chicago Press, 1970) and Thomas S. Kuhn, *The Copernican Revolution* (Cambridge, MA: Harvard University Press, 1957). Copernicus's paradigm-shifting publication was Nicolaus Copernicus, *On the Revolutions of the Heavenly Spheres* (Nuremberg, 1543), trans. and commentary by Edward Rosen (Baltimore: Johns Hopkins University Press, 1992). Kuhn's original notion of a scientific paradigm encompassed a social, psychological, and historical picture of scientific practice. He later developed this idea into a more explicit conception of scientific practice in Thomas Kuhn, "Second Thoughts on Paradigms," in *The Structure of Scientific Theories*, F. Suppe, ed. (Urbana: University of Illinois Press): 459–482, in which he replaced the equivocal term *paradigm* with the more socialized *disciplinary matrix*. Scientific revolutions take place at varying speeds: the "paradigm shift" from Newtonian mechanics to general relativity, for instance, happened relatively quickly, as compared with the slow shift from general relativity theory to quantum mechanics (see Max Planck's quotation in this chapter). A helpful analysis of the varying interpretations of Kuhn's conception of paradigms and paradigm shifts is in T. J. Pinch, "Kuhn—The Conservative and Radical Interpretations: Are

Some Mertonians 'Kuhnians' and Some Kuhnians 'Mertonians'?," *Social Studies of Science* 27, no. 3 (1997): 465–482.

Wittgenstein's second treatise was published in Ludwig Wittgenstein, with G. E. M. Anscombe, ed. and trans., *Philosophical Investigations* (Oxford, UK: Blackwell, 1953, rev. 1997). *Philosophical Investigations* provides compelling illustrations of language games and the fundamental problem of coordination. Wittgenstein's paradox concerns how we learn to "go on in the same way" when we follow a rule, even though there are many possible rules that describe our past behavior. An influential interpretation of Wittgenstein's work, often referred to as *Kripkenstein,* is Saul Kripke, *Wittgenstein on Rules and Private Language* (Cambridge, MA: Harvard University Press, 1982).

Wittgenstein was not alone in making the move from logic toward pragmatics. The pragmatic view of language was gaining popularity in the 1920s at the University of Cambridge; see, for instance, Frank Ramsey, "Facts and Propositions," *Proceedings of the Aristotelian Society* (supp. vol.) 7 (1927): 153–170. However, Wittgenstein's conception of "meaning as use" was both novel and revolutionary. The end-of-century poll of philosophy professors can be found in Douglas P. Lackey, "What Are the Modern Classics? The Baruch Poll of Great Philosophy in the Twentieth Century," *The Philosophical Forum* 4 (December 1999).

Chapter 9

The theory of tipping points was first applied to understanding patterns of residential segregation by race in Morton M. Grodzins, "Metropolitan Segregation," *Scientific American* 197 (1957): 33–47. The idea was later broadened to include general topics relating to "critical mass" dynamics in collective behavior in Thomas Schelling, *Micromotives and Macrobehavior* (New York:

W. W. Norton, 1978); and Mark Granovetter, "Threshold Models of Collective Behavior," *American Journal of Sociology* 83, no. 6 (1978): 1420–1443.

In Kanter's classic studies of critical mass (including Rosabeth Moss Kanter, *Men and Women of the Corporation* [New York: Basic Books, 1977], and Rosabeth Moss Kanter, "Some Effects of Proportions on Group Life: Skewed Sex Ratios and Responses to Token Women," *American Journal of Sociology* 82, no. 5 [1977]: 965–990), she brought the idea of tipping points to the sociological literature on gender and organizations. This work was further extended and applied to gender and politics in Drude Dahlerup, "From a Small to a Large Minority: Women in Scandinavian Politics," *Scandinavian Political Studies* 11, no. 4 (1988): 275–297. A useful application of critical-mass theory to changes in higher education can be found in Stacey Jones, "Dynamic Social Norms and the Unexpected Transformation of Women's Higher Education, 1965–1975," *Social Science History* 33 (2009): 3. Although the term *critical mass* has been generically used in the research that follows from Kanter's original studies, Kanter and Dahlerup used different terms: *tilted groups* and *critical acts*, respectively. There remains considerable debate about the application of tipping points in gender studies, and the specific factors—such as cohesiveness among the activists—that determine how effective a critical mass may be in tipping social norms, as discussed in Sarah Childs and Mona Lena Krook, "Critical Mass Theory and Women's Political Representation," *Political Studies* 56 (2008): 725–736; and in Drude Dahlerup, "The Story of the Theory of Critical Mass," *Politics and Gender* 2, no. 4 (2006): 511–522. In chapter 10, I explore some of these factors in the discussion of social tipping strategies.

Our experimental study of tipping points is published in Damon Centola et al., "Experimental Evidence for Tipping Points in Social Convention," *Science* 360 (6393), 2018: 1116–1119. We identified two key parameters—memory and population size—that govern the critical mass needed to trigger a tipping point. These findings extended my early theoretical work on tipping points, in Damon Centola, "Homophily, Networks, and Critical Mass: Solving the Start-Up Problem in Large Group Collective Action," *Rationality and Society* 25, no. 1 (2013): 3–40; and Damon Centola, "A Simple Model of Stability in Critical Mass Dynamics," *Journal of Statistical Physics* 151 (2013): 238–253; as well as our previous experimental study of coordination dynamics and social norms, Damon Centola and Andrea Baronchelli, "The Spontaneous Emergence of Conventions: An Experimental Study of Cultural Evolution," *Proceedings of the National Academy of Sciences* 112, no. 7 (2015): 1989–1994. Excellent early work in evolutionary game theory on coordination dynamics can be found in Peyton Young, "The Evolution of Convention," *Econometrica* 61 (1993): 57–84; and Glenn Ellison, "Learning, Local Interaction, and Coordination," *Econometrica* 61, (1993): 1047–1071. Classic economic work on equilibrium selection can be found in John Harsanyi and Reinhard Selten, *A General Theory of Equilibrium Selection in Games* (Cambridge, MA: MIT Press, 1988).

Studies of revolutionary "surprises" come from Timur Kuran, "The Inevitability of Future Revolutionary Surprises," *American Journal of Sociology* 100, no. 6 (1995): 1528–1551; and Timur Kuran, *Private Truths, Public Lies: The Social Consequences of Preference Falsification* (Cambridge, MA: Harvard University Press, 1995). Related observations about unexpected organizational change can be found in Rosabeth Moss Kanter, *The Change Masters: Innovation for Productivity in the American Corporation* (New York: Simon & Schuster, 1983). Excellent work on the Fifty Cent Party in China is in Gary King et al., "How the

Chinese Government Fabricates Social Media Posts for Strategic Distraction, Not Engaged Argument," *American Political Science Review* 111 (2017): 484–501; and Gary King et al., "How Censorship in China Allows Government Criticism but Silences Collective Expression," *American Political Science Review* 107, no. 2 (May 2013): 1–18. The Ai Weiwei interview is reported in Ai Weiwei, "China's Paid Trolls: Meet the 50-Cent Party," *New Statesman*, October 17, 2012.

Chapter 10

Interesting work on the introspection illusion comes from Emily Pronin et al., "Alone in a Crowd of Sheep: Asymmetric Perceptions of Conformity and Their Roots in an Introspection Illusion," *Journal of Personality and Social Psychology* 92, no. 4 (2007): 585–595, which was applied to climate-change interventions in Jessica Nolan et al., "Normative Social Influence Is Underdetected," *Personality and Social Psychology Bulletin* 34 (2008): 913–923. Related work on illusory self-perceptions in economic decision-making can be found in Daniel Kahneman, *Thinking, Fast and Slow* (New York: Farrar, Straus & Giroux, 2011).

Prominent contributions to the growing literature on "seeding strategies" for spreading social contagions include David Kempe et al., "Maximizing the Spread of Influence through a Social Network," *Theory of Computing* 11 (2015): 105–147; Yipping Chen et al., "Finding a Better Immunization Strategy," *Phys. Rev. Lett.* 101 (2008): 058701; and Chanhyun Kang et al., "Diffusion Centrality in Social Networks," in *2012 IEEE/ACM International Conference on Advances in Social Networks Analysis and Mining* (2012): 558–564. The snowball seeding strategy was presented in chapter 6, "Diffusing Innovations that Face Opposition," in Damon Centola, *How Behavior Spreads*, and was formalized using the measure of "complex centrality" in Douglas Guilbeault and Damon Centola, "Topological Measures for Maximizing the Spread of Complex Contagions"; which provides a general method for identifying the most influential locations in a social network for spreading social contagions.

Detailed accounts of the Malawi experiments are found in Lori Beaman et al., "Can Network Theory–Based Targeting Increase Technology Adoption?," *NBER Working Paper No. 24912* (2018); and Lori Beaman et al., "Making Networks Work for Policy: Evidence from Agricultural Technology Adoption in Malawi," *Impact Evaluation Report 43* (New Delhi: International Initiative for Impact Evaluation, 2016). The classic study of hybrid corn, which helped to establish the modern field of research on innovation diffusion, is found in Bryce Ryan and Neal Gross, "The Diffusion of Hybrid Seed Corn in Two Iowa Communities," *Rural Sociology* 8 (March 1943): 15; all quotations are from this study. For a clear network analysis of this spreading process, see Peyton Young, "The Dynamics of Social Innovation," *Proceedings of the National Academy of Sciences* 108, no. 4 (2011): 21285–21291.

The rapidly growing literature on neighborhood effects in the spread of household solar power includes Bryan Bollinger and Kenneth Gillingham, "Peer Effects in the Diffusion of Solar Photovoltaic Panels," *Marketing Science* 31, no. 6 (2012), 900–912; Varun Rai and Scott Robinson, "Effective Information Channels for Reducing Costs of Environmentally-Friendly Technologies: Evidence from Residential PV Markets," *Environmental Research Letters* 8, no. 1 (2013): 014044; Marcello Graziano and Kenneth Gillingham, "Spatial Patterns of Solar Photovoltaic System Adoption: The Influence of Neighbors and the Built Environment," *Journal of Economic Geography* 15, no. 4 (2015): 815–839; Johannes Rode and Alexander Weber, "Does Localized Imitation Drive

Technology Adoption? A Case Study on Rooftop Photovoltaic Systems in Germany," *Journal of Environmental Economics and Management* 78 (2016): 38–48; Hans Christoph Curtius et al., "Shotgun or Snowball Approach? Accelerating the Diffusion of Rooftop Solar Photovoltaics through Peer Effects and Social Norms," *Energy Policy* 118 (2018): 596–602; and Samdruk Dharshing, "Household Dynamics of Technology Adoption: A Spatial Econometric Analysis of Residential Solar Photovoltaic (PV) Systems in Germany," *Energy Research & Social Science* 23 (2017), 113–124. In Germany, the remarkable early success of the 1,000 roofs program spawned the 100,000 roofs incentive program (1999–2014), which built upon the critical mass dynamics that were already under way, by adding new incentives that would help to accelerate social tipping nationwide. The solar-panel figure in this chapter depicts the increase in photovoltaic watts per capita (from $wpc < 0.1$ to $wpc > 0.1$) from 1992 to 2014. An animated map can be found at https://en.wikipedia.org/wiki/Solar_energy_in_the_European_Union.

Chapter 11

Network approaches to understanding creativity and innovation were applied to the Broadway-musical industry in Brian Uzzi and Jarrett Spiro, "Collaboration and Creativity: The Small World Problem," *American Journal of Sociology* 111, no. 2 (2005); and Brian Uzzi, "A Social Network's Changing Statistical Properties and the Quality of Human Innovation," *Journal of Physics A: Mathematical and Theoretical* 41, no. 22 (2008): 224023. Related network ideas were applied to innovation in high-tech engineering and management firms in James March, "Exploration and Exploitation in Organizational Learning," *Organizational*

Science 2, no. 1 (1991): 71–87; David Lazer and Allan Friedman, "The Network Structure of Exploration and Exploitation," *Administrative Science Quarterly* 52, no. 4 (2007): 667–694; and Ray Reagans et al., "How to Make the Team: Social Networks vs. Demography as Criteria for Designing Effective Teams," *Administrative Science Quarterly* 49, no. 1 (2004): 101–133. Related work applying similar network ideas to the study of scientific discovery is in Roger Guimera et al., "Team Assembly Mechanisms Determine Collaboration Network Structure and Team Performance," *Science* 308 (2005): 697–702; and Lingfei Wu et al., "Large Teams Develop and Small Teams Disrupt Science and Technology," *Nature* 566 (2019): 378–382. Similar observations about the productive balance between coordination and creativity in scientific discovery can be found in Thomas Kuhn, "The Essential Tension: Tradition and Innovation in Scientific Research," in *The Third (1959) University of Utah Research Conference on the Identification of Scientific Talent*, C. Taylor, ed. (Salt Lake City: University of Utah Press, 1959), 162–174.

Information on the Netflix Prize can be found at https://www.netflixprize.com/. Resources for understanding the broader field of data science and data-science competitions can be found at https://www.kdd.org/. Details of the Annenberg Data Science Competition are found in Devon Brackbill and Damon Centola, "Impact of Network Structure on Collective Learning: An Experimental Study in a Data Science Competition," *PlosOne* (2020). Excellent cultural and economic studies that highlight the historical role of social networks in the process of innovation are in Jared Diamond, *Guns, Germs, and Steel: The Fates of Human Societies* (New York: Norton, 2005); and Thomas Piketty, *Capital in the Twenty-First Century* (Cambridge, MA: The Belknap Press of Harvard University Press, 2014).

Chapter 12

Studies of how framing effects impacted the interpretation of NASA's data about climate change (via a report from the National Snow and Ice Data Center) include Kathleen Hall Jamieson and Bruce Hardy, "Leveraging Scientific Credibility about Arctic Sea Ice Trends in a Polarized Political Environment," *Proceedings of the National Academy of Sciences* 111 (2014): 13598–13605; and Douglas Guilbeault et al., "Social Learning and Partisan Bias in the Interpretation of Climate Trends," *Proceedings of the National Academy of Sciences* 115, no. 39 (2018): 9714–9719. Classic work on motivated reasoning comes from Leon Festinger, *A Theory of Cognitive Dissonance* (Stanford, CA: Stanford University Press, 1957). Related work on "status quo bias" can be found in William Samuelson and Richard Zeckhauser, "Status Quo Bias in Decision Making," *Journal of Risk and Uncertainty* 1 (1988): 7–59.

My students and I have conducted several additional studies of network bias and collective intelligence using both centralized and egalitarian networks. These studies include: Joshua Becker et al., "Network Dynamics of Social Influence in the Wisdom of Crowds," *Proceedings of the National Academy of Sciences* 114, no. 26 (2017): E5070–E5076; Douglas Guilbeault and Damon Centola, "Networked Collective Intelligence Improves Dissemination of Scientific Information Regarding Smoking Risks," *PLoS ONE* 15, no. 2 (2020): e0227813; and Joshua Becker et al., "The Wisdom of Partisan Crowds," *Proceedings of the National Academy of Sciences* 116, no. 22 (2019): 10717–10722. Research on the sources of distrust toward mainstream medical care among African American women—in particular, as a result of involuntary sterilization programs in the 1950s and 1960s—can be found in Rebecca Kluchin, *Fit to Be Tied: Sterilization and Repro-*

ductive Rights in America, 1950–1980 (New Brunswick, NJ: Rutgers University Press, 2009). Useful research on the downstream effects of this history on the uptake of preventive health measures among vulnerable populations can be found in B. R. Kennedy et al., "African Americans and Their Distrust of the Health-Care System: Healthcare for Diverse Populations," *J Cult Divers* 14, no. 2 (2007): 56–60; and E. B. Blankenship et al., "Sentiment, Contents, and Retweets: A Study of Two Vaccine-Related Twitter Datasets," *Perm J* 22 (2018): 17–138.

The contagion dynamics of misinformation regarding vaccine safety is discussed in Damon Centola, *The Complex Contagion of Doubt in the Anti-Vaccine Movement*, and Damon Centola, *Influencers, Backfire Effects, and the Power of the Periphery*. A key policy challenge for COVID-19 vaccination programs is that false information can easily be tailored to target specific biases within different communities, whereas accurate information cannot. This gives rise to a potential asymmetry in the simple/complex contagion dynamics of misinformation versus accurate information, particularly when accurate information is novel or difficult to understand; see Neil Johnson et al., "The Online Competition between Pro- and Anti-Vaccination Views," *Nature* 582 (2020): 230–233.

Useful accounts of Forssman's work and his Nobel Prize include Renate Forssman-Falck, "Werner Forssman: A Pioneer of Cardiology," *American Journal of Cardiology* 79 (1997): 651–660; and H. W. Heiss, "Werner Forssman: A German Problem with the Nobel Prize," *Clinical Cardiology* 15 (1992): 547–549. Several excellent studies of how social networks and social norms influence physicians' prescribing behavior include James Coleman et al., "The Diffusion of an Innovation among Physicians," *Sociometry* 20 (1957): 253–270; Craig Pollack et al., "The Impact of Social Contagion on Physician Adoption of 354

Advanced Imaging Tests in Breast Cancer," *Journal of the National Cancer Institute* 109, no. 8 (2017): djx330; Nancy Keating et al., "Association of Physician Peer Influence with Subsequent Physician Adoption and Use of Bevacizumab," *JAMA Network Open* 3, no. 1 (2020): e1918586; and my commentary on Keating et al., Damon Centola, "Physician Networks and the Complex Contagion of Clinical Treatment," *JAMA Network Open* 3, no. 1 (2020): e1918585. Our study that uses egalitarian networks to address implicit bias is Damon Centola et al., "Experimental Evidence for the Reduction of Implicit Race and Gender Bias in Clinical Networks" (working paper; Annenberg School for Communication, University of Pennsylvania, Philadelphia, 2020).

Important studies in the rapidly growing body of work addressing implicit race and gender bias in medical decision-making includes Kevin Schulman et al., "The Effect of Race and Sex on Physicians' Recommendations for Cardiac Catheterization," *New England Journal of Medicine* 340, no. 8 (1999): 618–626; William Hall et al., "Implicit Racial/Ethnic Bias among Health Care Professionals and Its Influence on Health Care Outcomes: A Systematic Review," *American Journal of Public Health* 105, no. 12 (2015): e60–e76; and Elizabeth Chapman et al., "Physicians and Implicit Bias: How Doctors May Unwittingly Perpetuate Health Care Disparities," *Journal of General Internal Medicine* 28 (2013): 1504–1510.

A riveting account of the Oakland A's' remarkable 2002 season is in Michael Lewis, *Moneyball: The Art of Winning an Unfair Game* (New York: W. W. Norton, 2004).

Index

About the Author

Damon Centola is a professor in the Annenberg School for Communication, the Department of Sociology, and the School of Engineering and Applied Sciences at the University of Pennsylvania, where he is director of the Network Dynamics Group. His widely cited work has been published across several disciplines in the world's leading journals, including *Science*, *The Proceedings of the National Academy of Sciences*, *Nature Human Behaviour*, the *American Journal of Sociology*, and *Journal of Statistical Physics*. Popular accounts of Damon's work have appeared in the *New York Times*, the *Washington Post*, CNN, the *Wall Street Journal*, *Wired*, *Time*, *The Atlantic*, and *Scientific American*.